INTRODUCTION

As the Author of Gontierism, It is my endeavour to introduce You to the structure of our collapsing society and the reconstruction of *A New World Order. Since the dawn of *Consciousness, Man has gone in search of Truth...only to find His way blocked by some perverted measure of control. The forms of Control that stood to boycott the revelation of His search was wide and varied. Those who were in Control of His Social Structure had a Psychological method in curbing all endeavours to the success of His conscious awakening of a new dawn. Where-ever His search for Truth and Justice led Him...He would be confronted by some psychological obstacle under the guise and pretension of, inter-alia, Science, Religion, Judicial Laws and Secular Hospitals.

Although all these disguises of so called Knowledgeable Truth Wore the same fashion of attirement {They all dress up looking like Mother Grundy in her Black or White Night gown and expect the members of their respective Society to address them as either, Father, Your Honour, My Worship, Honourable Doctor and so on}. His search for Truth and enlightenment through the medium of His own religion proved fruitless... unless He was expected to recall to memory and count...the one fruit of Eden... which was nothing more than Two Bites of the Whole. His religious search for God was always met with... "It is a Mortal Sin to question the Mysteries of God". Even though God only became a Mystery by choice of their own perverted Teachings. For that which was Pure and most conducive to the Creative forces of Life was cut off from the mind's of men and allowed to be swept under the carpet of Lies...where it was intended by those in control to allow sleeping dogs to lie. However, unbeknown to them... the sleeping dog has long awoken and His bite is the sounding of their own barking. It suffice to say...Unless You forget all the Worldly Knowledge You have Acquired in Your own Life time and become as ignorant as a Child...You shall never ever attain the Divine Wisdom and Knowledge of the Almighty Creator who resides in the Kingdom of all the GODS. It has been written:

> "*Those who do not Know, and Know that they do not Know, Help them... for they are... but a child in arms.*
>
> *Those who know, but know not that They Know...awaken them...for They are... but asleep.*
>
> *Those who do not know and Know not that They do not know...avoid them...for they are...but the fools of yester-year.*
>
> *Those who know and know that They know...follow them...for They are the real Masters of Our Universe*".

CHAPTER ONE

THE BASIC CONCEPT OF LIFE:

In all of Life, there exist two fundamental principles of existence, the one principle is Negative(-), whilst the other is Positive(+), To cancel either 'One' of these Divine principle would be paramount to the destruction of our whole existence. Although the Negative principle is always concealed by the shadow of its own nature, it does in Truth, share a most harmonious relationship of intercourse with the Positive principle.

For the 'One'(1) is the Light, while the 'Other'(0) is the Shadow of that same Light. No Shadow can exist without a Light, No Light can exist without a Shadow. If the Light was indeed Superior to the Shadow, the Light would have eliminated the Shadow a long time ago. Likewise, if the Shadow was Superior to the Light, the Shadow would have also extinguished the Light, a long time ago. However, Neither the Light nor the Shadow endeavour to eliminate 'one-another', as They are Harmonically eclipsed in the romance of their own union. This statement will be attested to... during the pages of this book and all other books that is bound to follow the release of this publication, ...via the Internet.

THE PERVERTS OF SCIENCE:

They have the tendency of making the Negative look like the Positive...whilst making the Positive look like an optical illusion. They will argue that Scientific-Truth is the debatable and incontestable proposition expressed in Mathematical Terms while maintaining that Nonsense is the debatable and uncontestable proposition expressed in every-day languages. They insinuate that all Truth and Justice can be calculated and expressed in terms of FIGURES, as FIGURES never lie. What They don't tell You...is that although FIGURES never lie... Liars can FIGURE. So, let us figure the figures our self.

THE PERVERTS OF RELIGION

They will stand up high amongst their congregation and propound the WORD of God. Knowing all the Time... that They know very little about the WORD that They are propounding. Every Religion will claim that their respective Spiritual Leader is the True "Son-of-God" and it is their religion that shows the way of the Light. Yet none can define the Physical form of Light. They call their Gods By many names...so as to cause confusion amongst the mass. Even though the Almighty Creator had "One Son"...only! They will play around with the Sacred Vowels and Consonant of His Name in order to mispronounce and misspell His True Name, in the "false hope" that HE HIMSELF will not recognise HIS OWN DESTINY.

EXAMPLES:

CHRISTIAN Names applicable to God:

1)   Iesous, Jesu, Jesus, Messiah, Immanuel, Christ, Begotten, The Omega, Jehovah, Jehowa, Yahveh and so on

Moslems / Muslims Names applicable to their "ONE" True Prophet:

2)   Muhamad, Muhammad, Mohamad, Mohomet, Mahomet, Mahommet, and so on

And so it goes with all the Sciences, Philosophies and Religions of our Planet Earth. Therefore, In order to overcome our chains of Antiquity and gain the self-realization of Truth, Justice, Love and God, We have to rediscover the missing link between Man and His Creator. Although in the very beginning their was the WORD and the WORD...WAS GOD, it is difficult to explain God to You in terms of our everyday Vernacular {**Mother's Tongue}, as Both Science and Religion will contest any proposition of Truth expressed in everyday languages.

To Define the WORD, "GOD" in terms of Mathematics will only add to Your Confusion while at the same Time enhance the Control of Science over Society which will eventually lead to the destruction of planet Earth. What we need is a new standard of communication that will allow us to define the WORD and its very beginning in terms of GODS and DEVILS.

Although this study is not about religion... but rather about TRUTH and JUSTICE, it is impossible to define TRUTH and JUSTICE with the exclusion of the Creative Principle... universally referred to as GOD.

THE CREATIVE PRINCIPLE
Scientific Symbols of the Logo

Creation began from the void of Nothingness. Therefore, Symbolically speaking, the Creative force is best represented by the Logo symbol of Zero {0}. From Nothing {0}, came Something, now what ever that something was, It was Part and Parcel of that Nothingness {0} that came from the Void {0}. As this something was the First-thing that came out of the Void {0} of Nothingness, It is best represented by the Logo symbol of One {1}. Both together (0+1), They stand to represent "The Whole" of Life.

However, there is much more behind the TRUTH of "Zero and One", for besides being the Binary-code, of our Inter-web, They are also the tools of Scientific Manipulation of our own Genetic code.

A Ω

THE ALPHA AND OMEGA
Religious Symbols of the Logo

The Alpha and Omega are Symbolic Symbols which refers to, inter alia, The existing Alphabetical Order {*Codex Nasaraeus} of any Alphabetical Order and not exclusive to the Greek Alphabet... as Science and its associated philosophies would like You to believe.

The Letter{s} pertaining to the sound of any Language{s}, is the Metamorphosis of That related Alphabet to that particular Vernacular. Therefore, as not everybody can speak Greek nor Aramaic...but many can speak English...I have chosen to use the Roman Alphabet to demonstrate to You...the Power of Gematria.

The Symbol of Alpha (A) and Omega (Ω/O), are the Sacred Logo of the WORD...of GOD, incarnate. There is no difference between the Symbolic Logos of "O+1" or "A & O", They are both the same Divine Entity of the same Creative Force that came into existence out of Nothingness {O}.

Although the "A & O" Symbols are Secular (*Words), and the "0+1" are Judicial {*Numerical}, both sets of Logos are applicable to the same "Law & Order" of Control. It must be borne in mind, that the Symbol of "1 + 0" are only Numerical in terms of the Mathematical Logos. However, In terms of the Logo-word, They represent the Letter 'I' and the Letter 'O', and are the Soul Mate of "A & O".

For over Two thousand years, Ancient man has manipulated the physical constant of both Logos {"A & O and 1+ 0"} in order to maintain the continuous existence of their own so-called Superior race. In the beginning of our Language {Logo}, Our Vocabulary was very limited as our Needs and Wants were very basic. A simple 'Yes or No' was more than sufficient to maintain the existence of our everyday requirement. As our Needs and Wants began to increase, so did the physical constant of our Alphabet {**Roman Alphabet}.

The Sacred Logos continued their extension of growth with the progressive growth of Consciousness. Once *Ancient man {*Dual-man/*Cain and Abel} discovered that His own likeness was the Semblance of the Logo-Image {*God Science} He became resentful of His own inferior being. His endeavour to become like God...was the beginning of His own undoing. He Bit-off God from His Umbilical-Being...not knowing that His Superior Endeavour of being like God was the destruction of His own Consciousness as well as the reduction of His own Image. Hence, the birth of the Beast...in the form-image of Dog was born. Instead of being like GOD, He became the reversal of His own Thoughts. I believe that it is Time for the Beast to rise from sleep, and become the entity of His own potentiality.

THE SECRET OF LIFE:(- ><+) or E=(M/C)^2

Many modern Physicists, Scientists, Mathematicians, Occultists and so on, have gone in search of Life. Their motivating factor for finding Life...was to manipulate Life, for their own selfish needs. However, Life being Life, Life learns from its own tragic experiences of Truth.

Life can never allow modern scientific mad-men to discover the realities of Her Majestic Simplicity; as Life is well aware of its own beginnings and ends without allowing the Evil-Cycle of existence to continue on its monotonous Historical cycle of evil repetition. It is for this reason alone that the TEXT you are reading, was designed. The Simplicity of the reconstruction of the Lost Logos (*The Skeleton) of Alpha & Omega will allow You to see what our Scientific Society has been doing with our Genetic-Roots (*Codex Nasaraeus).

NB:

ALPHABETICAL ORDER = 150
AN ALPHABETICAL ORDER = 165

THE ROMAN ALPHABET:(*Word for Word).

The 26 Letters of the Roman Alphabet, are The 26 Soldiers of Our Universe. They Protect Mankind from Destroying the Evidence of Their Own History. Their Purpose and Function is to stand Up-Right in the face of God...so that when Judgement Over Mankind is Pronounced... They can swiftly seal-off the Gates of Hell.

A=1	N=14
B=2	O=15
C=3	P=16
D=4	Q=17
E=5	R=18
F=6	S=19
G=7	T=20
H=8	U=21
I=9	V=22
J=10	W=23
K=11	X=24
L=12	Y=25
M=13	Z=26

NOTAS:

The Relationship shared between Numbers and The Letters of the Alphabet is called Numerology (*Natural Science). The Greeks and Jews (Modern & Ancient) refer to this ART as "GEMATRIA". This science works as follows:

1) Choose any WORD, NAME, or SENTENCE.

2) Allocate each Letter of Your Chosen WORD, NAME or SENTENCE, with the Number Value applicable to the Above Key.

3) Add the total up and compare the Number Value of Your Total to The Number Value of the Numerical Dictionary.

This will define the meaning to You... as all WORDS are relative to God Himself. Please remember, that a "Single Asterix (*)" Symbol next to any WORD, NAME, SENTENCE(s) or NUMBER(s) indicates that You will find the Numerical Value defined for You in the NUMERICAL DICTIONARY that Comes within this TEXT.

You may increase its Numerical Vocabulary by inserting your own Calculation along the same Line of interpretation. A "Double Asterix (**)" indicates that the WORD has been defined by means of our everyday usage of an English Dictionary. This is done to indicate to you whether the WORD defined is applicable to the NUMERICAL DICTIONARY (*) or The Oxford Dictionary, The Collins English Thesaurus, and The Etymological Dictionary (**).

EXAMPLE No. 1:

T=20	A=1	G=7
H=8	L=12	O=15
E=5	P=16	D=4
	H=8	
A=1	A=1	H=8
L=12		I=9
P=16	A=1	M=13
H=8	N=14	S=19
A=1	D=4	E=5
B=2		L=12
E=5	O=15	F=6
T=20	M=13	
	E=5	
	G=7	
	A=1	
98	98	98

TRY TO DECIPHER THE FOLLOWING *24 TASK-LIST BY YOURSELF:

*THE CENTRE	*ENERGY ACT	*AGELESS ARK
*PROPHET	*NUCLEAR ACT	*A NUCLEAR END
*A STORY	*BIBLE LOGOS	*NEWS DEMO
*SCROLLS	*BIBLE ATOMS	*NEWS BEGIN
*DELIVERER	*BIBLE LANGUAGE	*HADE'S NEWS
*SYMBOLIC	*LIFE – and – TIME	*NEWS PLACE
*GEMATRIA ACT	*LIFE – and – THE DEAD	*NEWS HEX
*JEWISH ACT	*AGELESS BIBLE	*NEWS FEED-BACK

After having deciphered the above *24 "TASK-LIST" the observant Student of this Study will Notice that everything is *RELATIVE. (*NUMBERS). Therefore, when Albert Einstein Split The ATOM...all He really did...was to split the LOGO. By Splitting an *ATOM or *LOGO you create another *ATOM/*LOGO. This is how current News is produced by N.A.S.A.

Example:

A	1	L	12	
T	20	O	15	
O	15	G	7	
M	13	O	15	
	49	+	49	= 98
	X 2		X 2	
	98		98	

NOTAS:

"I Am GOD" = *49 and 4 x 9 = *36 (*Lode/*Field/*OHM/*Law/*ANU (**Sanskrit word for *ATOMS).

When an Atom (*Logo) is split into two, the one part becomes the energy and the other part becomes the particle. (*ENERGY = *God Son) & (*Particle = God Father)

	49	+	49	= 98

Energy =   74
Particle =   84
                158 = *North + South

Every Time that a scientist splits an Atom cell - from its natural state of rest... it screams out..."A...God Died" or "Deal-a-God". They are crucifying the Godhead a Thousand Times. If You think that is funny... or perhaps Something...to sweep under the carpets...then just You wait for the return of that Atomic Image which is non other than the *LORD, Himself. To calculate every letter of the Logo for You... would turn this TEXT into a monotonous study. Therefore, where any calculation is required, I shall place an Asterix (*) Symbol to indicate its respective Numerical Value. You may refer to the NUMERICAL DICTIONARY for the extension of that definition. I trust You will find the latter Numerical Dictionary most enlightening.

RELATIVITY
*Imaginary Space/*Imaginary Brain

As Albert Einstein was the First Physicist to Split an Atom Cell which resulted in Him being Blown-up by His own Petard, allow me to reconstruct the "Same Albert", for You, out of the remains of a *BOMB-PETARD = *96 and see if I can relate Him to the *Metaphor of *HIS NAME = 69, in terms of *RELATIVITY or the *RE-INCARNATION of *EINSTEIN-BODY/*A. FRANKINSTEIN.

*A. EINSTEIN, *ALBERT'S IDEA, *BOMB PETARD, *AN ATOM BOMB,
*AN ATOM CELL, *HYDROGEN, *NEW CHEMICAL, *SELF CHEMICAL,
*WAR CHEMICAL, *THALLIUM (**a Highly Poisonous, Colourless and Tasteless Chemical dubbed the "Homicide's Dream"), *MUSTARD, *TINIEST, *DUST-CELL,
*BIGGEST RACE, *TRUE LIFE, *A REAL BOMB GAS, *REALISTIC, *NAZI'S GAS,
*NAZI'S RACE, *NAZI'S CODE, *THE ODESSA, *GERMAN S.S.,
*GERMAN BALANCE, *GERMAN DEATH. *ADOLF SCIENCE, *FATHER CHANGE,
*SAME FATHER, *JEW FATHER, *A GERMAN SEAL, *JEW SCIENCE,
*GOLD SCIENCE, *COAL & FIRE GAS, *THE RECORD, *THE GENETIC,
*HUMAN MEAT, *MOON TEAM, *MOON ANGLE, *NET and GRID, *SHARK-NET,
*HUMAN-NET, * INTER-WEB, *WEB-NET CODE, *ON-LINE CODE, *BINARY-CODE, *W.W.W.-CODE,

To continue along this vein of thought... would be a never ending Story. However, a quick calculation of the above, will confirm the true definition of RELATIVITY.

The name, *RELATIVE-ATOM, or RELATIVE-LOGO, indicates the direct relationship shared between each aspect of life. Irrespective of whether that aspect can be viewed objectively or subjectively... all things... all matter... and all of Life, is attached to the *UMBILICAL-CORD *UMBILICAL MIND...of GOD.

*THE MIRACLE OF LIFE
*147
*THE PLANT = *96

Consider the Following. It takes an Oak tree Fifty Years before She Bares Her First Fruits. In the First Year of Her FRUITAGE, She bares FIFTY THOUSAND ACORNS. Out of all these thousands of Acorns...only "ONE", will be allowed to germinate itself into a full-grown Oak Tree. In order to do this, the Acorn...falling off its MOTHER'S Tree, must land directly on its MOTHER'S leaf, in order to Germinate.

Should The falling Acorn Hit a foreign object, such as the ground, the soil, a stone, and so on, before...landing on its MOTHER'S leaf, then Her Chances of being Germinated, has been ruined. Out of the Fifty Thousand Acorn..."ONE", does get to fall off the TREE and land on its MOTHER'S Leaf. However, this is not the end of the Story, as there is still more to follow. After falling off the ACORN TREE, all the acorns on the ground are subjected to becoming food for the scavengers that live off acorns, such as Squirrels, Foxes, Bears and so on. These scavengers arrive and eat every Acorn that is laying on the ground...except, that isolated "ONE" that made a direct landing on its Mother's Leaf. Its survival was not determined by the survival of the fittest, but rather by the protection of "Mother-Nature" (*North & South).

As for all the scavengers who did come to dine on the fallen acorns, not one of them could see... that "ONE" acorn laying on its Mother's Leaf - as it was afforded Protection by *MOTHER-NATURE (*Organic Growth) Her-self.

Consider the *MIRACLE of Your own Birth. As You know, the Moon has a direct influence over a females periodic cycle. Although, the Moon takes exactly "27 Day...7 Hours...42 Minutes" to circumnavigate Planet Earth...

Science stumbles over accurate calculation and prefers to round off Truth with so-called *ROUND-FIGURES...that have no bearing on the narrow gauges of Life itself.

They choose to say that it takes approximately "28 days Only". However, after completing a full Ratio of its given orbit, it inseminates all existing life with a seed of its own Nature. Should this egg be fertilised within "27 Hours...7 Minutes...and 42 Seconds after its arrival in the female's womb, the *Pattern of Life, will begin its course of Life until its state of maturity, where delivery of birth takes place.

However, Should the seed within the Female's womb remain unfertilised after the pre-scribed period of fertilization (* 27 Hrs... 7 Min... 42 Sec.), then the Womb will reopen itself and dispose of its unwanted *Gift-of-Seed. This means that that, disposed seed, will never ever experience the blessed joys of Life...with all its Ups and Downs. Now, imagine that that, seed, was You. And Your Mother-can-be, decides to bluff Your Father-can-be, that She had a Splitting Head-ache and was in no mood for sex...and decides to retire early to bed that Night...without sex. That would mean that Your chance of ever being born would amount to nothing more than awash-away dream.

However, Imagine on that same Night You were waiting to be conceived, and Your Father-can-be, tells Your Mother-can-be, that He has to work the Night Shift Train...but decides to skip work and visit the Ladies of the Night at some Brothel, You Would Have Lost Another Chance at seeing Life. However, Once again...lets imagine that both Mom-and-Dad-can-be, retires to bed in the full union of their romance. Now, here is the conclusion of Your Miracle Birth. Every Time a male {Your Dad-can-be) ejaculates His Semen, He ejaculates approximately "250 Million Cell-eggs" that want to mate With You... (The *Other/*Twin, half of You)... sitting in the Womb. Unfortunately, out of these eager "250 Million Cell-Eggs" Only "ONE" can touch You.

As soon as the Touch takes place, a chemical reaction takes place simultaneously... and seals-off Your Egg-Union, from the rest of the eager cells of ejaculation. This means, that on Your Father's side alone, You had to fight "250 Million other cells" in order to unite with Your Soul-mate, which is the composition of:

½ Mom + ½ Dad = YOU.

Although in all truth, You are half of Your Mom and half of Your Dad, THEY are not You. You are *AN INDIVIDUAL within Your own Rights. Therefore, You cannot be divided. As Your Soul-Mate is the Shadow of Your *OWN EXISTENCE (*Atomic Nucleus, *Characteristics, *The Dead Activity, *Radioactivity, *Polarization, *Self-Realisation, *New Realisation.)

*THE RELATIVITY OF BIRTH:(*252)
*Natal Blood Transfusion
*Mathematical Consistancy

PLEASE NOTE THE FOLLOWING RHYTHM OF:

69_cum_96

*A PLUS(+)...*HUSBAND...*AND A MINUS(-)...*EACH MOTHER...*WAS GOD...
*TO YOU...*THE CHILD...*FROM SPACE...*THE WOMB_BAG...*HER EGGS...
*HIS SEED, *HER ORIFICE...*THE PENIS. *THE COME...*A REAL LIFE...
*REALISTIC... *LIFE-MODE...*BEGIN-LIFE CODE...*MEDICAL DANGER...
*DR. DOOM... *NURSES...MIDWIFE...*NURSE-AIDE...*CLINIC-BODY...
*CLINICAL-AIDS... *DEATH'S TEAM...*BIRTH TEAM...*HUMAN TEAM...
*UMBILICAL-ACT... *A UMBILICAL END... *LIFE BEGIN...*LIFE UP...*H.I.V. Bug...
*FLU-BUG BASE...*RED H.I.V.BUG...*FAT FLU-BUG,

*CODE OF BLOOD:*96 (*LUMINOL**Chemical Agent used to trace-Blood during
*Forensic Test (*153).

There are Four (4) *Groups ...*Of Blood. Viz., A + B + AB + O.;

There is also *THE FACTOR=Rh. This factor is medically referred to as: *The
Rhesus Factor, Which is none other than the *Electro-Magnetic-Field. All of Life,
comes equipped with the Latter "Rh-Factor". This Factor, is a Negative (-) and
Positive (+) Current. It's the "A and O" of our *Blood-Cycle (*96). The First (1) and the
Last (0) *OF RED BLOOD (*96).

*RED BLOOD CELLS (*126). They carry the Oxygen of the Blood, providing *THE
WHOLE (*96) body with *THE CLEAN-AIR (*96).

*WHITE BLOOD CELLS (*164). They are the Completed *Alphabetical Nuclear, often
referred to as: *THE ALPHA AND THE OMEGA. They constitute the Beginning and
the end of our 'A + O' Blood Symbols. If You remove either "ONE" of the Symbols
from the *Blood Cycle, You instantaneously destroy the *BODIES IMMUNE SYTEM
(*230) which is the *AIDS ELECTRICAL SUPPLY; or if You Prefer me to be more
direct- it's…

*THE BLUE-BLOOD SUPPLY... *THE MIND BLOOD SUPPLY...
THE LIVE PAIN SUPPLY... *THE BINARY MIND VISION... and so on. Ref: *230.

The White Blood Cells are the *26 Soldiers (*Rh Soldiers) of our Blood's Circulation System. Their Function is to *Combat-New...*Bacteria $>E=(M/C)^2$, such as the Viruses of the "H.I.V. Classification".

THE INTRODUCTION OF AIDS:

In the Western parts of *SOCIETY, *THE PUBLIC, were requested to donate their Blood "Once" in every Three (3) Months. Due to a sudden Blood Shortage...*Members of...*Society are now requested to donate "Once" every Second (2ⁿᵈ) Month. However, in the poorer parts of the World, such as Africa, You cannot persuade a Black-man to give anything away for free... let alone His Blood. Therefore, the 'only' way to obtain Blood from a Black-man, was to purchase it from Him. Hence, the beginning of the *BLOOD-TRADE (*96).

Offering a Black-man Money, in exchange for His Blood, led the Black-man into the false belief that *GOLD ran through His *VEINS (*69). Instead of going back to the Blood Bank after the pre-scribed period of Two (2) Months, to donate more Blood, He preferred to *RETURN (*96) immediately, to the back of the *QUEUE (*69), so as to sell more of His Blood while the going was good...on the *Sale of Blood/*AIDS in VEIN. The Members of the Blood Bank, who were collecting the Blood, did not seem to mind this most 'unethical practice' of continuously returning back to the queue...after each donation.

Instead of refusing their repeated Blood Sale and sending them home until Two (2) Months had expired, They chose to keep a "blind-eye" and exacerbate the pending disaster. The Members of the Blood Bank would drain their required amount of Blood from the respective donor... place the donated Blood on *A VIBRATOR and allow the Blood to separate itself in it's *Mathematical order of pure *ARITHMETIC. That is to say, that when Blood is placed on a *SEPARATOR (*113), the *SIX-and-NINE (*113) *SYNDROME (*113) of the *H.I.V._NUCLEAR (*113) begins it's *STANDARD-CELL (*113) *RESISTANCE (*113).

When blood is Vibrated, it separates itself into its respective Colour Composition. The Red Blood is *RETURNED DEAD...back into the *VEINS of the African Blood Donor, minus His *White Blood Cells (*Human Aids Cross). You can well imagine for Yourself what the end result has on the Donor's Immune System. If You continually remove the *WHITE CELLS (*Polarity), from the Natural flow of Blood, You remove its *Polarity and *Cancel its Resistance to Foreign Cells.

In short, By removing Your White Blood Cells, You remove Your *Bodies Soldiers...thus allowing diseases to attack the *Human Meat (*96). As for the *White Blood Cells...which was removed from its Natural *Life Orbit (*96), well that, simply gets converted into *New Chemical (*96) *Drugs (*69) for resale as... inter Alia,

(HERE IS YOUR *TASK-LIST (*Calculation))

1) The Dead Pill (*The Dead Clone)
2) Doom Pill (*Medical Pill)
3) Time Pill (or... *Pill Time)
4) Aspro Base
5) AZT Pill (*Genetic Name)
6) M.K. Ultra
7) H.I.V. Vaccine
8) The Aids Bible (*Dr Doom)
9) The Aids Baby (*Sarafina)
10) Aids Genetic
11) Genetic Seed (*An Apple a Day...?)

THE TREE OF LIFE (*The Skeleton) & *THE TREE of KNOWLEDGE:

There are Two Trees in Life that have existed since *Eden's Garden. Many Books have been written on *THE TREE of LIFE...and very little on the *TREE of...KNOWLEDGE.

A quick calculation of the latter and former will tell You why.

While The Tree of Life provides *INFORMATION,... *THE TREE of KNOWLEDGE provides *THE RESURRECTION of *The Whole Dimension. The Tree of Life is better known as the *CABALA (*20)... whilst the Tree of Knowledge is better known as *DAGGA (*20). Together, They create the *MIND (*40...as 2x20=40).

Many Masters of the *Occult (*74 x 9 = ?) have written an account of the CABALA. Their so-called KNOWLEDGE on the subject is based on pure hearsay. They speak about meeting *THE HIGH PRIEST (*The Devil's Son)...along the way, as well as *THE DEVIL HIMSELF (*The Son of Satan). Had They actually climbed-up the Tree, Themselves, They would have known better, for the Devil Himself awaits "No-Man" along the path of Life.

In Life, the Devil awaits You, at the *BOTTOM (*THE DEVIL) of His Tree, and not on Top, nor half-way up. It must be borne in mind, that *THE DEVIL OF LIFE was *THE DEVIL of EVE (*BIOLOGY of LIFE).

*DR. DOOM:

Consider the Following: You are feeling Sick, so You go and pay *Dr. Doom a Medical Visit in Order to find out, what is 'medically wrong', with You. Instead of *Doc Doom giving You a 'full-medical-check-up', as You were expecting him to do, He catches You 'off-guard' on Your arrival, with the following statement. "Good morning, and what seems to be the matter with You? This question has the ability to *Over-ride Your *Cerebellum, Where the Brains Stores its information. You suddenly forget that You are there to be examined, by Dr Doom and not there for a "self-diagnosis" in order to determine Your condition of Health. However, after having completed Your "self-diagnosis" on His behalf, (even though You may not be really ill...but just went there in order to score a few days off work and obtain a so-called *DOCTOR'S CERTIFICATE...for the days off work.}

Dr Doom will now approach You with His stethoscope... wrapped around *His Neck (*69) in order to appear *Medically Official (*145) in Your Sight. (This type of *Psychology (*145) is most conducive in re-establishing His control over You... once You've completed Your "self-diagnosis" of poor health.

Due to His own lack of *Knowledge (*96) pertaining to *Human Vice (*96)... He will now begin to probe You...here and there, with His stethoscope (pretending to be a sound specialist,) Dr Doom Will *Medically Confirm (*162)" that You are indeed, very sick and require a few days off work. He will then *Reward (*69) You for *Each Visit (*96) with a *Listed-code (*96) of *Drugs (*69), as well as the *Solicited (*96) *Sick Note (*96), as required *By-Labour (*96).

The Whole Medical Profession is a Psychological game of *Mind over Matter/*Matter over Pain. They play games with Your mind as They Know that any *Message* (*69) received by the *Faculties (*96) of *The Brains (*96), via the *Audios (*69) of Your *Basic-Sense (*96), is *Conducive (*96) to the *Metaphor (*96) of a *Sick-Voice (*96)... *In Sound (*96). What this teaches *Us (*40), the *Mind (*40) of *Pain (*40), is that if Your *Free Sense (*96) allows Dr Doom to convince You that You are indeed unwell and suffering from some *Basic Disease (*96), then that exact disease will befall You, on the following grounds:

        a) *I Believe
        b) *Message
        c) *Doc Doom
        d) *Prints
        e) *In Voices
        f) *Pictured
        g) *On Mind

There is no difference between a so-called *Modern (*69) *Medical Pill (*96) to that of *Basic Medicine (*96) handed *To You (*96) by *A Witch-Doctor (*139) who knows all about the *Chemical Reaction (*139) of the *Pituitary (*139) Gland caused by *The Genetic (*96) of any *Plant Seed (*96) placed within a body of *Human Meat (*96). Death is nothing more than the Psychological changes pertaining to the Pituitary Changes of Body Chemistry.

The Changes Occurring in one body within the presence of a foreign body is totally conducive to *The Sight (*96) of the *Beholder (*69). If I Kill You, in the presence of others, then those who saw You Die, will accept the *Message of Death Mode (*165...69 + 96= *165) and You will therefore remain *Invisible (*101) to them all...who saw You Die. You, on the other hand, will immediately wake up in Bed, in another Time Frame of mind. You will believe that You had just suffered from *A Nightmare (*96) or a *Dreamless Night. I shall continue the story of *Mr Death (*69) beyond the Forbidden Page of Wisdom, as Death and Life has been my companion since my Birth.

THE NUMERICAL DICTIONARY

* 9 =   Dad,

*10 =   Dada,

*11 =   Bi, Fad,

*12 =   Bee,

*13 =   Age, 'I.D.', He,

*14 =   Ma, Dead, Fag, Dia[**Irish & Scotish for God],

*15 =   Face, A Dead,

*16 =   Deaf, Cage,

*17 =   Acid, Ice, Back, El, Aged,

*18 =   Head, Hade, Mad, Dam, Me, Die,

*19 =   Adam, And, 'D.N.A.', Jah, Idea, Egg, Ra[**God of Ancient Egypt],

*20 =   Abel, Able, Dagga, Cabala, Caged,

*21 =   'I.C.I.', Edge, Beam,

*22 =   Alah, Ali, Arab, Ape, Fig, Coca, Died, "Im"{**plural of respect in Hebrew},

*23 =   End, I am, In, Ago, Re, Deck,

*24 =   Cat, Act, Chaff, Blade,

*25 =   Sea, "Pi", All, Area, A Act, A Chaff, Mecca,

*26 =   GOD, Eli, Mega, Och, Elah, 'I.Q.', Card, Flag, Lie, Aud, Bear, Mid, Data, Hide, Eat, Dog,

*27 =   Cain, Fu, Job, Code, Race, Lama, Red, Gas, Hand, Bike, Mahe, Hod{**8 in Cabala's Tree of Life}, Off, Headed,

*28 =   "OM", Man, We, Air, Call, Lamb, Is, Case, Read, A Code, Dio, Eden, Race,

*29 =   See, A Man, Black, Page, Bind, Ref, Lake, It,

*30 =   Bible, Baby, Day, Ark, Arch, Peace, Bread, Mamba, Him, Map,

*31 = Dagne, Old, Cash, Land, Jacob, Rage, Abijah, Safe, Her, Bell, Echo, Coal, Fall,

*32 = Life, Eve, M/C2, Bomb, Leo, Cock, Madam, She, Ram, Again, Cell, Jail, Arabia,
        Rabbi, Pig,

*33 = Aids, Gay, Fags, Find, Cheap, Magic, Bird, Seed, Rama, Amen, 'A life', "A-Cell",
        "A-Bomb",

*34 = Allah, One, Free, Dark, Fair, Faces, Hate, Cold, Grace, Basic, Binah, 'A Gay',

*35 = Image, Eye, Naked, Abram, Hagar, Rice, Aum, Atma (**Soul in Hindi & Sanskrit),

*36 = Law, 'OHM', Child, Come, Lode, Field, "S.A.P", 'S.o.B', Oil, His, Chip, Here, Heer, Juda, Feet, Hair, Coco, Anu (**Sanskrit word for Atoms),

*37 = Hell, Hades, Begin, Up, Side, Cheat, Seal, Rand, Called, Hex, Edom, Place,
        Dies, Demo, "E-M/C2", Feed-Back, Flame,

*38 = Death, Late, Dood, Same, Alike, Change, Balance, Adolf, Hated, Jew, Fire, Africa, Gold, Rich, Road, Plead, Alpha, Boat, Noah, Gland,

*39 = Ten, Angel, Angle, Vice, Dieu, May, Belt, Cobra, Belief, Cried,

*40 = David, Buddha, Mind, Hole, Pain, Food, Rape, Idol, Eloh, Dead-Data, Liar, Seek,
        Film, Nile, Dumb, Dogma, Bow, Blue, Obadiah, Jude, Harm,

*41 = Mom, Home, Key, Lock, Clue, Omega, King, Alien, Fuck, Apes, "U.S.A", Abaddon, Cow, Figs, Defeat, Awake, He-man, Dream, Good, Fun, Joke, Box, Blind, A liar,

*42 = Sin, New, Bitch, Lady, Boy, Fish, Nine, Five, Self, Hemp, Female, War, Gun, "U.F.O", 'A-Alien', Rebel, Radar, Tele, T.V., Rain, Aleph,

*43 = Mark, Wife, Goat, Arse, Was, Saw, Ears, March, Harp, Book, Choice, Define,
        Charm, Manna, "R.I.P", Left, False, Hot,

*44 = Abraham, Talk, Shake, Brain, Anno, Faith, Hope, Set, Week, Anti, Space, Cut, Kill, Judah, Old-age, Adonai, Hidden, Mask, Oath, A Choice, A Book, A Mark, Cancer,

*45 = GODS, Zen, Path, Bridge, Knife, East, Daniel, Shem, Anger, Fox, Lies, Filii, Bears, Flags, Leader, Wail, Milk, Cards, A cut,

*46 = Papal, Branch, Body, Drain, "G.S.T", Hands, Pipe, Hero, Dove, Deceased, Cry,

Mad-man, "S.A.R.& H", Greek, Aramaic, Bladder, Apex,

*47 = John, Seer, Time, Omen, Monad, Doom, Beast, Tri, Judge, Rock, Calls, Force, Save, Isaiah, Sarah, Yang, Legend, Dios, Caesar, Malachi, Lot, Middle, Radio, The Dead, Epoch,

*48 = James, Yin, Son, Cycle, Blood, Sex, Evil, Live, Tree, Ring, Craft, Thief, Long, Rude, Chord, Build, Wall, Veil, Pages, Pole, Amos,

*49 = Atom, Lord, "I am God", Danger, Green, Pro, Luke, Days, Tit, Aaron, Garden, Deus, Caffeine, Born, Poem, Sing, Sign, Logo, God-Made, In God, God-end, Apogee, Phase, Eight, Model,

*50 = Ma and Pa, Sacred, Circle, Vein, "I.N.R.I", Bells, Drug, Graph, Chart, Lands, Nato, Tomb, Paul, Ezra, June, Lion, America, Bush, Fight, Judo, Wind, Snake,

*51 = Reader, "A.E.I.O.U", The C.N.A, "The A.N.C", Michael, Homo, Mars, Indian, Top, Lent, Daily, Rome, Falcon, Preach, Avoid, Great, Fuse, Insha, Wave, Rise, Wine, Gifted, Feast, Issac, Seder, 'A circle',

*52 = Devil, Lived, Pope, Earth, Six, Xis, Seth, Heart, Form, Last, Flood, Terah, Salt, Birds, Names, Pride, Mass, Alter, Ship, Speak, Door, "Eli-Eli", "GOD-GOD", Seeds, "The Egg", Riddle, Pesach, Abracadabra, Nero, African,

*53 = Look, Nose, Run, Chicken, Basic Egg, Sheep, Velma, Womb, Blur, Mirage, Zol, Dagga-name, Dagga-seed, Magic-dagga, The Dagga, The "D.P", Grave, Coffin, Atlas, Saul, Many, Divide, Sabbath, Axis, One Egg, Free Adam, One "D.N.A", One Adam, One Idea, Cyber, Free Idea, Basic Idea,

*54 = Sun, Chemical, Love, Play, Eyes, Voice, Roof, Vagina, Rider, Ants, Tribe, Islam, Geneva, Man-God, French, Note, The Edge, Race-bike, Hand-bike, Gas-bike, Allon, Search, Trek, Bodies, "Acid-Head", Fanatic, Mind-dead,

*55 = Sky, Cloud, Grey, Less, Heaven, Satan, Watch, Pass, Diabolic, Laws, Awaken, The Ape, Trap, Escom, Wages, Fields, "Ohms", Dead-key, Dead-lock, Dead Clue, Dead Mom, Dead Home, Dead Fuck, A dead hole, A dead mind, Burn, Wire, Fused, A chemical,

*56 = Friend, Wolf, Shock, The end, Three, Light, Equal, Shell, Yoke, Seals, Ether, Rule, Created, Will, Poet, Paper, Attack, Member, Drink, Hindu, Alert, Karate, Index, Down, April, Deaf & Dumb, Sides, Comet, Flames, Black-Ball, Latin, A dead-lock,

*57 = Mandy, Human, Moon, Birth, Shark, Xmas, Bless, Mary, Ascribed, Wheat, Gemini, Lingo, Jews, Balances, Changes, The Act, The Cat, Divided, Roll, Steal, Boast, Sore, Dagne Aud, Nahum, Quod, Deaths, Sleep, Alight,

*58 = Science, Micro, Scope, Father, Albert, Night, Star, Two, Angles, Angels, Muse, Exit, Steam, Adult, God-Life, God-men, Abimelech, Zodiac, Roy, Ampere, Phone, Penned, Mudra (**Indian-dance), Sedated, A Human,

*59 = Dragon, Sickle, Slave, Shiva {**Lord of the Dance}, Koran, Donate, Minds, Dogmas, Copy, Double, Direct, Tasbih, Brass, Idols, Finger, Solid, Bicycle,

*60 = Pray, Holy, Pure, Verbal, Vow, Believe, Word, Magnet, Order, Police, Battle, Robber, Peace-day, Mob Peace, Mafia Peace, Bible Peace, Baby peace, Tune, Desire, Four, Diocese, Active,

*61 = N.E.W.S., Roman, Church, Anglican, Heathen, Miracle, Atomic, Mush, Room, News, Ascribed, Sins, "U.F.O's", Chakras, To Mega, God-Image, You, God-Eye,

*62 = Papacy, Jehowa, Cardinal, Hebron, Queen, Sense, Black-magic, Black-seed, Ruin, Looked, Hour, Forehead, Action, Rest, Vote, Ballot, Books, Torah, Gloria, Gott, Adonis, Elohim, Critic, All Failed, Doubt, Medicine, Mauve, Plasma, Cosmic, Digital, Signal, Pause,

*63 = Divine, Diety, Godly, Plant, Saint, Roger, Genetic, Penis, Eleven, Friday, Konrad, Nehemiah, Crowd, Public, Trip, Flash-Back, Record, Brains, Cancer D.N.A., Shakes, Weeks, The Bible, "Y.H.W.H", The Map, Aids-Baby, Baby-Seed, Porn, Obscene, Witch, Stare, Smoke, Backward, Whole, Mahadevi, Pilate, Limit,

*64 = Peter, Coward, Dust, Zero, Israel, Poor, Lazy, True, Sammael, Domini, Zion, Watt, Unit, Bright, Ohmere, Infant, Piggy, Anti-dagga, Dagga-brain, Cabala-brain, Captain, Dagga-oath, Cabala-oath, A-limit, A stain, A dagga mark,

*65 = Solar, Centre, Seven, White, Horse, Cosmo, The Life, Token, Show, Music, Breast, Alphabet, Finish, Mental, State, Beyond, Perigee, Life Seed, Magic Life,

*66 = Queer, Judges, Women, Neron, Mankind, Cain and Abel, Wedding, Curse, Swear, Bury, Ancient, Envy, Alcohol, Sugar, Saves, Times, Monads, Legends, Pro-acid, Green-acid, Atom acid, Acid-danger, Lost, Liver, Forces, Family, Figure, Twin, Freedom, Mad cycle, Head cycle, Crime Head, Back-a-Crime, Evil Hade, Radium, Fishes, Length, Dual-man, Ammonia,

*67 = Water, Urine, Alchemy, Good and Bad, Evidence, Hurt, Mantra, Soul, Receive, Copies, Theos, Netsah (**7 In the Cabala Tree of Life), Mediaval, Touch, Ruth, Ishmael, West, Parole, Trees, Cycles, Blood-D.N.A., Mandrake, Honey, Pinis,

*68 = Diabolical, Language, Quella, Eminence, Pardon, Tixo, July, Nuns, Married, Atoms, Quark, Yesod[9], Decipher, Signs, Albumen, Ageless, X-ray, The Eye, The Image, Agrippa, Sweat,

*69 = Bishop, Knight, Check-mate, Jigsaw, Husband, Whore, Archangel, Message, Text, Red-tape, Released, Pandora, Ghost, "O.T./N.T", Jehovah, Yahveh, People, Animals, Darwin, Jungle, The Law, The S.A.P., The S.O.B., Piglet, Cat and Dog, Pedigree, Tombs, Tuth, Snakes, 'I Believe', Mom and Dad, Worm, Graphs, Circles,

Drugs, Heroin, Modern, Mechanical, Labour, Fatigue, Broker, Forks, Umbilic,
Dynamic, Antenna, Arsenic, Helium, Spacing, Rifles, All Space, Sea Space, Modimo,
Volt, Primal, Brain Area, Jeremiah, Hand-gun, Foist

*70 =   Darrell, Shadow, Adam and Eve, Lilith, Yahweh, Homo-Adam, Incest, Anti-
Och, Proof, Suicide, Readers, Fig tree, Galaxy, Naked Image, Naked Eye, Eye-Image,
Post, A Red-Tape, Stop, Robot, Falcons, Essence, The being, Demons,

*71 =   Temple, "I Think", "I Doubt", Zeus, Moses, Talmud, Qur'an, Googol,
The Balance, The Change, The Same, The Jew, The Fire, The Gold, The Alpha,
Orion, Ovum, Sperm, Chapter, Tear-gas, Popes, Devils, Celebrate, Catholic, Babylon,
Desert, Bowls, Barrier, Tube-End, Blood End, In Blood, Crime End, Sex-End, In-Sex,
Recycle, Tree-end, In-Ring, Ring-in, Crime-end,

*72 =   First, Origin, World, Money, Hitler, Reborn, Chickens, Looks, Slut, The
Cobra, The Vice, The Angle, Live cat, Evil cat, Sex cat, Tom cat, Marriage, School,
Hashish, The Dead Sea, Radius, Magnetic, Moody, Gentile, Monday, Shaitan, A
Barrier, The Team, The Meat, Aids Team, One Jew, Free Adolf, Jew Hate, Dark Jew,
Fair Jew,

*73 =   Number, Count, Sacrifice, Children, Paradise, Kingdom, The Mind, Stone,
The Buddha, The Food, The Pain, Life Key, Home Life, The Hole, Sexy,
Orgasm, Living, Sound, Good Life, Circus, Unbalance, Eye Balance, Empiric,
Ezekiel, Joseph, Egypt, Front, Shrine, Perfect, Prefect, Lungs, Vaginas, Commit,
Flying, Surface

*74 =   God Son, The King, The Omega, Jesus, Messiah, Muhammad, Lucifer,
Duiwel, Escom's, Nuclear, Energy, Burns, The Clue, The Home, The Key, The Lock,
Cross, Point, Donkey, The Joke, "I.V.X.L.C.D", Joshua, Hazrat, The Dream, Bitter,
Occult, Heavens, Clouds, Traps, Photo, Moves, The Cow, The Tika, Gematria,
Parables, New Life, Fish Life, Self-life, Sin life, War life, Gun-cock, Jewish, English,
Eighty, Between, Dialogue, Drug act, Opium, The Wide, Preacher, Hexagon, Ruler,
Proud, Hippy, Families, Fruit, Tempt, The Fuck, Refuse, Parent, Gospel, Hade's Seal,
Elohite, Queen bee, Angular, Aurora, Stuck, Aids Fuck,

*75 =   Diameter, Doctor, Madness, Suffer, Eternal, Paranoia, Distance, Critical,
Nobody, Analogy, Analogical, Infra red, A cross, One King, Sun beam, Electric,
Reform, The New, The Self, Mandrax, Hari-kari, Marry, Lawful, Law Vice, Law
Team, Deaf and Dumb, Death seal, Death & Hades, Death & Hell, Fire & Hell,
Octagon, Poets, Write, Cults, The Sin, Comets, Lights, Spiral, Immune,

*76 =   Master, A Doctor, Divorce, Split, Salary, Scholar, Invoke, Anti-bomb, Anti-
Life, Anti-jail, Xmas, Revenge, Driver, Addition, Safety, Graffiti, Magazine, Contact,
Moon Egg, Human-Egg, Birth Egg, Prick Egg, A Puss, Human Adam, Kosher,
Human D.N.A., Human Idea, A Human Head, Prove, Humans, Exotic, The Book,
Divided D.N.A., Inertia, Analogue, Lingual,

*77 =   Adam Kadmon, The God-Head, Christ, God's Life, God's Agenda, Yehowa,
Power, Disciple, Identical, Hexagram, Glory, Taught, Elixir, Zaboor, Allegany,
Atnatu, Moslem, Rehoboam, Zodiacs, Forbidden, Judaism, Muses, Valley, Fathers,

The Oath, The Mask, The Hidden, Court, Scopes, Nights, Stars, Things, Matter, Stands, The Week, The Brain, Rama Karma, Law Key, Law Home, Law Clue, Law Lock, "Mind-a-Law", Mind-a-Child, Child Dream, Child Key, Home Child, Mom & Child, Funeral, Exist, Orbital, Chemist, Vibrate, Known,

*78 =   Genesis, Start, Embryo, Hade's Home, Earth God, Devil God, God Lived, Porno, Pope God, Pope Lie, Pope Dog, "I am Satan", Crucified, The Path, God's Name, Sabachtani, Mental-age, White I.D., Slaves, Rouse, God's Aids, Acquired, Alcoholic, October, Calculate, Mistake, Accessible, Repent, Selfish, A Chemist, Lock-up, Fuck-up, Hannukah, Ellipse, Galaxies, Solids, Electro,

*79 =   Mother, Nature, Moeders, Mommy, Granny, Virgin, Words, Sword, Scroll, Listen, Hymns, Magnets, Navigate, Nirvana, "In the End", Murder, Secular, Mortal, Zechariah, My Dream, Same Dream, Dream Alike, Begin a Dream, Begin a Home, Stomach, Cyber-God, My Home, My Key, My Lock, My Clue, My Mom, Holy Ra, Believes, Alpha & Omega, Flower, Super, Loving, Your, Disobey, Death Dream, Death Home, Death Key, A Death Hole, Balance a Mind, Change a Mind, Yahuwa, Bacillus, Dead-Centre, Life of God,

*82 =   Saints, Records, Minute, Rainbow, Sexual, Clothes, Free-Sex, Plants, Free Blood, Erudite, Tauraat, Revised, Young, Tongue, Innocence, Apartheid, Backwards, Genetics, Utopia, Life-Span, Image of God, Eye of God, Hippies, Echo-Wave, Crowds, Public-Idea, Sacred Life, Bush Life, Life Circle, Primate,

*83 =   Wisdom, Dowism, Bhagavad Gita, Sabbath Day, Bible Sabbath, Bread Sabbath, The Hadith, Faithful, Spring, Book of Adam, Mark of Adam, Book of D.N.A., Author, Monkey, Psychic, Perceive, Circuit, Creative, Gifted Life, Gifted Eve, Narcotic, South, Negative, Divine Dagga, Dagga Plant, Cabala Plant, The Circle, Deficiency, The Lion, The I Ching, Germany, Gestapo, Concrete, Real Time, Real Monad, Time Law, Time Field, Law Legend, Law Judge, S.A.P. Judge,   S.A.P. Monad, S.A.P. Force, The Dead-Law,

*84 =   God Father, God Science, God Star, Dog Star, Hade's Time, Begin Time, Time-Up, A Real Time, A Real Legend, A Law Judge, A Real Judge, Hell Judge, Al Qur'an, Sunday, Cosmos, Moabites, Pluto, Centres, Whites, Horses, Tokens, Colour, Catatonia, Invent, Lawyer, Half Moon, Half Human, Human Race, Human Hand, Harness, Human Code, A Law of God, A Child of God, Cronos, Forward, Repeats, Lecture, Abstract, Chlorine,

*85 =   The Pope, The Devil, The Earth, The Six, The Xis, Insha Allah, Sentence, Biology, Bi-energy, Nought, Bottom, Creation, Malkuth[10], Churches, "I Split", Burning, The Riddle, Aids Riddle, Name Riddle, Magic Riddle, God Shiva, Circular, Matrix, Sacred Image, Sacred Eye, Naked Circle, Script, Presence, Identified, Biological,

*86 =   Brother, Voodoo, Compass, Pyramid, Tri-angle, Trigram, Symbol, Formula, Souls, God's Key, God's Home, Holy God, Pure God, Magnet God, Pharaohs, Mantras, Convict, The Black Cat, Infinite, Omega Path, Home Path, The Atlas, Key Leader, Home Leader, A Mind Leader, Temurah, Oppose, Fraction, Above Key, Statue, King Above, Above Home, Mom Above, The Sabbath, Chicken Seed, The

Chicken, The Run, The Look, Free Salt, One Earth, Allah Lived, Lived Free, One Pope, One Devil, The Blur, The Mirage, The Grave, Epistle, Anabolism (**The constructive processes within the Protoplasm...which eventually becomes a Living Matter), Police Dog, Blind's Dog, Pure Dog, Roman Sea, News Area, All News, Hade's Logo, Logo Feed-Back, Atom Feed-Back, Logo Seal, Hell Born, Begin a Crime, Crime Balance, Death Crime, Same crime, Gold Crime, Crime Change, Blood-Change, Blood Balance, Sex Change, My Son?, For a Girl?, Like-a-Son?, Diabolical Head, Death Trade, Gold Trade, Trade Balance, 'Exchanged a Dead',

*87 =   Justice, Nothing, Twelve, The Sun, The Chemical, The Love, The Eyes, Priest, The Images, Natural, Donour, The Search, The Trek, The Knock, The Voice, Muslim, Birthday, Birth-date, Baby Birth, Moon Day, Mad People, Unique, Lotus, Initiate, In-breeding, Different, Person, Languages, Russia, Time Scale, Mind of God, Church God, Mind the Dead, Mind Judge, Mind Monad,

*88 =   Gontier, Guldvog, Begotten, Iesous, Immanuel, Dream of God, Vision, Life & Light, Hormone, A Priest, Sanity, Smoking, Marijuana, Cigarette, Inflammable, Volts, Electrical, Apostle, Empathy, The Laws, Policeman, Thieves, Left Path, Volume, Crime Scale, Crime Mind, Sex Mind, Evil Mind, Live Mind, Eclipses, Kometes, Doctrine, One Sun, One Love, One Voice, Free Voice,

*89 =   Solveig, Life and Death, Unity, Therion, Titus, August, The Hindu, Hindu Seed, Religion, Fig Trees, Regulate, The Black Race, Summer, Winter, Provide, Yesus, The attack, The Past, The Light, The Friend, The Wolf, The Yoke, The Will, Shadows, Memory, A holy Man, Tribune, Anatomy, Incubus, Study, A Cigarette, Nicotine, Complete, "I Love God", Wycliffe, Musician, Alleluya, Mystic, Osiris, Virus, Parasite, Insects, Sequence, A Police man, Church Man, News   Man, Key of God, Di-Electric, Dynamics, Photon, Complex, Massive, Nameless, Fungus, Hologram,

*90 =   The Moon, The Birth, Human Name, Human Seed, Human AIDS, One Light, Dark Light, Fair Light, Holy Bible, Holy Baby, Holy Map, Holy Day, Holy Date, Matthews, January, Sister, Thunder, Locust, Opposed, Sphinx, Eye Object, The Naked lead, The Naked Ape, Book of God, Epilogue, Missing, Mosque, Oxygen, Autumn, Vertical, Genetic Code, Brethren, Object Image,

*91 =   Radiation, Fission, Formulae, Theory, Darkness, Future, Objective, Honour, Creature, Phoenix, Live Charm, Evil Charm, War Lord, New Lord, New Atom, New Danger, War Danger, Self Danger, Mirror, Men's Mind, Life's Mind, Life's Hole, Life's Food, The Star, The Father, The Science, THe Scope, The Micro, The Zodiac, Tattoo, Genealogy, Glitter, Prison, New Born, Born New, Self -Born, War Born, Fish Atom, Spirit, Emotion, Delirium, Democratic, Asteroid, Change of Life, Death of Life, Balance of Life, The Calendar,

*92 =   'I am who I am', "Am I who I Am", Numbers, Counts, Identify, Picture, Life's Key, Life's Clue, Life's Home, Mom's Life, King's Life, Electron, Horror, Reverse, Latitude, Altitude, Circulate, Sea-water, Pentagon, Nakedness, Heavenly, The Koran,

Yellow, Telegraph, Rhythm, The Copy, The Double, The Third, The Dragon, The Slave, Philemon, Messianic, Celeritas,

*93 =   Sacred Book, Sacred Mark, Child Birth, Law Birth, Human Law, Editorial, Saturn, Harvest, Parents, Regulated, Love Angle, Love Team, Love Mate, Chemical Team, Voltare, Lost race, Disturb, Coloured, Physical, Penalty, Convent, The Vow, The Word, The Pure, The Holy, Holy Name, Holy Seed, Gospels, Errors, Propaganda, News Media, News Life, News Agenda, Conquer, Nazareth, Lived and Died, Died and Lived, Angel Gabriel,

*94 =   Unicorn, Black & White, Six & Nine, Nine & Six, Six & Five, Third Eye, Third Image, Eight Fold, Esoteric, Guilty, Likeness, Relation, Inspired, Churchill, The News, Micro Chip, Science Law, Science Field, Micro-Ohm, Death and Hades, Death and Hell, Fire and Hell, The Old Bible, Maximum, Human being, Human Hell, A Human Child, A Human Law, Doctors, Cemetary, Friction, November, Reforms, Harmony, Matzos, Uranus, Covenant, Iscariot, Appolos, Mind's Eye; Mind's Image, Man & Woman, Jehovite, Passive, Distances, Bull-Shit, The Eye God, The God Image, The Naked God, Resonance, Vertex, Magnitude,

*95 =   Tribute, Life Record, The Bible Life, Divine Life, Diety Life, Godly Life, Saint Life, Bomb Record, Plant Life, Plant Cell, The Baby Life, The Baby cell, Life-Trip, Love Key, Love Clue, Love Fuck, Pregnant, Sun Key, Sun Home, A Sun Hole, Chemical Key, Chemical Lock, Fanaticism, Pentagram, Hierachy, Hierarchical, Invokes, The Black Magic, The Black Name, The Black Bird, Halloween, Flash-back Life, Tuesday, Drivers, Convicted, Revenges, Scholars, Result, Masters, The Action, Proves, Neptune, Promise, Gomorrah, Almighty, Whole Life, Whole-cell, Nucleus, Discover, Magnet image, Magnet eye, Holy image, Holy eye, Naked word, Active image, Geometric, Number Deal, The Axiom,

*96 =   Freemason, Satanism, Courts, Judicial Code, Judicial Race, Judicial Job, The Malleable, The S.A.P. Code, The S.A.P. Race, Blue Light, Uniform, Whistle, Gun Hand Code, The Public, Society, Moslems, Star Balance, Death Science, Gold Science, Same Science, Same Father, Father Alike, A. Einstein, Decimal and Digit, Same Albert, Hydrogen, War Chemical, New Chemical, Mustard, An Atom Bomb, An Atom cell, Jew Father, Jew Science, Jewish Lead, Cross Lead, Messiah Deal, "I'm Jesus", "I'm Messiah", "I'm Lucifer", "I'm Energy", "I'm The Omega", Father Alpha, "A Son of God", "I'm God Son", Code of Crime, Code of Blood, The Genetic, Blood Cycle, Live-Blood, Evil Blood, Race of Blood, Groups, "A,B,A+B,O-Blood Code",
'H.I.V. Map Code', H.I.V.Vaccine, "M.K. Ultra", 'A.Z.T. Pill', Doom Pill, Drugs Code, Dr. Doom Code, Mr Death Code, Funerals, Stella Base, Durban C.B.D. Code, Mr. Rich Hand, Visa Cards, Mr Africa Code, Rhodes Code, Smith Code, Hendrik Code, Timol Code, Hector Code, Mandela's Code, "A 27 Years", "A Long Time", Madiba's Time, Madiba's Legend, Madiba's Omen, S.A. Master, The Naked Man, Double Mode, Stores, Knowledge, Faculties, The Brains, Cerebellum,
A medulla base, A Root Base, The Spine, The Butt, The Bum Base, Male Orifice, The Penis, The Bone Base, In Muscle, Sacred Branch, The Limb Base,
The Feet Base, Back-ground, Home-Soil, Mom's Child, Mom's Law, Numerical,

In Number, Worded Code, In Stone, Text Hand, Was God Hand, Oscillate,
Look Left, Left Wing, Divided Angle, Kyk Tyd, Doing Time, Oos & Wes, Ons Son,
Ons Wet, Red Sun Face, Sun Tail, Sun's End, Doom's Day, "Y.2.K. Science",
'Y.2.K Calendar', "Y.2.K. Star", Alpha-Bravo, Noah's Team, Team's Boat,
Doom's Ark, Hot and Cold, Atlantis, Return, A Promise, February, Boastful,
Pymander, The Avatar, The Medusa, Snakes Code, The Hair Base, Snake Park,
"A Snake Pit", A-Black Cobra Code, Fat Worm, Fat Red Lady, Fat Whore, Play-Boy,
Play Bitch, Play Lady, Singable Code, Operama-Code, Beethoven, Musical Head,
Off-Beat Key, Music Echo, Time's Atom, Time Speed, Speed Monad, High Revs,
Slow Code, Slow Race, Model "T" Race, "T"-Shape Base, Hand Cart Race, New
Engine, Toyota, Isuzu, Fairmont, Auto Team, Auto Vice, Auto Garage, Hoopers,
Barons Code, Samcor Code, Auto-Net, Human Net, Shark Net, Web-Net Base,
"Inter-Web", Binary-Code, W.W.W.-Code, Digital-C.D. Code, Density, Vibrates,
Invariance, Coincident, Conjugate, Adam in Love, Chemical in Idea, Danie Craven,
Mind Light, A Hierarchy, A Dog Pedigree, "Elan Vital {**The Creative Force of
Life), Vital Life, Projected, Genius of, Genius at, That Alone, Algebra Circle,

*97 =   Supreme, Control, Over-Hell, Begin-Over, Red Stop, Serpent, Injury, Fuse
Link, Police Hell, A Police Law, Blood of Man, Man of Crime, Born Thief, A Police
Child, Crime Born, Son of Man, Sex Atom, Sex Lord, Foreskin, Protect, Nuntis, A
Liars Seal, Gene Marker, Broad-Sheet, The Zero, The Unit, Fair Ratio, Godly One,
Divine Allah, Rouses, Hinduism, Hindu King, Scandinavia, Gethsemane, Holy Hell,
Holy Hades, Man Prayed, Orderly, Equator, Kyrios, Sukkot, Mangu-Mola, Yu Huang,
Present, A Date and Time, Protein, Uranium, Atom Cycle, Blood Born, A Playboy, A
Fat whore, A Sexist, A Red Bishop, A Red Knight, Plagiarise, The American,
American Name, American Seed, American Aids,

*98 =   Alpha and Omega, The Alphabet, The Centre, Prophet, God Himself,
        Life and Time, Life and the Dead, The Dead's Agenda, Life's Monad,
        Muhummed, Deliverer, A Serpent, Angel of Death, Angle of Death,
        Balance of Angle, Change of Angle, Balance of Ten, Change of Ten,
        Change of Team, Police Change, Police alike, Police Death, Same Police,
        Same Order, Change Order, Balance Word, Change Word, Death Vow,
        Holy Death, A balance of balance, Symbolic, Criminals, Mission, Scrolls,
        Lysergic, Mortals, Rosetta, Virgins, Chosen One, Chosen Fair, Free chosen,
        Exorcise, Film Star, Film Science, Film's Team, Aryan-Team, Falsetto,
Soprano,
        Crystal, The Head of God,

*99 =   Judgement, Nero Caesar, Up-right, Thirteen, Letters, Mustapha, Ascension,
        The Octave, Current, Minarets, Bhagavat Gita, The Woman, The Queer,
        The Judges, The Twin, The Dual Man, Artistic, The Fishes, Cain and Abel
seed,
        The Ancient, The Times, The Curse, The Wedding, Sun Path, Love Path,
        Chemical-path, God's Love, East Sun, Green Bush, Green Circle, Danger
Circle,
        Atom Circle, Sacred Atom, Atom Graph, Logo Chart, Sacred Logo, Sacred
Lord,
        Sacred...I am God, "I'm a sacred God", Elliptical, Fossils, Thought, One
Centre,

Free Centre, One Alphabet, Dark Centre, One White, Dark White, White Hate,

*100= Star War, Science War, New Science, New Star, New Father, Father Self,
Sin Father, God and Satan, God's Sky, God's Heaven, God Jesus,
Messiah God, The Omega God, The God King, The God Mom,
God and Heaven, Star Fish, Analysis, Styles, Holy Buddha, Holy David,
Mind Word, Magnet Mind, Pure Mind, Holy Food, Pure Food, Inflation,
Mezuzah,
Breviary {**Roman Mass Book}, Hospital, Wednesday, Parousia, Holograph,
Telescope, Primary, Time-Machine, The Dead Machine, Machine Monad,
Boundary, Sacred Circle, A Sacred Lord,

*101= Skeleton, Immortal, Invisible, Calcination, Compound, Vis-a-Vis, Body and
Bone,
Division, Suction, Magnetism, M/C Squared, Nuclear Code, Energy Code,
Gospel Code, Nuclear Gas, Side-by-Side, Both-Sides, Hade's by Hell,
Grave-Yard, Dogmatism, Blasphemy, Last Days, Ultimate, Minutes, Interval,
Doubtful, Gateways, In-accessible, Lock and Key, Home and Key, Mom's
Home,
Mom's Key, Mom's Lock, Mom's Clue, Omega's Key, King's Omega,
Offer & Wave, Vertices, Identikit, Melchizedek, Magnet Key, Magnet Lock,
Magnet Clue, Singular, An Angel of God, The Albumen, Blood of Life,
Cycle of life, Tree of Life, Tree of Eve, Sex of Eve, Life of Sex, Red Cross,
Cross Base, Hand-Cross, The Market, Full Circle, Three Gods, God's Light,
God's Past, Three Path, The Dead Race Code, Time Race Code, Race Time
Code, Sun Time, The Married, The Dead Love, Chemical Monad, The Icon
Code, Lingulate, English Code,

*102 = Vicarius, Name in Papal, Seed in Papal, Said in Aramaic, Said in Greek,
Name in Greek, Seed in Branch, Branch in Name, Aids in Greek, Evil Love,
Sex Love, Sex Chemical, Love Cycle, Blood Chemical, Sun Cycle, Love Evil,
Love Tree, Love Ring, Geography, Inner-Self, Lecturer, Version, Authors,
Grammaton, Time's Law, Time's Child, Ancient Child, Ancient Law, Judges
Law,
Judges Child, Queer Child, Queer Law, Doom's Law, The Snakes, The Worm,
The Husband, Principle, Space Warp, Brain Warp, Brain Science,
Cancer Science, A Book Science, Gravity, Dimension, Voltaire, The Drugs,
Nitrogen, The Law Aids, Sacred Heart, Scared Heart, Slavery, Exorcised,
Flash-Light, Straight,

*103 = Diffusion, Satellite, Moon-Body, Human-Body, Birth-Body, Solomon,
Mercury,
Apocrypha, Student, Politics, Swatsika, East Star, Star-path, God's Science,
Star Gods, The Fig-Tree, Adam and Eve Seed, The Naked Image,
The Eye-Image, Sun Atom, Chemical Atom, Chemical Danger, Green Sun,
Green Chemical, New News, War News, New Church, Church War, Church
Sin,
Church Boy, Church Lady, News Lady, News Bitch, New News, Circumcise,

Love Lord, Love Danger, Numbering, Numerals, Enlightened, The Naked Eye,
Colours, Fussion, Blown-up, Hell Blown, Sun Sign, Love Sign, A Cupid Sign,
The Demons, Time Flow, The Dead Flow, Wolf Monad, The Dead Wolf,
The Dead Past, Past Time, The Dead Will, Free Wealth, Wealthy Dad,

*104 = Big-Brother, Marxist, Head Brother, Mad Brother, Brother Hade, Anti-Word,
Anti-Vow, Anti-Order, Anti-Police, Police Brain, Police Cancer, Experience,
The Googol, Subtract, Last Flood, Earth Flood, Last Pope, Devil Pope,
The Aids Death, The Said Death, The Amen Balance, The Name Change,
Pervert, Pope's Name, Pope's Seed, Pope's Aids, Jerusalem, Integrated,
Scripts, Blue Movie, In the Blood, In the Sex, Aids in Sex, The Sex-end, End
the   Cycle, In the Son, The in-Sex, Observer, A Pope's Life, Electronic, Digital
T.V.,
Digital War, War Signal, New Signal, T.V. Signal, Tele-Signal, Signalling,
Mafia Cross, Mafia Energy, Baby Cross, Baby Messiah, Baby Jesus,
The Bible King, The Bible Key, The Bible Clue, A Devil's Life, Eve's a Devil,
Life's a Devil, Back To Earth,

*105 = Pyramids, Tri-angels,Tri-angles, Time's Angle, Formulas, Fractions, Times
Ten,
Chapter-One, One Chapter, Free Chapter, Desert Camel, One Desert,
Cold-Desert, Desert Hate, Free Desert, Desert Allah, Allah Temple,
Camel Temple, Opposes, Plagiarism, The Evil Act, The Live Act, The Blood
Act,
The Crime Act, The Sex Act, The Sex Cat, The TOM cat, Hierograph,
Pantheism, Neurotic, The Black Book, The Book Ref., See the Book,
The Book Page, The Page Mark, Mark the page, The Black Mark,
Mark one man, Free Man March, Mad person, Saviour, God in Three,
Horizon,
The Mirages, The Looks, The Chickens, The First, The Origin, The World,
Free the Eggs, Free the Adam Egg, The one D.N.A. egg, Radio-Star,
Radio Science, The Dead Star, The Dead Father, Monad Father,
Science Monad, Father Time, Time Science, Time Scope, Time Star,
Time Warp, Time Loop, A body warp, Wrap a body, Nano meter, Man Power,
Bureacracies, "A BIG-bother", Brother Adam, God in Light, Light Lord,
Light Atom,

*106 = Human Lord, Human Atom, Birth Atom, Human Danger, A Human Cycle,
"A-Human Crime", A Human Blood, A Moon Cycle, Musical Beat, Musical
Air,
Musical Man, Genesis Man, A Christ Man, Ref. Adam Kadmon, Identity,
Chronicles, Arithmetic, Mathematical, The Number, The Children,
Name Sacrifice, The Kingdom, Name in Vein, Aids in vein, Persons,
Birthdays,
Birth dates, Name Number, Century, Muslims, Adultery, A Life Number,
Infinity,
Holy Body, Holy Dove, Holy Branch, Holy Pipe, Pure Body, Magnet body,
Police Body, Police Hero, Police Girl, News Path, God's News, Bridge-News,

News Fox, Times Table, Collective, His Man hood, Pendulum, Initiates,
Exorcism, Acceleration, Air Travel, Travel Man, Born Human, A Travel Race,
Al'uzzas, Shavuot,

*107 = Circumcised, Penis Cut, Divine Cut, Vow of God, Word of God, The Messiah,
The Omega Name, The God Son, The Live God, The God Tree, The God
Cycle,

Jesus Name, The Cross, Energy name, Energy seed, The Energy, Aids Cross,
Hormones, Breath of Life, Doctrines, Cross Name, Cross Seed, Treasure,
Atonement, Eternal Life, Theology, Theological, God the Son, Second Time,
Second Beast, Holy Monad, Magnet monad, The Dead Word, Police Force,
Magnet Force, Pure Force, Holy Force, A Slave Force, Right Path, Under-
dogs,

Photons, Quantum, Nuclear Aids, Nuclear Seed, Nuclear-Name, Repellent,
Begin Man-hood,

*108= Holy Vehm {**Freemason's order of Initiation}, Police Cycle, Police Son,
Police Crime, Police Sex, Police Blood, Police Tree, Police Ring, Evil Police,
A Police Monad, A Police Judge, A Police Legend, One Dead Police,
Police Yard, Funerary, Sin Figure, Self Figure, Judges Self, New Judges,
War Judges, Lady Judges, Sun Rider, Fish-Figure, Figure-Nine, Five Figure,
Sequences, Rastafarian, Descendants, Worship, Religion, "Oikoumene",
Anno Domini, The Diameter, Interior, The Distance, The Arrow, The Skull,
The Doctor, Geometry, Geometrical, Invariant, Full-Moon, Seychells,
'I am The Pope', 'I am the Earth', 'I am Earth Seed', "Am I the Devil?",
God created God, Instinct, The Deaf and Dumb, Good and Evil, The Lord
God,

The God Atom, The North, Live Magnet, Magnet Cycle, Word Cycle,
Magnet Blood, Musicians, Friendship, Generation, Magnetic Field, Collision
Magnetic Ohm, World Field, World Law, First Law, Law Origin, Bi-direction,

*109 = The Hidden Life, The Hidden Agenda, Hidden Centre, Omni-Star, Omni-
Science,   Omni Father, Light of Life, Life of Light, Life Matter, Christ Life,
Adam Kadmon Life, The God Head Life, Binary Mind, The Brain Cell,
The Brain Life, Cell Matter, Life's Stand, Sun shine, Sun Burn, Star wave,
Science Wave, The C.N.A. Science, Homo Star, Homo Science, Homo Father,
Saturday, Ammonites, Magnet Atom, Lode Stone, Mosques, Written,
Rasoldavel, Inspires, Purity, Word Atom, Holy Atom, Pure Atom, Police
Lord,

Police a crime, Scorpion, Mulungu, Locusts, Court-Agenda, Court-Cell,
Taught again, The Deaf and Blind, Child Sacrifice, Child Count, Law Count,
Law Paradise, Child Paradise, Umbilic-cord, Jehovah Mind, The Law Mind,
Mind on-line, The Driver, Buddha on-line, Food on Mind, Food on-line,
Pain on mind, Mind on Mind, Mind see Mind, Mind Page Mind, Mind-ref.-
Mind,

*110 = The Christ, The God-Head Name, Adolf Hitler, Sun Light, Chemical Life,
Chemical Agenda, Fish eat Fish, Fish eat Self, Self eat Self, Self ate Fish,
Dawn of Time, Dawn of the Dead, New Logo D.N.A., NEWS LOGO,
The Dead Diety, News Atom, New Language, War Language, Self Language,
A Language Key, "A Language Omega", A Home Language, Saint John,

Young-Man, Tradition, Something, Father Earth, Earth Science, Pope Father,
Timothy, Summary, Vibration, Mirrors, The Moslems, The Scopes, The
Power,
The Glory, The Zodiacs, The Sciences, Father's Name, Apollyon, Meteorite,
The Forbidden, The Said Oath, The Aids Oath, The Magic Oath, Such is Life,
Space and Time, Godly of God, Area of Zero, All of Zero, Pi of Zero,
Sea of Israel, Zero Body, Israel Branch, God's Centre, God's Alphabet,
Centre Path, Centre Bridge, God in You, The Muses, The Identical, Time-
Trax,
Tritium, Meditation, News Atom, Lie in News, Asteroids, Partless,
The Light Beam, The Light Edge,

*111 = Computer, The Crucified, The Genesis, The Start, Electrons, Life's Keys,
News Circle, Life's Locks, Under Danger, Under Atom, Life's Dreams,
Eve's Vow, Life's Word, Life's Omegas, Witchcraft, Divine Craft, Diety Craft,
Godly Craft, Diety Cycle, Diety Blood, Divine Blood, Divine Son, Diety Tree,
Divine Sex, Godly Thief, Police Cells, A Police Circle, Homo Police, Kaffir
Police,
Kaffir Vow, Kaffir Word, Pure Kaffir, A Kaffir Slave, Indian Police, African-
Coolie,
African Liars, A Indian Slave, African Makula, Split Image, "Who's Who?",
White Body, White Hero, White Branch, White Girl, White Dove, Body
Centre,
Obituary {**Relating to the Death of a Person...a Death Register}, Illusion,
Number Balance, Number Change, Same Number, Perfect Balance,
Perfect Change, Perfect Death, Death Sacrifice, Death Count, Gold Count,
Rich Count, Number Africa, Count Africa, Count Balance, Perfect Alike,
Count Alpha, Sacrifice Change, Sacrifice Africa, Gymnastic, The Mental Age,
The White Age, The White I.D., Strength, Sorceries, Calculation, The Devil
God,
The Earth God, The African God, The Pope God, The Pope Lie, The Pope
Flag,
God Name Lived, AIDS Lie Lived, African Aids Lie, The African Dog,
African Bark code, Insanity, Pictures, "Here and There", Exotic-Image,
Exotic-Eye, Master Eye, Master Image, A Free Master, Free-a-Master,
A Fair Master, Master Aum, Rice Master, Heaven and Hell, Formulate,
Death Sacrifice, Late Sacrifice, Dodo Sacrifice, The Aids Path, Queer Path,
Judges Bridge, Judge's Lies, The Embryo, Human Chemical, Birth Chemical,
Human-Love, Moon & Sun, Human Voice, Rhythms, Book of the Dead,
Mark of the Dead, Mark-of-Time, Mark of the Beast' {*111 x 6 = 666},
Mark of Time, March of Time, March of The Dead, Mark of Monad,
Greek Alphabet {"A & O"}, Alpha and Omega 'I.D.', Alpha and Omega Age,
Zero Time, Israel Time, Sun Birth, Chemical Birth, Moon's Image,
Human Chemical, Oxidation, Free Christ, One Christ, Allah Christ, Stands
Free,
Stands One, Free Matter, Coat of Arms, Linguist, Numericom,

*112 = Christ Image, Christ Eye, Glory Image, Victory, Imagination, Delirious,
Potential,
Eternally, Coloureds, Dichotomy {**A division into two parts}, Door-Keeper,

'A place called Hell', A place called Hades, Rotation, Propagandas, Telepathy,
Mathematics, Liturgical, Divinity, Our Father, Our Star, Our Scope, Our
Micro,

Our Science, Chemical Science, Chemical Father, A Chemical Birth,
A Prick Chemical, A Human Chemical, Alpha-Omega Name,
Alpha-Omega Seed, Alpha-Omega Aids, Aids Nature, Gay Nature, Nature
Seed,

Secular Aids, Magic Words, Magic Nature, Nature's Dead, Dead Mothers,
Ma's Mother, Granny Name, Earth Magnet, Pope Vow, Change Jesus,
Alike Jesus, Jesus Death, Moves Alike, Death Cross, Messiah Death,
Nuclear Balance, Nuclear Fire, Energy Balance, Energy Fire, "Escom's Fire",
East and West, Cross change, Electric Hell, Electric's Head, Hade's Diameter,
Critical Balance, Critical-Side, Critical Seal, Distance Flame, Critical Feed-
Back,

Doctor Dies, Doctor Hell, Hex-Doctor, Doctor Edom, Suffer Hell,
The Dead Centre, The Dead White, White Monad, White Doom, Time Centre,
Doom Centre, The Dead Alphabet, Alphabet Monad, The Life of God,
Pyramid God, Mega Pyramid, Pharoah's God, Pharoah's Data, Holographic,
Unknown, The Hidden Image, The Hidden Eye, The Mega Mirage,
The Mirage lie, The mirage data,

*113 = Six and Nine, Black and White, Patterns, Human Past, Moon-Light,
Apocalypse,

Prediction, Exorcist, Resistance, Standard Cell, Life Standard, Solar Pole,
Petro-Net, Petro-Team, Petro-vice, Centre Ring, Ring Centre, Alphabet Cycle,
White Blood, White Son, Centre Cycle, Crime Centre, Blood Centre, World
Key,

World Lock, World Clue, First King, Magnetic Key, Mom First, Salvation,
Universe, Inquiry, Dagne and Roger, Sacred Diety, Godly Circle, Historian,
Ten Horns, Third Eyes, Third Images, Liars Images, Mind's Images, Mind's
Eye,

The Buddha Mind, The Mind-Mind, Zero Speed, Dust Atom, Green Dust,
Lord Israel, Earth's Sin, Earth News, Devil's Sin', Dying Love, Dying Sun,
Three in one, Mutation, Perverted, The Sixth, The Pope Man, Call the Pope,
Call the Devil, The Earth Air, Iron Oxide, Adversary, The re-birth, The
Entrance,
The Baptism, Lingually,

*114 = Yin-and-Yang, The Faces of God, Your Image, Your Eye, God meets God,
Nature Image, Magnets Eye, Mother Image, Mother Eye, Naked nature,
Virgin Image, Naked Virgin, Earth Queen, Queen Lived, Queen & Pope,
Pope Queen, Under Pope, Under Earth, Lived Under, Devil Under, First Lady,
First Bitch, First War, Fish First, New World, World War, Hitler War,
A Hitler Dream, First Gun, New Money, Life Bag Money, Bag Life First,
War Origin, Second Love, Love Word, Police Chemical, Word Chemical,
Magnetic fish, Self First, Birth and Death, Moon Birth, Human Birth,
A Human Light, Perpetual, History, Ancestors, Family Tree, Family Cycle,
Family Blood, Family Sex, Family Son, A Family Time, A Family Legend,
A Family monad, Free Dead Family, Spitting, The End of Hell, The End Of
Up,

Begin of the end, End of Hade's Name, End of Hade's Aids, The Lost Face,
Dead Lost One, Lost one Dead, The Beginning, A Zulu Name, A Zulu Magic,
A Zulu Aids, Turn a Deaf Ear, The Aids Ring, The Aids crime, The Natal
Aids,

The Blood Aids, Prisoner, Frequency, Conquest, Horoscope, Cavitation,
Continent, Synagogue, Holy Islam, Allah Entrance, One Entrance,
Free Entrance, Dark Entrance, Free The Beast,

*115 = Trinity, Combination, The Image of God, The Eye of God, Genetic Coding,
Figure Eight, Twin Atom, Ancient Atom, Ancient Lord, Number Nine,
Number Five, New Number, New Sacrifice, New Kingdom, God is a Word,
God is a Vow, God is You, Church is God, God is News, God is a Magnet,
God is a Police, Consonant, Living Fish, Self Living, New Living, New
Paradise,

New Sound, Self-sacrifice, Homo Sapien, West Pole, Water Cycle,
Water & Blood, Blood Water, Occultism, Messiahism, Energy Key,
Nuclear Home, Escom's Key, Positive, Negative Life, Negative M/C2,
Crucifying,

The Anointed, Anointed Seed, Anointed Name, Flower Child, Flower Law,
Secular Law, Nature Law, Nature Child, Mother & Child, Child Mother,
Child Nature, Virgin Child, Virgin Law, The Free Sex, The Fair Sex,
Aids Free Blood, Free Gay Blood, Alchemy Blood, Oscillates, The Life Span,
Satanic Sex, Satanic Blood, Satanic Craft, Satanic Crime, Satanic Son,
Sulpher,

Proverbs, Commandment, The Denied Dream, The Denied Key,
Denied the Clue, Denied Aids Clue, Robben Island, Star Birth, Human
Science,

Human Father, Human Scope, Human Micro, Moon Science,

*116 = Jesus is Dead, The King is Dead, Don King is Dead, Muhammad is Dead,
The Boxer's D.N.A., Messiah is Dead, Mom is the King, The Child of God,
The Child of Aud, The Law of God, The God of Law, No Justice, New
Messiah,

Survive, Holy-Attack, Thursday, The Holy End, The Magent End,
"I Am The Word, Serpents, Laws of David, The Magic Circle,
Deaf...Dumb and ... Blind, Egyptians, Eternity, Nuclear-War, Chemical
Valence,

Star Science, Muse Science, Muse Father, Angel Sciences, Angle Sciences,
Angel Sciences, Polarity, Inflammble-Man, Inflammble-Air, The Book of
Adam,

The Mark of Adam, The Mark of Ra, The Sabbath-day, Angel of Light,
Angle of Light, Micro-Scope, Deuterium, Centrifugal, Primal Time,

*117 = Testament, Statement, Torture, Prophets, Holy-Human, Human Word,
A Angel of Light, Progress, You Will, Visualise, God the Father, God the
Star,

Israelites, News Paper, Publishing, Film Stars, Mary of Magdala, Borne In
Mind,

Christ Mind, Christ Pain, Mind Matter, Food Matter, Buddha-Christ, Master
Key,

Master Lock, Holy Fires, Magnets Death, Robin Island, Protons, Mathematician,
   Communicate, Social Science, Comrade Science, Liars Science, Aryan Star,

*118 = Concentrate, Conscious, Thoughts, Life's Manra, I believe in God, Fifty Six,
   Compass-Life, Pharaoh's Life, The Creation, God's Number, Dictionary,
   The Nought, Next-of-Kin, Find the Devil, Pyramid Life, Life Symbol,
   The Life of Life, The end of Omega, The Death of God, Incarnation,
   Time Barrier, Desert Monad, Space & Energy, Space Cross, Isotopes,
   Micro-Soft, Word Science, Magnet Science, Worded Logo, The Law Logo,
   The Chip Logo, Bill Gate's Cash, Bill Gate's Land,

*119 = Star-of-David, The Angel-of-God, The Angle of God, Family Ties, Artificial Gene,
   The Symbol, The Holy God, The WorD...God, The Magnet God, Attractive,
   Dagne Gontier, Dagne Guldvog, The Holy Data, The Magnet Data, Foundation,
   Blue Blood Gene, The Sacred-Law, The Pyramid, Vulture, The Above Key,
   The Dream Above, He is the above, He is the Path, He is the Zen,
   He is the Leader, He is the Gods, Undeniable Life, Confession, Salt-Water,
   Pursues, Ishmael and Isaac, An Original Idea, An Original Adam,
   An Original Egg, "An Original D.N.A.", Human Disease, Birth Disease,
   Biological Hate, Medical World, Beast World, Monad Origin, Time Origin,
   World Time, Magnetic Beast, The Dead World, Human Medicine, Birth Medicine,
   Death's Medicine, Medicine Cancel D.N.A., Jews Medicine, Sleep Medicine,

*120 = Vocabulary, 'Rosh Hashanah', Leviticus, Ecclesiastes, Christians, Lost Note,
   Lost Love, Love Lost, The Truth, Lost Voice, Twin Sun, Zodiacal Sign,
   Lost Tribe, The Planets, Planet Earth, Earth Language, Understand,
   Under Science, Communism, Secularism, Word's Clue, Word's Key, Nature Key,
   Murder Clue, Home Mother, A Virgin Rape, Enormous, The Holy Dance,
   The Magnet Code, The Magnet Dance, The Word Code, The Pure Code,
   The Pure Race, The Police Dance, The Police Hand, The Police Race,
   The Police Code, The Mad People, The Mad Bishop, The Mad Knight,
   The Head Bishop, The Judicial Head, A Judicial Circle, Judicial Homo,
   Judicial Kaffir, Initiation, Bar-Mitzvah, The Muslim, Darrell and Dagne,
   Atmosphere, Mad Man Energy, Messiah Body, Nuclear Body, Nuclear Branch,
   Body Energy, Moves Body, Christ Book, Christ Mark, Power Mark,
   War in Heaven, War in Sky, Rain in Cloud, Sin in Heaven, Self in Heaven,
   Self end Satan, Illuminati, Unidentified, Chemistry, Mad Cross Man, Body Cross,
   God's a Cross,

*121 = Revelation, The Vision, The Begotten, The Immanuel, The Dream of God,
   The Key of God, The Clue of God, The Home of God, Cross of God,
   Messiah of God, God of the King, Anti-Christ, A Christ Mark, Christ Brain,

Brain Matter, Brain's Science, Sciences Brain, Godly Science, Divine Science,
Diety Science, Godly Father, Anti-matter, Attraction, The Blind...can see!,
The Blind Monad, The Dead Cross, Time Cross, Jesus & The Dead,
The Icon Legend, Adam Kadmon Brain, The God Head Brain,
"A Computer Dad", The Earth Field, The Earth Ohm, The Pope Law,
The Pope Child, The Anti-Godhead, Poverty, Live and Love, Sun's Cycle,
Crime's Chemical, Possessed, Pressure, Principles, Synoptic {**Affording a
general view of "The Whole".}, Equilateral, Oscillating, Twisting, Bible
Theory,
Bible Honour, Bible Future, Future Day, Bi-directional, Unification, Triology,
Time Stuck, Doomology, Monadology, Second Coming, Holy Coming,
Coming Pure, Coming Vow, Holy News, News Word, The Lake of Fire,
Midian Desert, The Left Path, The Goat Bridge, The False Path,
The False Gods, Dimensions, Copy rights, Liars Rights, Liars Mind-key, Liars
Mind Lock, Aryan Mind Key, Turbulence, Combustible, By Friction, The
Pure Air,
The Holy Man, The Word...Man, The Holy Call, The Holy Lamb, The Police
Man,
Begotten name, Marijuana Seed, Marijuana Name, The Last Child,
The Last Law, Things Hidden, The Exodus, Fish Nature, Sin Nature,
New Nature, God Almighty, Yourself, Your Sin, Your War, Virgin Lady,
Virgin Boy, South Africa, Same Monkey, Monkey Change, Like a Monkey,
Negative Change, Negative Balance, Adolf Germany, The Africa Lion,
'*122 = Mushroom, Prophesy, Machine People, Cyber People, Cyber Text, News
Room,
Rome Editor, Kaffir Editor, Homo-Editor, Invention, The Ark of Noah,
The Ark of Death, The Day of Death, The Bible of Noah, The Change of
Bible,
The Bible of Alpha, The Change of Baby, The Change of Day, Homo Aids
Death,
Homo Seed Balance, Homo Seed Change, Homo name Change,
Homo Gay Balance, King and Queen, King of Kings, Figure Three, Light
Figure,
Ancient Light, Ancient Past, Woman Past, Wolf Woman, Red-tape Machine,
Cyber Knight, Cyber Check-mate, Lie...Stale-mate, The Only End,
Judgement end, The Ancient 'I am', The Woman...I am, "I'm One Woman",
The Unity, Millennium, Arithmomania, Noah's Cosmo, Cosmo's Death,
Come Like a Thief, Law alike Thief, A Law like Crime, "A Amnesty Act",
The Freedom end, The Judges End, Change Jury, Same Jury, Fire Jury,
Jury Alike, A Hade's Jury, Homo Advocate, Handiworks, The Bush Team,
The Sacred Ten, The Sacred Angle, Umbilical Cord, Umbilical Line,
Umbilical Food, Umbilical Mind, Umbilical Pain, Minds Record, Records
Mind,
Three Times, Quartz's, Implosion, Symphonic, An Orchestra,

*123 = The Holy Bible, The Book of God, The Mark of God, The Genetic Code,
The Divine Code, The Godly Code, The Diety Code, The Godly Race,
The Holy Baby, The Pure Baby, The Baby Word, The Holy Ark,
The Magnet Arch, The Bible Word, The Police Baby, The Police Bible,
The Police Mob, The Mafia Police, Cracking Bible Code, Ancient Bible Code,

Ancient Bible Race, Comparative, Pro Jesus, Pro-Nuclear, Atom Energy,
Nuclear Atom, Nuclear Danger, Green Energy, Atom Cross, Cross Danger,
A Blood Cross, A Crime Cross, Epilogue, Circumference, Beginning and end,
Beginning's end, The Image of Allah, The Image of One, The Eye of Allah,
Eye of the Camel, Desert-Earth, Water-bag Body, Holy Saint, Shadow of Life,
Eighty-eight, Seven Star, Centre Star, Science Centre, Alphabet Science,
White Star, The Earth Balance, Change the Earth, African Aids Death,
In African Blood, End African Sex, End African Trade, In Earth Blood,
Blood end Earth, Super Space, Super Brain, Cancer Nature, Secular brain,
Torsional, Classic Catch - 22, Linguistic, Hieroglyph {**Any difficult character to
read},

*124 = God's Word, Linguiform, Immanence of God, Passport, Sufferings, Fornication,
The Arse Sex, The Goat Sex, The Goat Blood, The Live Goat, The Evil Goat,
The Blood Book, The Crime Book, The Evil Book, The Evil Mark,
Time's Calendar, Calendar's Monad, Caesar's Calendar, Warps Time,
Caesar's Science, Caesarean Birth, Water Birth, A Queer Birth, Technology,
The Live Charm, Holy Peter, Police Peter, Judge Christ, Court Judge,
Court Legend, Court Time, Left and Right, Polarities, Cold nor Hot, Photograph,
The Mirror, The Theory, The Darkness, Name Theory, Aids Theory, Gay Theory,
Conviction, Life's Number, Life's Sacrifice', Cell Numbers, Immunity,
Darrell's Image, Darrell's Eye, The Balance of Life, The Change of Life,
The Death of Life, The Phoenix, The Fire of Life, The Life of Africa,
The Road of Life, Depression, Hierographs, Definitions, Dead Key Message,
The Dead Law Key, The Dead Law Lock, Magnet Dust, Pure Dust, Dust Word,
The End of Time, The End of The Dead, The End of Doom, End of the Monad,
End of the Seer, End of the Legend, Lazy Police, Cosmology, The Law of Allah,
The Law of Basic, Basic of the Child, Name of One Child, Faces of Law Name,
Faceless Chemical, Faceless Love, Faceless Islam, Faceless Sun,
*125 = Mystery, Solution, West Star, Water Science, Alchemy Science, Micro Alchemy,
East Pole Life, The Middle Bridge, The Middle Path, The Time Path,
Bridge The Time, The Electron, The Numbers, Own Numbers, Name Numbers,
The 'I am who I am', The Twin God, The Lost God, The Ancient God, Circulation,
The Middle East, Inversion, The Only God, Judgement God, Up-right God,
Judgement Data, Up-Right Flag, Colour Blind, Blind Colour, Colour Clue,
A Blue Colour, Mind a Colour, The minimum, The Holy life, The Pure Life,
The Magnet Cell, The Life Word, The Word...Life, Alphabet Word,
Alphabetical Image, Human Language, The Human Image, Human Atoms,
Moon Atoms, Moon's Speed, Human Planet, Diabolical Human, Planet Birth,

Human Root, Birth Root, Umbilical Mark, An Umbilical Man, Primate Manna,
Primate Mark, Primate Book, Primate Wife, Monkey Lady, Monkey Boy,
Monkey Bitch, New Monkey, Monkey War, Monkey Sin, Monkey Self,
A Monkey Mom, A Monkey Clue, A Monkey Key, A Monkey King,
'A - Alien Monkey', A Monkey and Ape, A Monkey Fuck, A Primate Bitch,
A Lady Primate, A Boy Primate, A He-Man-Primate, A Monkey Joke,
Baboon Master, A Baboon Doctor, A Baboon Puss, Darwin's Feed-back,
Darwin's Flame, Darwin's 'E=M/C2', Jungle's Mode, Animals Past,
Animals Friend, The Equal Bone, Animals Member, Jungle Rule, Animal Indexs,
Animal D.N.A. Index, Science's Crime, Science's Sex, Science's Blood,
D.N.A. Blood Science, Father and Son, Arab Numerals {**1 & 0},
Holographical,
Time Travel, The Dead Travel, A Dead President, President Face,
John Kennedy, The Christ Face,

*126 = Roman Alphabet, Words of God, Nature of God, Human text, Human Message,
Birth Text, Umbilic Text, Umbilical Brain, Brain's Record, Diety's Brain,
Mother of God, The Sacred book, The Sacred Mark {**A & O}' The Body of God,
Mirror Image, Face of the Human, Light Shadow, Forty Nine, Worm Wood,
The Human Law, The Whole Bible, The Godly Bible, The Divine Bible,
The Convent, Gay Convent, The Pope Key, Colossians, Mountains,
The Law of Ohm, Speed of Light, Atom of Light, The Sacred Choice,
The Drug's Act, End Free Drugs, Hypnosis, The Lost Race, The Lost Code,
The Ancient Code, Mankind Name Code, Code-name...Mankind,
Face of the Moon, Red Blood Cells, Homo Blood Code, Kaffir Blood code,
Indian Blood Code, Homo Sex Code, A Nato Crime Code, A Blood Chart Code,
A Red Blood Chart, Regulated Aids, Regulated Name, Parent's Name,
Parent's Seed, Aids Propaganda, The Propaganda, Coloured Name,
Coloured Aids, Editorial Aids, The News Media, The News Agenda,
The News Life, Cock The News, The Cock News, "Cock-a-dood-li-doo",
Conquer Aids, A Messianic Aids, A Messianic Name, Originator, First Love,
World Sun, Magnetic Love, Magnetic Chemical, Magnetic Voice, World Voice,
Hitler Voice, Histler Image, Dictator Law, Law Dictator, The C.N.A. Write,
The A.N.C. Reform, The A.N.C. Death Seal, A Lawful Circle,
A Mandela Law Team, The A.N.C. Law Team, An Electric Field, An Electric Law,
Editorial Magic, The Editorial, An Electric Chip, 'I'm Electronic', Electronic Lead,
Change Human Echo, Human Death Land, Human Gold Land,
Human Land balance, Human land Change, Africa...divided land!, Positron,
Neutrons, The Magic Word,

*127 = Saint Peter, The Key of Life, Symbolism, Key Symbol, Symbol Key,

The Dream of Life, The Mind's Eye, The Mind's Image, The Third Eye,
The Third Image, Vatican City, One third Free, Communist, Enlightment,
Intelligent, Nought & Nine, New Biology, War Biology, Sin Biology,
The Lost Man, The Ancient man, Judgement-man, Up-Right Man, Ministry,
The Maximum, Compilation, The Law Father, Father The Child, Primal
Father,

*128 = Human Sperm, Coward Peter, Zero-dust, The Holy Image, The Magnet Image,
The Pure Image, The Word Image, The Holy Eye, The Tree of God,
The Son of God, The Blood of God, The Cycle of God, Brother-hood,
Brother-lady, Ceremonial magic, Ceremonial Name, The Black Magic Name,
The Black Woman, The Black Queer, Queer Queen, The Seal of Hell,
The Seal of Hades, Noah and the Boat, The Live Omen, The Live Monad,
The Live Beast, The Evil Beast, The Sex Beast, The Crime Beast,
Aids Sex Monad, Aids Time Cycle, Aids Blood Legend, The Crime Judge,
Judge the Sex, The Yin & Yang, Multiply, Master's Name, Master's Seed,
Gomorrah Aids, A Doctor's Aids, Hierarchy Aids, Hierarchy Name,
Master's Name, Court Cells, Court's Agenda, Life's Court, Life Matters,
Congregation, The Public Agenda, The Public Life,

*129 = Gontierism, The Book of Life, Light Bringer, Electricity, Escom's Wire,
Satan's Trap, Satan's Dead Key, Satan's Dead Clue, Satan's Dead-Home,
Congella's Omega, Congella's Home, Congella's Lock, Umgeni's Omega,
Umgeni's Defeat, Satan's Laws, Social Suicide, Liars Suicide, Escom's Judas,
Critical Chemical, Infra-Red Chemical, Infra-Red Sun, Sun Distance, Sun's
Light,
Sun's Past, Light Sacrifice, The Seal of Fire, Hell's Sacrifice, Escom's Wages,
The Seal of Death, Hade's Name of Death, Pandora's Box, Pandora's Camera,
Camera-man's Camera, Hade's Picture, Big-Pictures, Hollywood, First
Human,
Human Origin, World & Moon, Virtual God, Virtual Data, Mecury God,
Oscillation, Repulsion, Disorderly, Meteorites, Being...Born Anew, A New
Born Being, The Eye of David, The Image of David, The Image of Mind, The Eye
of Mind, House of Mind, House of David, Language of Mind, The Seal of
Balance,
The Seal of Change, The Seal of Africa, The Rand of Africa,
The Change of Rand, The Side of Africa, The Place of Change,
The Place of Death, The Balance of Hell, The Demo of Africa,
Begin of Africa Aids, Nelson Mandela, Mother America, Bush Nature,
Sacred Nature, The A.N.C. Genesis, Sacred Words, The C.N.A. Genesis,
Homo-Genesis, Um-Fanegiso, Begin A New Atom, Begin A War Atom,
A New Atom Feed-back, Explosion, Destroyer, Experiment, Ninety-Nine,
Begin a New Year, Judgement Day, Judgement Bible, Judgement Ark,
Current-Bible, Current Day, Current Mob, Current Mafia, "Om is Sound",
Light Sound, Past Sound, Man is Sound, Wolf Sound, Pearly Gates,
The Adam Christ, Adam Kadmon's Name, Holy Ghost, The Holy Child,
The Magnet Field, The Magnet Ohm, Theory Balance, Fire Theory,
Death Theory, My Theory, Balance Darkness, Same Theory, Under Water,
Soul Under, Cycles Under, Under Parole, Digital Soul, Digital Alchemy,
Digital Evidence, Papacy Touch, Blood's Plasma, D.N.A. Blood Plasma,

Cosmic Soul, The Middle Way, The Time Way, The Middle Danger,
The Time Atom, The Atom Monad, The Beast Logo, The Dead Atom Name,
The Genetic Seed, The Genetic Name, The Aids Genetic, The Blood Tree,
The Blood Cycle, The Blood Sex, Aids Blood Cycle, The Blood Trade,
Aids Blood Trade, The Natal Blood, The Natal Cycle, The Evil Trade,
The Live Blood, The Code of Blood, "A + B + AB + O-Blood Code Name",
The Red of Blood, The Knowledge, Aids Knowledge, The Freemason,
A Freemason Agenda, The H.I.V. Vaccine, H.I.V. Aids Vaccine, The M.K.
Ultra,
"A.Z.T. AIDS Pill",

*130 = Pythagoras, Pythagorean, Mysticism, A Mystic Mind, A Mystic Hole,
The Inner-Being, Altered State, Altered Centre, Hierographical, State Centre,
Washington, The Black Market, Lord of the Dance, Hippocrates, Radar
Vision,
New Vision, Self Vision, Begotten Sin, Promised Land, Industry, The Serpent,
Serpent Seed, Name Control, Aids Control, Aids Gene Marker, The Son of
Man,
The Sex of Man, The Cycle of Air, The Blood of Lamb, The Lamb of Blood,
The Call of Blood, Plasma Dolly, Sheep Matter, Hitler Science,
Sheep & Lamb Clone, Sheep & Man Clone, Sheep & Man Atom,
A Sheep & Man Sex, A Sheep & Man Blood, Changes God's Lamb,
Adolf's Paradise, Adolf's Children, Changes Children, Angel of Death Cell,
Angel of Death Agenda, Ten of Same Cell, Ten of Alike Cell, Digital Dolly,
Digital Language, Electronic Data, A Electronic Area, Television, T.V.
Vision,
Electrical T.V., 'illusions', Protector, The Equator, The Angel of Hell,
Corinthians,
Gymnastics, Begotten Sin, God and the Devil, God and the Pope,
God and the Earth, God and Bi-ology, Astrologer, The Supreme,
The Divine One, "Elixir of Life", Matter of Life, Life of Matter, Christ of Life,
Life of Christ, Life of Adam Kadmon, Life of The God-Head, Electrical
Charge,
Power of Life, D.N.A. Science of Life, Science of Adam & Eve,
Father of Adam & Eve, Glory of Life, Pinis & Penis,

*131 = The Holy Death, The Pure Death, Crucifixion, The Holy Balance,
The Word Change, Change The Word, The Same Word, Pray the Same,
Pray alike ... Amen, The Magnet Balance, The Police Balance,
Same Police Name, Police Alpha Name, A - Alpha Bravo Cop, The Criminals,
Criminal's Name, Criminal's Aids, Parallel-o-Gram, The Atom of Man,
The Lord of Man, The Danger of Man, The Speed of Man, The Man of Speed,
The Speed of Air, The Atom Speed, The Danger Speed, Combustion,
Diversity, West and East, The Divine Image, The Godly Image, The Diety
Image,
The Naked Saint, The Naked Penis, The Cover Image, The Naked Cover,
Cock-Condom Image, Free Foreskin, One Control, Basic Control,
The Image of Self, The Image of Sin, The Image of Nine, The Image of War,
The Image of Fish, Holy Qur'an, The Chosen One, One Chosen Name,
Name Chosen Free, The Balance of Ten, The Balance of Angle,

The Angle of Balance, The Change of Ten, The Vice of Change,
The Team of Africa, The Angel of Death, Door-Keepers, Pope-Keepers,
African Keepers, Devil Keepers, Earth Keepers, Bitterness, Human-Cross,
Moon Energy, Human Messiah, Mary & Jesus, The Garden of Eden,
The Garden of Man, The Green Atom, The Green Garden, Human Energy,
Hydrogen Bond, Triune God Head, Birth Energy, Birth Parent, Human Parent,
The Baby of Time, Time of the Bible, Legend of the Bible, The Time of Day,
The Day of Doom, Doom of the Mafia, Day of the Epoch, Time of the Ark,
Day of the Beast, Ark of the Beast, The Ark of Time, The Ark of The Dead,
The Ark of Doom, Noah's Cross, Noah's Messiah, Theosophy, South Pole,
Faithful Cycle, Faithful Son, Faithful Sex, Life Span Cycle, Record's a Crime,
Echo Wave Cycle, Homo Land Sex, Monkey Sex, Monkey Son, Monkey Blood,
Live Monkey, Arse-hole Sex, Sex Deficiency, Blood Deficiency, Negative Sex,
Negative Cycle, Negative Blood, Negative Crime, The Lion's Page,
The Bush Sex, One Man's Loin, Angel of Light, An Angle of Light, Messiah Birth,
Messiah's Death, Change Parent D.N.A., The Alpha and Omega, God's Symbol,
God's Pyramid, The Death and Dream, Intuition, Imaginations,

*132 = Triple Six, Three Sixes, Science Energy, Nuclear Science, A Number Science,
Two Parts, The Key of Hades, The Key of Hell, Cross of Hell, Begin of Nuclear,
Feed-back of Energy, Feed-back of Jesus, Back-feed of Lucifer,
Flame of Nuclear, Place of The Omega, King of the Place, Star Energy,
Micro-Energy, Micro Photo, Parent Science, A Perfect Science,
A Children Science, Prick & Puss, A Flying Star, Moon Distance,
Moon Diameter, Moon Analogy, Birth Analogy, Analogical Birth,
Divided Distance, Divided Diameter, Doctor's Death, Doctor's Gold,
Rich Doctors, Africa's Doctor, Africa's Diameter, The Last Monad,
One African Hero, The African Doom, The African Legend, The African Monad,
The Earth Time, The Earth Beast, The African beast, The Last Time,
The Last Dead Name, The Last Name Dead, The Flood Legend,
The Flood Monad, Ever Lasting, Lasting Circle, Last Bush Baby,
Sacred Earth Baby, Twin Octave, Lost Octave, Ancient Octave, Queer Judges,
Woman Judges, Ancient Judges, Cain and Able Twin, Septuagint, Astrology,
Trumpets, Quotation, The Lost Name, Pseudonym, Chronological, Chronology,
Freedom's Bi-Law, Earth's News, Roman Popes, Unforgivable, Popes' Sins,
The Divine Law, The Diety Law, The Godly Law, The Godly Child, Controller,
The Divine Tao, The Law Ratio, Catholic Church, Satan is Alive, Satan is Lord,
Heaven is Alive, Air-Cloud Atom, Mars & Venus, Michael & Venus,
Real Earth Space, Real Earth Brain,

*133 = Number Order, Children Order, Holy Number, Holy Sacrifice, Pure Children,

Police Children, Ancient Evidence, Tribune God Head, Tribune Brain, North
Star,

The Death Hour, The Same Hour, Change The Hour, Change The Queen,
Fire The Queen, The Death Queen, The Alpha Hour, The Fire Action,
The Same Action, The New Science, Puss Science, Doctor Science,
A Doctor's Death, A Human Puss, Diameter Star, Star Distance,
A Moon Distance, Electric Science, Lawful Science, Spiral Science,
Lawful Father, Deaf and Dumb Science, The New Science, The War Science,
Critical Science, Analogical Science, Science Analogy, Madness Science,
Human Head Science, Infra-Red Star, Horoscope, Micro Distance, World
News,

Magnetic News, First News, News Origin, Reborn News, News in Atom,
News Radius, The Dead-sea News, Marriage News, Church Marriage,
First Church, Church Origin, Money Church, Church Money, Roman Money,
Roman Origin, First Roman, The Good and The Bad, Temptation, Evolution,
The Grave Yard, Poor People, Prisoners, Witnesses, Witness-Act,
Christiandom,

Denomination, "Go...accordingly", Synagogues, A Messiah Science,
A Energy Science, A Nuclear Science, A Nuclear Star, Father a Messiah,
The Messiah Data, The Messiah God, The Energy Data, Condensation,
Virginity,

Homo-sexual, The Sabbatic Goat, Late Einstein, Government, God's Vision,
Mega's Vision,

*134 = THE SKELETON, The Tree of Life, The Cycle of Life, The Blood of Life,
Live Voodoo, Evil Voodoo, Voodoo Blood, Compass Cycle, Pyramid Cycle,
Live Tri-Angle, Blood Symbol, Blood Formula, Live Symbol, Evil Symbol,
Crime Symbol, A Biological Cycle, A Biological Blood, A Biological Son,
A Biological Sex, Live Mantras, Convict Crime, Holy God Cycle, Holy God
Son,

Blood Brother, Holy Jesus, Holy Messiah, The Holy Omega, Holy Cross,
Pure Energy, Pure Cross, Magnet Energy, Word Energy, The Omega Word,
Alpha and Omega Law, Live Souls, Evil Souls, Souls Cycle, Blood and
Water,

Pharaoh's Son, Pharaoh's Veil, Compass Pole, South Top, South Wave,
A Negative Circle, A Negative Chart, A Negative Graph, Abstract Circle,
A North Star, A North Science, A Diameter Science, Different Time,
The Dead Person, Unique Time, Unique Monad, Justice Monad, Justice Judge,
Natural Judge, Natural Time, Wall Statue, Crime Statue, The Grave Wall,
Convict Wall, The Atlas Cycle, Divide The Wall, Lord God Shiva, Circular
Logo,

Sacred Logo Image, A Sex Biology, The Chicken Blood, A Blood Biology,
A Live Biology, A Evil biology, Information, Reformation, Church Sacrifice,
Church Children, Global Warming, The Red Cross, The Energy Code,
The Nuclear Code, The Jewish Code, The Jewish Race, The Gospel Code,
The Gematria Code, Gematria Name Code, Living Church, The English Code,
The Messiah Code, The Magnet Key, The Word Key, Living News, News
Sound,

Empiric News, News Front, Surface News, News Shrine, Church Shrine,

A World News, A News Origin, A Magnetic News, Under the Dead-Sea,
All under the Dead, Under-World, World Under, World Queen, Magnetic
Queen,
First Queen, Money Queen, Queen's Nose, Queen's Mirage, Queen's Look,
A Queen's Pride, A Queen's Ship, A Pope's Queen, Cyber Queen's,
Queen's Divide, Queen of Rome, Queen's Atlas, Queen's Grave, Queen's
Coffin,
First Papacy, World Papacy, Papacy Origin, Papacy Money, First Cardinal,
Cosmic World, Cosmic Origin, Magnetic Plasma, Plasma Origin, Digital
World,
Magnetic Signal, World Looked, Magnetic Mauve, Atomic Number,
New Rhythm, New Electron, New Numbers, War Electron, War Penta-gon,
The Third War, The Liars War, The Mind Wars, A War Theory, A New
Theory,
A New Honour, A Self Honour, A Self Theory, The Lock And Key,
The Love of God, The Sun of God, The Chemical of God, The Voice of God,
Commandments, Manuscript, Mother and Child, Nature's Law, Nature's Child,
Umbilic Centre, The Cosmo Law, The Child Alphabet, Lost Language,
Family Language, Ancient Language, "A Alphabet LogO",
Sacred A & O Language, Nought & Eight, Biological Atom, The Earth Logo,
The African Logo, The Logo Speak, African Aids Logo, The Abracadabra
Logo,
Brain Logoism, Brain Logo Key, The Mind of Buddha, Brain & Brain Logic,
I'm a Computer, War Horror, The Liars War, Gun The Liars, The Liar's Gun,
Pollution, Reverse War, Reverse Self, Text in War, End War Text,
End War Essay, The Harm of Dogma, The Pain of Mind, The Mind of Dogma,
The Mind of Mind, The Buddha of Mind, The Food of Buddha,
The Food of Mind, The Voice of God, Lord of Israel, The Green Earth,
Green Grass Edge, Shadow's Path, Darrell's Bridge, Darrell's Path,
Darrell's Knife, Encounters, Science Fiction, Science Master, Exotic Science,
Revenge Science, Science Magazine, Adult Magazine, Scope Magazine,
Exotic Scope, Exotic Cunt?, Science Analogue, Scope Analogue,
Cunt and Prick, Moon and Star, Birth Matter, A Master Birth, A Birth Master,
A Human Master, Human D.N.A. Science, Human Egg Science,

*135 = The Birds And bees, The Facts of Life, The Baby of Adam & Eve,
The Fact of Adam & Eve, Baby Seed of Adam & Eve, Covenant Box,
Covenant Key, Covenant Fuck, Black & White Fuck, Immorality, Esoteric
Fuck,
A Esoteric Mind, Relation Fuck, The News Home, The News Key,
Death and Hades Key, Doctors Home, Doctor's Fuck, Alien-Doctor's,
U.S.A. Doctors, Doctor's Joke, Micro Chip Key, A Micro Chip Mind,
Cemetery Key, Unicorn Key, Man & Wo-man Clue, Man Fuck Woman,
The Lost Child, The Lost Law, Current Law, The Key of Mind, The Key of
David,
The Key Of Buddha, The Home of Food, The King of Food, The Open Door,
The African Bush, The Dagga Plants, Burning Bush, Moses' Grass,
Earth Wisdom, The Holy War, The Police War, The New Police, Police the
Self,
In Life and in Death, Songs of David, Stone-Mason, The Lord of Life,

The Atom of Life, Chemical Atom Bomb, The Sacred Earth, Symphony
Brain of Adam and Eve, Mount Sinai, Book of Thoth, The Inner Self,

*136 = Virgin Mary, Mother Mary, Nature Birth, Human Nature, Moon Nature,
Human Mother, Birth Mother, Stomach Birth, Saint Joseph, Divine Children,
Godly Children, Gontierist, Circumcision, The Holy Mark, News Papers,
Testaments, Statements, Tree of Good and Bad, Cycle of Good and Bad,
Changes Words, Human Words, Equilibruim, Gravitation, A Trip to Hell,
Profession, Nonentity, Linguistical,The Numbering, Antiquity, Marijuana
Tree,
Begotten Tree, Missing Son, Begotten Son, Electrical Cycle, Electrical Blood,
Missing Cycle, Missing Blood, Missing Tree, Photo-graphic, Surface Limit,
Mad Scientist, Head Scientist, A.Einstein Mind, Mathematicians, Veil a Truth,

*137 = Saint Lucifer, Diety Cross, Divine Cross, Godly Energy, Nuclear Plant,
Escom's Plant, Koeberg Plant, Energy Plant, Green Marijuana, Green Fungus,
A Live Fungus, A Complex Tree, A Complex Cycle, Photon Atom, Sperm
Donor,
Di-Electrical Atom, A Nameless Tree, A Nameless Crime, A Electrical Cycle,
Electrical V.I.R., A Volt's Cycle, A Volt's Blood, A Blood Hormone,
A Life & Light Cycle, A Light Life Cycle, Life and Death Cycle, Complete
Cycle,
Blood Virus, Mystic Cycle, Mystic Blood, Memory Cycle, The Past Cycle,
The Last Flood, The Earth Flood, Dead Sea Scrolls, Dead Sea's Words,
Number Israel, Count Israel, Sacrifice Israel, Israel Children, Zero Count,
Enough Evidence, The Holy Faith, Holy Christ, Word Matter, Holy Matter,
The Holy God Head, Active Adam Kadmon, Active Matter, Police Matter,
Police Court, Anonymous, Non-descript, Name of Wisdom, Hall of Wisdom,
Characteristics, Electric Train, Under Electric, Authority, God Created
Heaven,
God Created Satan, Satan Created God, The Birth of God, Nought & Six,
Washington D.C., God's Sacrifices, Turn Back Time, Turn Time Back,
The Dead Turn Back, The Human Time, The Human Monad, The Human
Beast,
The Human Judge, Judge The Human, Human Aids Doom, Human Aids
Epoch,
Human Aids Legend, Human Aids Monad,

*138 = Train Driver, Digital Addition, Digital Split, Digital Analogue, Analogue
Signal,
Distance Signal, Train Safety, Cosmic Safety, Astronomer, Your Finger,
Your Toes, Horizontal, "I am Trinity", The Life Sacrifice, The Children's I.D.,
The Children Agenda, White Children, White Sacrifice, Artificial Genes,
Blue Blood Genes, Witch Doctor, Plant Doctor, All Bush Plant, All Drug
Plant,
Marijuana Bush, Mandrax Plant, Sea-Bush Plant, Genetic Doctor,
Obscene Doctor, Diplomatic Law, The Snake's Law, The Snake's Bone,
The Snake's Ohm, The Snake's Lode, The Snake's Field, Snake Poison,

Electrical Circle, Limit Distance, Plant Members, Poison Bush, Bone Principle,
Child Slavery, Gravity Field, Vicarius Law, A Body and Bone Law,
A Body and Bone Field, Human Body Image, Naked Human Body, Missing Son,
Missing Blood, Missing Sex, Evil Missing, Missing Chord, Missing Trade,
The Human Trade, The Human Blood, The Human Tree, The Live Human,
The Moon Cycle, The Birth Cycle, The Birth Trade, The Birth Crime,
The Birth Blood, The Natal Birth, Human Sex Seed, Human sex,
The Human craft, The Monad Science, Aids Monad Micro, Aids Monad Science,
Aids Doom Science, The Dead Aids Science, The Micro Monad,
The Micro Beast, The Science Omen, Seed Science Monad, The Holy Bridge,
The Holy Path, In the Image of God, The Sacred Laws, The Law's Circle,
Symmetry, The American Dream, The American Key, The American Lock,
Fuck The American, Fuck American Aids, The American Fuck,
The American Home, American Cross, American Nuclear, American English,
The American Joke, American Families, American Parent, American Ruler,
Homo Clinton, Clinton's Agenda, Clinton's Life, Clinton's Cock, Clinton's Bomb,
Clinton's M/C2, Clinton and Madam, Playboy-Lady, New Play-boy, Play-War Boy, War Playboy, Lady-Play-Bitch, Lady-Play-Boy, Fat-Boy & Fat Lady,
Singable Fat Lady, Fat Lady-Whore, Bishop & Knight, Bishop & Whore,
War Code Message, Binary Text, New Chemical War, Hydrogen War,
Mustard War, Red Japan War Code, Mayday Text, Mayday Message,
Alien Calling Mate, The Pyramids, Vultures, The Beast of Hell,
The Dead Name of Hell, God Our Father, The Saviour, God our Science,
Our Science Lie, Our Science Data, Our God Father, Perspective,
Spirit of God, Theory of God, God of Honour, God of Darkness, Phoenix Monad,
Phoenix's Ash, The Night Monad, The Night Time, Fluid Motion, Earth Motion,
Major Problem, Human Problem, Birth Problem, Human Mind Lock,

*139 = Sixty Nine, Sixty Five, Ninety Six, Chemical Reaction, Chemical Biology,

Biological Chemical, Biological Love, Biological Sun, Sun's Corona, Excitations,
Solar Energy, Energy Centre, Nuclear Centre, Cross Centre, White Messiah,
Micro-Tower, White Parent, White Families, Solar Cross, A White Kingdom,
Competition, Jewish Alphabet, English Alphabet, Eight-Fold Path, The
Pendulum, Plain Truth, Plain Justice, African Justice, African Priest, Pope &
Priest, African In-breeding, African Person, Unique Person, African Languages,
Pope's Logos, Pope's Language, Earth's Language, African Head-People,
Global Economy, Virtual Law, Virtual Field, The Nuclear Cell, The Nuclear Bomb,
The Nuclear Agenda, Hydro-Dynamic, Hydro-Volt, Magnetic Water,
Water World, World Alchemy, Chemist Medicine, The Child Stop,
Stop the Come, Doctor Condom, Zuma's Finger, Zuma's Aids Lie,

Medical Pill Book, H.I.V. Vaccine Mark, Human Records, Birth Records,
Plasma Matter, Lazy Doctor, Cosmic Matter, Cosmic Christ,
The Cosmic God-head, Digital Matter, Under Matter, Zero Diameter,
True Diameter, True Distance, The Wheel of Life, The Holy Body,
The Magnet Body, Pituitary, Three in One God, "I am The Bible of Life",
'I Am The Ark of Life', The Holy Link, The Word Link, The Pure Link,
The Magnet Link, The Inner Link, Ancient Number, Ancient Sacrifice,
Freemasonry, Initiations, The Third Beast, The Liars Monad, The Third Judge,
The Slave Judge, The Slave Monad, The Liars Bull, Mafia Bull-Shit,
Mob Bull-Shit, A Pagad Bull-Shit, A Gang Bull-Shit, The Bull Dragon,
The Dragon Beast, The Third Doom, Ancient Egypt, The Muslims,
Punishment,
Sado-Maschoism, Hospital Team, Hospital Mate, Hospital Vice, Hospital Rat,
A Hospital Death, A Hospital Balance, New Science Team, New H.I.V.
Science,
Mind Current, Mind Thought, Food Thought, Pain Current, Buddha Thought,
The Ancient Buddha, The Ancient Mind, Atom Mind Graph, Mind Logo
Chart,
Mind Pill Chart, Food & Drug Lord, Food and Drug Mafia, Baby Food and
Drug,
The Aids Count, The Many Grave, The Many Coffin, Collective Aids,
Body And Bone Balance, Calcination, Skeleton Death, Skeleton Ash-Bag,
Immortal Death, Invisible Death, Invisible Change, Compound Balance,
Both Sides Balance, Both Sides Alike, Balance Side by Side,
Offer Balance Wave, Offer-Tide & Wave, Offer Tide Rise, Ultimate Balance,
Star War Team, Top Sport, Homo Sport, Kaffir Sport, Rome Sport, Text Stop,
Message Stop, Red Tape Stop, The Law Stop, The Robot Law, The Robot
Chip,
The Child Robot, Curri-Culum, The Dead Education, Education Time,
Education Monad, Education Doom, Children's Doom, Children's Time,
Children's Legend, Children's Epoch, A School's Force, School's Sex,
School's Crime, School's Blood, School's Evil, School's Tree, School's Veil,
School's Ring, Teacher's Word, Teacher's Vow, Teacher's Order,
Verbal Teachers, Verbal Nature, Verbal Words, Encryption,

*140 = Fermentation, The Breath of Life, The Holy Grail, The Holy Beast,
The Holy Monad, Mythology, The Word of God, The Doctrines, Testimony,
Copy Rights, The Right Path, The Right Bridge, The Papacy Path,
Under the Bridge, The Cardinal Bridge, The Eternal Life, Doctor White,
Diameter Centre, Electric Centre, Spiral Centre, Doctor Centre,
Death Seal Centre, Hade's Death Centre, The Lost Key, The Ancient Key,
The Ancient Box, The Ancient Home, The Judge's Home, The Judge's Lock,
The Judge's Key, Judgement Key, Current Key, Home Current, The Fishes
Key,
God's Holy Image, God's Holy Eye, The Second Beast, The Second Doom,
The Time Second, The Rich People, The Gold People, Temple People,
Temple Bishop, Temple Wealth, Catholic Wealth, Catholic Bishop,
Catholic Knight, Temple Whore, Business Men, Business Agenda,
Oikoumene Agenda, Funerary Life, Full Moon Agenda, Interior Life,
A Cash Worship, Geometrical Life, Geometrical Cell, Geometrical Bomb,

Life Collision, Cell Collision, Bi-Direction Cell, Police Crime Life,
Holy Vehm Agenda {**Freemason's order of initiation}, Police Crime Cell,
Police Blood Cell, Police Crime Agenda, The Verbal Monad, Atomic Time Cell,
The Dead News Agenda, News Time Agenda, Mush-Room Head,
Mad Mush-Room, News Room Head, A Bad News Editor, The Law Editor,
Basic Law Robot, The Temple Law, Mose's Text, Mose's Message,
Mose's Tombs, Mose's Chambers, Mose's Ghost, Mose's...saw God,
Mose's & Jehovah, The Desert Law, The Desert Oil, The Desert Field,
Nazi's Desert, Desert Jungle, Desert People, Desert Animals, Desert Camel
Eye,
A Free Desert Camel, I Love Power, I Love Christ, Diety Christ,
The Divine God Head, The Godly God Head, Nature of Mind, Mother of
Mind,
Words of Mind, Words of Buddha, Listen News, Listen Church, Church
Hymns,
News Scroll, Church Scroll, Secular News, Virgin News, Mortal News,
Nirvana News, Bottomless, Sky Bottom, A Holy Nirvana, A Holy Nature,
Sky Biology, Biological Sky, Biological Cloud, Astronomy, Pornographic,
Queen Genesis, Start Under, God Lived Under, Under Dog Lived,
Devil Under God, God Under Pope, Lived Under Lie, Slaves Under,
Slave and Queen, Lock-up Under, Lock-up Queen, Lock-up Papacy,
White I.D. Under, Cosmic Start, Atom Theory,

*141 = Relativity, The Fuck to Life, Family Doctor, Ancient Doctor, The Key To
Life,
Logo Rhythm, Logo Picture, Logo's Life Key, The Lock To Life, The Clue To
Life,   One Hole To Life, One Mind To Life, A Nuclear Family, A Clear Family
Image, The Image of Form, Form of the Eye, Form of the Image, Parent's Blood,
Parent's Tree, Chemical In-breeding, In-Breeding Love, Parent's Sex,
Natal Parent's, Blood's Cross {-+}, Electron Logo, The Koran Logo,
Blood's Energy, Son's Energy, Quantum Leap, One Breath of Life,
Free Chemical of Life, Love & Hate of Life, Life of One Sun, Love of One
Life,
Unique Love, Natural Love, Unique Search, Unique Voice, Justice Voice,
Natural Voice, Different Voice, Chemical Mind of God, Chemical Time Scale,
Begotten Cyber, Cyber Gontier, Earth Mystic, The Earth Past, The Pope Past,
The Earth Light, African Hologram, Devil Hologram, Pope Hologram,
The Dream to Life, The Holy Vehm {**Freemasonry order of Initiation,
*Chemical Reaction order of Chemistry}, The Dream to Life, Re-incarnation,
Transverse, False Prophet, Book Prophet, Philosopher, The Holy Chord,
The Pure Blood, Coloured Blood, Regulated Blood, Lost Blood Race,
Ancient Blood Race, Physical Blood, Coloured Cycle, Coloured Crime,
The Life of Satan, The Life Master, The Master Life, The Life Hidden Life,
The Hidden Bomb Life, The Hidden M/C2 Bomb, Omni-Science Life,
Omni-Bomb Science, Omni Life Star, Sun Shine Cell, Star Wave Cell,
Binary Mind Cell, Umbilic Cord Cell, Umbilic Life Cord, School Text,
School Message, The Child School, The Child World, The First Law,
The World Law, The Origin Law, Umbilic Mind Life, Umbilic Mind Agenda,
Mind Cell Text, Mind Cell Message, Lode Stone Cell, Lode Stone Life,

Lode Stone M/C2, Life Written, Written Life, Written Agenda, Life Word
Logo,
Holy Logo Life, Inspires Life, Life Taught Again, Life Taught Life,
Children Language, Nuns Children, Diabolical Children, Diabolical Sacrifice,
Children's Danger, Ageless Children, First People, First Bishop, World
Wealth,
Money Wealth, Mr Rich World, Gold & Cash First, Gold & Cash World,
World Bank Key, The Magnetic Chip, The Magnetic Field, Zero Matter,
Zero Power, The Forbidden Land, The Funeral Land, The Identical Land,
One Identical Map, The Orbital Land, The Orbital Echo, The Circle Science,
The "I" Ching Science, Creative Science, Creative Star, Creative Angles,
Queen Mother, Books Words, Cosmic Words, Cosmic Mother, Cosmic
Nature,
Magnets Plasma, Digital Words, Digital Nature, Bright Matter, Unit Matter,
Solar Master, Great Sphinx, South Star, Diameter Science, Puss Science,
The French Love, The Vagina Love, Note The French, The French Note,
The French Voice, The Love Voice, The Chemical Love, The Love Chemical,
Chemical Love Seed, Purgatory, Transport, Air Traveller, Imaginary Space,
Limitations, Distance and Time, The Cross Leap, The Energy Leap,
The Nuclear Leap, Nuclear Copies, Unclear Evidence, Unclear Water,
Nuclear Alchemy, Mediaval Energy, Water Energy, Urine Nuclear,
The Magic Lights, The Light's Name, The Light's Seed, Plutonium,
The Image of Pope, The Eye of Earth, African Religion, The African Past,
African Virus, African Parasite, Earth Parasite, African Mystic,
The Black African Race, The Black African Code, African Unity,
The African Wolf, The African Past, The African Attack, Rome Genetic Code,
Rome Genetic Race, Homo-Genetic Code, Kaffir Genetic Code,
Kaffir Plant Code, Complex Fungus, The Naked Homo-Ape, Homo-Brethren,
The Kaffir Birth, Homo Birth Seed, Kaffir Prick Seed, Homo Prick Aids,
Rastafarian Seed, Liars Sea-act, Sea Slave Act, Oikoumene Aids,
Oikoumene Name, Oikoumene Seed, Geometrical Seed, Geometry Seed,
Geometrical Aids, Generation Seed, Generation Name, Aids Generation,
Descendants Seed, "I Am The Pope Seed", Aids Colllision, Descendants Aids,
Placenta Text, Placenta Message, World Message, First Message, School Text,
The Child School, Placenta & The Child, Sever Placenta, Red-Tape Placenta,
The News Monad, The News Time, The News Legend, The News beast,
News Creator, News Letter, News Fossil, Real Space News, Real News
Office,
Child Brain news, Real News Cut, World War Code, First War Code,
Published Lies, Prints Lies, Doctor's Monad, The Dead's Doctor,
The C.N.A. Genetic Code, Perpetual Code, Ancestor's code, History Code,
A History Data, A History Lie, Birth and Death Code, Frequency Code,
Yin and Yang Code, Time and Crime Code, Prisoner Code,
Genetic Data Coding, Data Combination, The Life Span Data,
"26 Sacred Alphabet", A '26' Alphabet Logo, Alpha and Omega Mark,
Books Words, Books Nature, Nature's Book, Mother's Book, Mother's Choice,
Nature's Choice, Free Printing, Basic Printing, News after Date, Day after
News,

*142 = Cross of Time, Cross of the Dead, The Key of the Dead, The Home of the
Dead, The Clue of the Dead, Energy of the Dead, Force of Energy, Energy of Radio,
　　　The Home of Radio, Diabolical Energy, Language Energy, Jewish Language,
　　　English language, Diabolical Cross, Language Cross, Jewish Logos,
　　　English Logos, Nuclear atoms, Nuclear Logos, Unclear Atoms,
　　　Unclear Language, Nuclear Quark, Decipher Unclear, Unclear Signs,
　　　Signs Energy, X-Ray Energy, Nuclear X-Ray, Alpha and Omega Ray,
　　　The end of the Ages, The Pure Atom, The Holy Atom, The Word Atom,
　　　The Danger Word, The Word Logo, The Magnet Logo, The Pure Green,
　　　The Magnet Atom, Two Centres, Sciences Centre, Stars Centre, White Matter,
　　　Centre Matter, Christ Centre, The God Head Centre, White Christ,
　　　The Empiric Law, Seven Stars, Circumferences, The Deaf and the Blind,
　　　Justice in Life, Sky Justice, Nothing in Life, Subtraction, The Kingdom Law,
　　　Life Time Record, In and Out a Book, Current Book, Book Thought,
　　　The Original Act, Book Current, Judgement Book, The Ancient Book,
　　　The Judge's Book, A New Thought, Records Word, Divine Words,
　　　Divine Nature, Godly Words, Divine Vows, One New Octave, New Octave
Free,
　　　One News Judge, Free News Monad, Free News Time, One Church Monad,
　　　The Public Body, The Public branch, The Public Hero, The Diety Body,
　　　The Godly Body, The Public mad-Man, Freemason Body, Freemason's Code,
　　　A Freemason's Data, A Freemason's Lie, A Human's Centre, Skeleton Key,
　　　A Skeleton Hole, Body and Bone Key, Immortal Key, Immortal King,
　　　Red Cross Key, Bone...Body and a Mind, The Perfect Law, The Children
Law,
　　　One School Law, One World Law, One Magnetic Field, One Origin Law,
　　　One Origin Child, Iron Curtain, Pyramid Light, Light Symbol, Iron Statue,
　　　Pharaoh's Past, Sixth Sense, World Web-Line, World Web-Mind,
　　　First Baby-Mind, Adam and Eve Origin, World Stop, First Stop, World Robot,
　　　Money Stop, World Shadow, Magnetic Shadow, Magnetic Stop, Stop Hitler,
Darrell's Cyber, A Marijuana Zol, Date before News, Day before News,
　　　Linguistics,

143 = 　The Dawn of Time, The Time of Sin, The Time of Self, The Monad of Self,
　　　The Legend of Sin, The Beast of War, The Time of War, The Monad of War,
　　　The Legend of War, Legend of the Gun, Doctor of Doom, Doctor of the Dead,
　　　R.C. Doctor Monad, Ageless Skull, Diabolical Doctor, Doctor Language,
　　　Root Doctor, The Eye Doctor, The Naked Doctor, Nun's Doctor, Nun's Suffer,
　　　Ageless Doctor, Nun's Paranoia, Nun's Madness, No Girl Nuns?,
　　　Girl Nuns See?, A Nun's Man-Body, A Nun's Cross, Bishop Cross,
　　　Knight Cross, Jigsaw Cross, Check-mate Cross, Stale-mate Monad,
　　　The Dead Stale-mate, Life and Death Chess, Religion Chess, Chess Sequence,
　　　Chemical Sequence, Love Sequence, Catholic World, First Catholic,
　　　Catholic Origin, Catholic Money, Temple Money, Money Temple, First
Babylon,
　　　Temple Marriage, Nun's Death Seal, Nun's Change Mode, Nun's Cheat Death,
　　　Nun's Death Cheat, Nun's Begin Change, Black and White Mob,
　　　Black and White Mafia, Nuns Marry, Mafia's Relation, Mafia's Likeness,
　　　A Gang's Likeness, A Pagad's Likeness, The News Logo, The Mafia's News,

Mafia Bull-Shit-Bag, The Mafia's Church, Man and Woman Mob, Mafia's Pattern,

Donkey Knight, The Donkey Bone, The Nun's Sin, The Boy Nuns,
The New Nuns, The War Nuns, Nun's Immune, Deaf and Dumb Language,
The Nun's Gun, The Nun's War, The Husband Joke, The Nun's Lady,
The Lady Nuns, Fuck the Husband, Fuck the Bishop, Fuck the Romance,
Fuck the Knight, Fuck the Whore, Fuck the Fat Bitch, Fuck the Fat Lady,
Fuck the Red Lady, Fuck the Lady Red, Fuck the Fat Boy, Nun's Puss,
Critical Language, Language Analogy, Logo's Analogy, Analogical Logos,
Analogical Language, Analogical Signs, Atom D.N.A. Analogy, Maximum Speed,

Speed Resonance, Speed Pattern, Maximum Phase, Maximum Apogee,
The God in You, David & Solomon, Mercury Mind, Human mind Body,
First and Last, The Chicken and Eggs, The Human Chicken,
The Chickens Eggs, The Dodo Chicken, The Dodo Chicken Egg,
The Same Chicken Egg, Change The Chicken Egg, Changes The Chick Egg,
Changes the Chick D.N.A., Changes Chicken R.N.A.,
Changes Dead Chicken Egg, Earth's Origin, Earth and World, Earth's World,
Oscillate the Dead, Oscillate Time, Oscillate Omen, Oscillate Beast,
Oscillate Monad, The Face of Jesus, The Face of Messiah, The Face of Lucifer,

Duiwel Van die Ma, Ouma's Duiwel, Vader's Duiwel, Son Kyk Ons,
Blood of Jesus, Crime of Lucifer, Craft of Lucifer, Son of Lucifer,
Cycle of Energy, Ring of Energy, Trade of Nuclear, Nuclear War-Code,
Japan...Nuclear Code, Japan's Armageddon, An Atom Bomb Monad,
Mustard Omen, Hydrogen Force, Force...Time...Speed, Density Force,
The Dead Speed Time, Monad Speed Time, Brain Current, Brain Thought,
The Brain Octave, Artistic Brain, Logo Brain Chart, Logo Pattern, Atom Pattern,

Speed Pattern, Danger Pattern, Green Pattern, Garden Pattern, A Blood Pattern,

Pattern Phase, Apogee Pattern, God-made Pattern, Model Pattern, Pattern Sign,

Born Pattern, Born Black & White, Doctor's Logo, End Doctor's Lie,
End Doctor's Data, End Mega Doctors, A Doctor's Blood, A Doctor's Crime,
A Doctor's Sex, A Doctor's Abuse, Playboy Monad, Playboy Legend,
Self-Love Monad, Mechanical Energy, Modern Energy, Modern Lucifer,
The Devil Father, Atlantis Monad, Return The Dead, Dead Aids To You,
Doom To You, Serpent Body, Serpent Branch, Body Control,
Body Gene Marker, Ancient Body Gene, Queer Matter, The Queer Brain,
Court Judges, Court Woman, Dualman Matter, Man+ Wo Matter,
Adam Kadmon Curse, The God Head Curse, The God Head Twin,
The Mad God Twin, Adam Kadmon Twin, Family Court, Family Matter,
Freedom Matter, Christ Freedom, The God Head Freedom, Ancient Christ,
Christ Twin, Ancient Forces, Lamentations, The Forbidden Name,
Secret Number, Hethgrammaton, Secret Children, Killing People,
English People, Jewish People, Secret Sacrifice, Children Stop, Secret Kingdom,

Robot Children, Robot Number, Identical Twin, The Closed Door,

Sidereal Month, Honoris Causa{**An Hon. Degree}, Sol Kerzner, Circuit
Breaker,
Gold Bank Account, My Bank Account, Change Bank Account,
Balance Bank Account, Same Bank Account, Jew Bank Account,
Africa Bank Account, Death Bank Account, Die Vierde Kabinet,
World Wide Web, First Fuck Baby, Her First Rape, Her First Mind,
Her First Pain, The Queen Sex, The Queen Cycle, Finger Daughter,
Daughter's Rape, Rape's Daughter, Daughter's Pain, Dead Man's Record,
Dead Man's Switch,

*144 = The Book of The Dead, The March of The Dead, The March of Doom,
The March of Time, The Book of Time, God Lives in Man, Man Lives in
God,
God Lives in OM, God Lives in Air, The Twin Gods, The Twin Bridge,
The Lost Gods, The Lost Path, The Lost Bridge, "I am the Image of Life",
"I Am The Eye of Life", "I am The Image of Eve", King Solomon,
The True Judge, Peter The Judge, The Israel Judge, The Israel Monad,
The Israel Legend, Blind Colours, Yom Kippur, Three Wise Men, Inspiration,
Umvelinqangi {**Zulu God}, Imaginary Monad, Imaginary Beast, Imaginary
Time,
Imaginary Legend, Stuck in Time, Stop and Move, Stop's Cloud, Nuclear
Stop,
Energy Stop, Parent Stop, Messiah Stop, The Omega Stop, Nuclear Robot,
The Robot Key, The Home Robot, Darrell Nuclear, Darrell's Escom,
Darrell's Sky, Darrell's Cloud, Darrell's Watch, Darrell's Laws,
Darrell's Dead Key, Darrell's Dead Mom, Darrell's Trap, Darrell's The Ape,
Darrell Awakens, Adam and Eve Awakens, Parent Adam and Eve,
Anti-Clock-wise, Begotten Past, Complex Past, Light Complex, Nameless
Light,
Nameless Past, Past vision, Vision Light, Electrical Light, Electrical Past,
Policeman Past, Thieves Past, Blue-Crime Past, Blue Crime Light,
Blue Blood Wolf, Blue Light Crime, Blue's The Devil, The Devil's Food,
Liars Biology, Biological Liars, Slave Biology, Aryan Biology, Aryan Brain
Key,
Aryan Cancer Key, The African Slave, The African Liars, The African Coolie,
The African Makula, The African Manager, The Earth Liars, Slave the Earth,
The Last Liars, The Last Ayran, The Last Boers, The Earth Boers,
The African Boers, The Solid Earth, Poor Farmers, Poor Zulu,
Poor Afrikaan D.N.A., Zulu Infant, Bright Zulu, True Afrikaans, Mark of the
Beast,
March of The Monad, Time Control, The Dead Control, Free Public Time,
Free the Dead Public, The Computer, Electronic Mind, Mind Observer,
Food Observer, Pain Observer, Electronic Dogma, Electronic Liar,
Electronic Film, Electronic Line, Electronic Pain, Computer Aids,
Computer Magic, Voodoo Science, Pyramid Science, Science Formula,
Science Symbol, The Grave Science, The Grave Father, Pharaoh's Science,
Triangle Science, Triangle Star, Science Statue, Science Fraction,
A Matrix Science, A Biological Science, A Micro Biology, Sedated Souls,
A Biological Star, A Biological Father, The Atlas Science, Compass Science,
The Image of Satan, Famous People, No Body People, See Hero People,

The Alphabet Body, The Body Centre, No Deceased People, Ref. Dove
People,
See Stella Body, Rouses the Dead, My Soul Mate, My Soul Team,
Soul Death Team, The Law Doctor, The God of Israel, God of the Poor,
Synesthesia,

*145 = Dagne Aud Gontier, Proto-plasm, Psychology, Judge of Character, Third
Insight,
Doom of Character, Character of Doom, Character of the Dead,
Character of the Ma, Numerology, Biological Order, Biological Word,
Biological Magnet, Magnetic Number, Number Origin, First Number, Count
First,
Nostradamus, Character of Time, Prophet of God, The Holy Six, The Holy
Pope,
The Earth Magnet, The Devil's Key, The Devil's Home, The Pope's Key,
The Earth's Lock, The African's King, The Pope's Dream, The Pope's Clue,
Kinetic Energy, Limited Surface, Limited Kingdom, Sacrifice Limited,
Children Limited, Limited Living, Limited the Mind, Limited Flying,
Surface Radius, World Surface, Paradise World, Money Front, First Number,
School Children, Chicken's Sacrifice, School Number, School Count,
Perfect World, School Child Mode, Hade's Child School, Chronological Age,
Age Chronology, Everlasting-age, Age Controller, I.D. Controller,
Septuagint age, Triple Six Age, Three Sixes I.D., The Door Keeper,
Authorities,   The Earth keeper, The Devil Keeper, The African Keeper, The Devil in
Hell,
The Pope in Hell, Bottom in Hell, Bottom Order, The Devil Vow, The Police
Devil,
The African Police, The African Robber, The African Battle, African Aids
Battle,
African Police Name, Millennium end, In Prophesy, In Implosion, In Mush-
Room,
In News Room, Come in…like a Thief, King And Queen end,
End the Ark of Noah, In the Day of Noah, In the Day of Death,
End the Change of Baby, End the Death of Baby, Umbilical Cord end,
Umbilical Line end, Umbilical in Mind, Records in Mind, Adam and Eve's
Past,
Genetics in Mind, Genetic D.N.A. in Mind, Genetic Idea in Mind,
Genetic Adam In Mind, End Umbilical Food, Genetic D.N.A. in Food,
The Human Bone D.N.A., The Umbilic Birth D.N.A., Child Birth D.N.A. &
R.N.A.,
Child Birth Seed & Egg, Divided Blue Blood, Divided Mind Blood,
Divided Food Cycle, Divided Live Mind, Evil Birth Pain, Human Mind Cycle,
Human Tree Food, Human Life Beings, Human Life Begins, Coincidental
Law,
Manipulation, Faces of the Moon, Begotten Birth, Moon Light Cell,
Light's Shadow, Shadow and Light, Darrell's Past, Post and Past, Electric
Stop,
Doctor Stop, Analogical Stop, Madness Stop, Critical Stop, Stop Distance,
Stop Nobody, A Cross Stop, A Stop and Move, The Magnet Form,
The Earth Magnet, The Magnet Riddle, The Police Riddle, The Word Riddle,

Riddle The Vow, Race Against Time, Race Against the Dead,
Race Against Doom, Stuck in Tube, Reborn Children, Reborn Number,
Paradise ...Garden-end, Primal Addition, Green in Paradise, Lord in Paradise,
"I am God...in Paradise", "I Am God ...in Number", 'I am the Ratio God',
"I am the Whole God", "I am the Diety God", "I am the Divine God",
"I am the Godly God", Holy Script, Word Script, Pure Script, Magnet Script,
Synaesthesia, Cell Mutation, Life Mutation, M/C 2 Mutation, Bomb Mutation,
Human Past Life, Historian Life, Historian Agenda, Life Resistance,
Cell Resistance, Bomb Resistance, Standard Life Cell, Three in one Life,
Light in One Cell, The Rebirth Cell, The Life in Birth, Iron & Oxide Cell,
Black and White Cell, Black and White life, Dying Sun Cell, Universe Life,
A Baby Birth and Death, Birth and Death Echo, A Baby's Ancestor,
Perpetual Echo, History Echo, A Baby History, A Bible History, A Ark
History,
Land History, Land Continent, Frequency Echo, Land Frequency,
Solar Pole Cell, Solar Pole Life, Solar Life Cycle, Petro Net Cell, Blood
Control,
Crime Control. Crime Amnesty, Sex Serpent, Blood Serpent, Tree Serpent,
Live Serpent, Evil Serpent, Eve's Relation, Eve's Likeness, Homo Likeness,
Eve's Black & White, Black and White Life, Esoteric Homo, A Esoteric
Circle,
A Guilty Circle, America Hierarchy, Hierarchical Circle, Sacred Hierarchy,
Bush Hierarchy, One Hierarchism, Hate Hierarchism, Free Mind Arch Key,
One Baby Mind Key, The Sacred Books, The Sacred Torah, The Sacred Ruin,
The Sacred Hour, The Sacred Medicine, The Bush Medicine, Under the Bush,
The Queen Circle, Queen Monkey, A News Monkey, Cosmic Monkey,
Monkey Plasma, Monkey Signal, Digital Wisdom, Monkey Action, Monkey
Rest,
Monkey Hour, Under Monkey, Monkey Sense, Monkey Vote, Monkey Ballot,
Cosmic Author, Real Time Hour, Child Time Hour, Under Real Time,
Under Real Monad, Judge Under Law, The Dead Under Feet, Lode Stone
Field,
A Echo Resistance, Cosmic Psychic, Perceive Under, Psychic Signal,
The Cosmic 'I' Ching, The Cosmic Circle, The Cosmic Bush, Law Under
Rock,
Time Under Law, Doom's Day Logo,

*146 = The Holy Atlas, Heavenly Bodies, Heavenly Chemical, Heavenly Love,
Heavenly Sun, God's Holy Key, God's Holy Home, God's Word Key,
God's Pure Key, God's Magnet Key, Fish Meets Fish, Fish Meets Tail,
Darre'l Gontier, Fish meets Self, Self Meets Self, Boy meets Lady,
Boy meets Bitch, Lady meets Bitch, Bitch meets Bitch, Lady meets Lady,
Guns meet War, T.V. meets Tele, Radar meets T.V., Radar meets U.F.O.,
U.F.O. meet Church, U.F.O. meet News, You meet Self, God's Holy Dream,
The Apocalypse, Lucifer Himself, First Energy, Magnetic Energy, Nuclear
Origin,
First Cross, World Messiah, The World King, The First King, The King
Origin,
The Earth News, The African News, The Devil News, The Pope News,
The Pope Church, The Roman Pope, The African Church, The African's War,

The Devil's Sin, The Pope's Sin, The Pope's War, The Earth's War,
Big Brother War, War Experience, New Experience, Self Experience,
Pervert War, News Script, News Biology, Biological News, Biological Wars,
Wars Biology, New D.N.A. Biology, New Biological D.N.A., New Biological
Idea,
Plagiarism Key, Plagiarism Clue, A Neurotic Mind, Human Memory,
Birth Memory, Moon Memory, Changes Memory, Changes the Past,
Changes the Wolf, Changes the Light, A Umbilical D.N.A. Cut, The Christ
Child,
The Umbilic Cut, Ancient Child Brain, Woman...Brain...Child, The Human
Past,
The Moon Light, The Human Light, The Human Will, The Birth Yoke,
The Birth Shell, The Human Shell, The Death's Past, Balances the Past,
Changes the Past, Balances Life and Death, Human Life and Death,
Children Sacrifice, Living Sacrifice, Living Sound, Perfect Sound, Children
Front,
Sacrifice Shrine, Sexy children, All Sex Children, All Abuse Children,
Children Abuse All, A Magnetic Stone, A Reborn Stone, Children Reborn,
Manifestation, Divine Wisdom, Godly Wisdom, Diety Wisdom, Chinese
Dowism,
The Chinese 'I' Ching, The Chinese Circle, The Chinese Drug, Chinese
Narcotic,
Chinese Deficiency, Chinese Book of Adam, Chinese Book of D.N.A.,
Chinese Book of Idea, Chinese Psychic, Negative Chinese,
The Sacred China Man, Chinese Monkey, The Human Wolf, The Human End,
The Resistance, Monkey Penis, Genetic Monkey, Darwin Matter,
Monkey Record, The Baby Monkey, The New Baby Mom, Catholic Doctor,
Temple Doctor, Sperm Doctor, Ovum Doctor, Babylon Doctor,
Lawful Baby Fuck?, Children's Vagina, Post Prick Egg, Stop Human Egg,
Stop Human Idea, Stop Human D.N.A., Stop Human Adam,
Adam And Eve's Birth, Temple Death Seal, Nun's Genesis, Nun's Embryo,
Diabolical Embryo, Crucified Atoms, Crucified Quark, Decipher Genesis,
Genesis Signs, Soul Nature, Copies Mother, Mother's Blood, Mother's Tree,
Mother's Cycle, Mother's Sex, Mother's Son, Mother's Chord, Separated Birth,
Separated Human, Separated Moon, The Moon Past, The Moon Light,
Black Hole Matter, See Mind Matter, No Mind Matter, Mind Page Matter,
Black Mind Matter, The Black Colour, See the Colour, Black and Blue Father,
Father Policeman, Policeman Science, Policeman Star, Policeman Bravo,
A Alpha-Bravo Logo, Colour Action, Pure Racial War, Racial War battle,
Racial War Word, New Racial Word, New Racial Order, New Racial Vow,
United Nation, United Kingdom, United Children, A World Sacrifice,
An Adult Count, Count Children, Number Unbalance, A School Unbalance,
Commit The Mind, Aids Resistance, R.N.A. Resistance, Name Resistance,
Seed Resistance, Magic Resistance, The Face of Christ,
The Face of the God-head, The Face of Adam Kadmon, The Salvation,
Great Son of God, Blood of Christ, Tree of Christ, Cycle of Matter, The
Exorcist,
Mechanical Power, Modern Power, Volt Power, Volt Matter, People Matter,
Wealth Matter, Primal Power, The Third Eyes, The Mind's Eye,
The Buddha's Eye, The Mind's Image, The Six and Nine, Unicorn Image,

African Likeness, Earth Likeness, Pope Likeness, Devil Birth Begin,
African Cemetery, Inspired African, African Covenant, African Bull-Shit,
African Human-being, Pope Doctors, African Doctor's, African Man &
Woman,
African Micro-Chip, African Field Science, African Child Science,
African Law Science, African-Law Father, African Child Father,
Pope... child Father, African 'come' Science, Reforms R.N.A. & D.N.A.,
Black & White Devil, Black & White Pope, Black & White African,
African Unicorn, African Brain Circle, African Bush Brain, Exorcised Brain,
Brain Slavery, Drugs the Brain, Principle Brain, The Child Mind Begin,
Principle Cut, The Child Mind Dies, Umbilic Cord Seal, Umbilic Mind Seal,
Seal the Child Mind, Cheat the Mind Law, Cheat the Mind Chip,
The Child David... Dies, Bad Curri-culum, Bad Chemical Reaction,
Bad Solar Energy, Bad Pituitary, The New Baby Sacrifice,
Number the New baby, Number the New Day, Count the New Baby,
Self Count...the Baby,The Mind Judge's Bad, Sacrifice the Mind,
A New Counting, My Date of Birth, My Day of Birth, My Crucified Day,
My Baby Genesis, Same Bible Genesis, Dictates to Baby, Consistancy,
Dictates to Him, The Coming Form, The Devil Coming, The News Form,
The Roman Ship, Rocket Energy, Nuclear Rocket, False Moon Body,
False Satellite, Hot Mercury, False Time Flow, Set Space Warp,
Calendar Week Set, A False Calendar Week, Moon Hologram,
Human Hologram, Human Life and Death, The Human Past,
The Death's Past, The Death's Light, A Tribune Light, Moon Anatomy,
Human Anatomy, Human Incubus, Human Gene-Pool, Human Gene Science,
A Complete Past, A Complete Light, False Chemical Atom, Hot Chemical
Atom,
Hot Sun Atom,

*147 = Inter-Course, The Pure Love, The Magnet Chemical, The Chemical Word,
Computer Chip, Computer Law, Computer Ohm, Conjugate Wave,
Critical Radius, World Diameter, Magnetic Diameter, Poets' Origin,
Electric World, Electric Origin, The Dead Write All, The Dead Sea's Poet,
Atlantis Wave, Atlantis Rise, Atlantis Sea God, A Pymander Tomb,
A.E.I.O.U. in sound, Voices in Reader, Reader's Vowel, The C.N.A. Prints,
Red Tape by The C.N.A., Released by The C.N.A., The C.N.A. Nile Paper,
The C.N.A. Knowledge. Published Daily, Prints Daily, A.E.I.O.U. Characters,
The A.N.C.Characters, Pictured Daily, Genesis Text, Genesis Message,
Genesis Worded, Jehovah Genesis, The Law Genesis, Red Tape Genesis,
A Freemason Circle, Homo-Society, A Judicial Red Circle, A Red Suit Circle,
A Red Knight Circle, A Red Bishop Circle, Wave Oscillate, Wave Invariance,
An Atom Bomb Wave, An Atom cell wave, Hydrogen Wave, Uniform Wave,
A Constant Hole, A Constant Film, A Constant Mind, A Constant Line,
A Mathematical Line, A Mathematical Film, A Mathematical Mind,
A Mathematical Liar, A Constant Idol, Rise on Water, Waves Vibrate,
Wave Coincident, Wave Density, Homo-Destiny, Mars' Time-Speed,
Homo Time Lord, Judges Another, Ancient Venus, Judges' Mind Key,
Judge's Arrest, The Naked Homo Man, Physical Love, The Public Homo,
The Homo Elders, Mars Face Venus, Judicial Hand Rise, Judicial Hand Wave,
A Complex's Angle, A Complex Science, Liars Complex, Begotten Liars,

Physical Chemical, The Etheric Body, Language Nature, Secular Language,
The Body Language, Logo's Nature, Logo's Words, Determination,
The Yin And Yang, The Time and Crime, Grave Harmony, The History,
The Horoscope, The Past Science, The Pure Note, The Pure French,
The French Word, The French Vow, The Lost Chord, The Twin Cycle,
The Twin Son, The Twin Sex, The Blood Twin, The Lost Note, Past & Future,
The Birth and Death, The Magnet Voice, Congregation, The Human Birth,
Last Supper, Ninety Four, Surface Energy, Nuclear Count, Unclear Number,
The Wheel of David, The Axis of Mind, The Mind of Cyber, The Mind of
Chicken,
The Pain of Chicken, The Rape of Chicken, First Puss, Chicken's Puss,
Puss Origin, Chicken...arse...and...Cock, Adam and Eve's Science,
Cock's Knowledge, Eve's Return, Life's Return, A Life's Promise,
The Food of Chicken, The Atlas of Mind, Magnetic North, Static North,
Positive Life, Positive Cell, Figure Eight Cell, Lost Atom Cell, Ancient Atom
Cell,
Ancient Green Cell, Ancient Garden Life, Atom Combination, Speed
Consonant,
Twin Cell Atom, Genetic Cell Coding, Genetic Life Coding,
Genetic Bomb Coding, Plant Cell Coding, African Plant Cell, African
Hierarchy,
Robben Island Jail, Mandela's Lock-Up, Mandela's Home mode,
Mandela's Hell Home, A Mandela's Hell Hole, A Mandela's Mind Begin,
A Mandela Idol begins, Nelson Mandela Head, Pandora's Head Box,
Pandora's Sickle, Head Destroyer, Mad Destroyer, Pandora's Liars,
Pandora's Comrade, Pandora's Dragon, Pandora's Finger, Pandora's a Star,
Pandora's Films, Hollywood Head, Virtual God Head, Holy Ghost Head,
Pure Text Head, My Mad Theory, Vivisection, "Human Genetic Code",
Genetic Birth Code, Human Plant Race,

*148 = Thermo-Dynamic, The Magnets Field, The Magnets Law, Nuclear Weapon,

Nuclear Energy, Unclear Energy, Naked Angle Energy, Image Angle Photo,
Moves Eye Angle, Eye Dot Energy, Pupil Eye Dot, Change a Pupil Image,
Change a Photo Image, Change a Cross Image, Change a Parent Image,
The Human Father, The Human Science, The Birth Father, The Birth Science,
The Moon Science, The Moon & Star, The Two-Moon, The Double Light,
Dark Star Light, Fair Star Light, Light Faces Star, One Star Light,
Free Star Light, Twilight-Hole, Mind Twi-light, Earth-Hole-Light, Earth Mind
Light,
The C.N.A. Key Light, The C.N.A. Home Light, The C.N.A. Control,
The C.N.A. Gene Marker, The C.N.A. Land Marker, The C.N.A. Broad Sheet,
The C.N.A. Fuse Link, The C.N.A. Amnesty, Homo Control, Rome Control,
Kaffir Control, The C.N.A. Story, The C.N.A.State Agenda,
The Head Centre Agenda, White Kaffir Cell, White Kaffir Agenda,
White Homo Cell, White Kaffir Jail, A Bush Control, Genesis Shadow,
Adam and Eve Genesis, Egg and Cock Genesis, Tree of Life Monad,
Cycle of Life Monad, Cycle of Life Time, Cycle of Life Legend,
Blood of the Dead Life, Cycle of the Dead Agenda, Blood of the Body,
Cycle of the Hero, Blood of the Dove, Tree of the Dove, Branch of the Tree,

Umbilic-Nature, Text Nature, Worded Words, Nature...was God,
Mother & the Child, God Saw...Mother, Words...was God, The Magnet's
Chip,
Unique You, Unique News, Birthday News, Human Baby News,
Death's Baby News, In-breeding News, Natural News, Earth's Print,
African Prints, Pope Prints, Devil's Print, African Blood Craft, African Tree
Craft,
African Blood Cycle, Earth Blood Cycle, African Blood Tree, African Crime
Cycle,
African Knowledge, Devil Knowledge, Earth Knowledge, Catholic Funeral,
Temple Funeral, Morning Star, Missing Star, Missing Father, Missing
Science,
Missing Angles, Double Hologram, Hologram Copy, Mystic Liars, Mystic
Idols,
Liars Religion, Liars Anatomy, Direct Sequence, Light's Shadow, Past
Memory,
Memory Light, Cross Cloning, Cloning Energy, Nuclear Cloning, Destruction,
Escom's Energy, Koeberg Biology, Messiah Cross, Lucifer Cross, Jesus Cross,
The Omega Energy, Jesus & Lucifer, Diety Biology, Biological Diety,
Divine Biology, The Trinity, Trinity Seed, The Homo-Sapien, Homo-Sapien
Seed,
Homo-sapien Aids, Plant Biology, Penis Biology, Steroid Science,
A Human Steroid, A Prick Steroid, German Steroid, One Small Prick,
Doctor's Love, Puss Muscle, Puss Sacrifice, Muscle Doctor, Pussy Cat-Act,
A Tom Cat Doctor, A Body-Muscle Man, A Hero Muscle Man, Biological
Plant,
The Earth Plant, Earth on Water, Water on Earth, Uniform Earth,
Flood Lake Water, No Salt Water, See Flood Water, No Earth Water?,
Ship on Water, Cross-Cross, Pope on Water, Oikoumene Dogma,
Oikoumene Rape, African on Water, Descendants Line, Liar's Descendant,
Rastafarian Line, Rastafarian Nile, Oikoumene Nile, Liar's Memory,
Slave Memory, Koran Memory, Liar's Hologram, The Black Slave Race,
The Black Slave Code, The Black Comrade Code, Dumb Unity, Dogma
Unity,
Mind Sequence, Mind Virus, Mystic Liars, Slave Mystic, Mind's Parasite,
Parasite's Food, Religion's Idol, Liar's Religion, Regulates Mind,
Regulates Film, Regulates Food, Regulated Laws, Old Testament,
A Bible Testament, Old Statement, Land Testament, A Baby Statement,
A Ark Testament, Old News Paper, Old Past News, Old Latin News,
Old Shit News, Land Shit News, Past...News...Echo!,
African Ho Ho Ho-Ha Ha Ha, The C.N.A. Take-Over, Latin Church Bell,
Latin Telegraph, Light Telegraph, Paper Telegraph, Black Race Telegraph,
Black Ball Telegraph, Black Ball Rhythm, The Paper Copy, Copy The Past,
Double The Past, Editorial Laws, Copy the Light, Editorial Watch,
Editorial Dead Key, Dead Editorial Clue, Regulated Watch, Propaganda Laws,
Satan...Died and Lived, Jesu...Died and Lived, News Media Watch,
Watch News Agenda, Watch News Life, Same News Atom, Watch M/C2 News
{**NEWS...means...North, East, West & South...it indicates to us the Current
Flow of *The Magnetic Field / *Relativity}, Scriptures, Literatures,
Hypotenuse,

Able To Stretch, Provocation, Protestant, Guy Fawke's Day, Lucifer Cross,
Jewish Cross, Jewish Parent, English Cross, Cross a Number
{**1+0=A+O...First
and Last/Alpha & Omega), The Child's Teacher, The Laws' Teacher,
The Wicked Teacher, Puranic Legends, Puranic Monads, Puranic Times,
Inner Life Light, Inner Past Life,

*149 = The Inner Light, Electric Energy, Diameter Energy, Infra-red Energy,
Critical Energy, Eternal Energy, Madness Unclear, Madness Energy,
Messiah Madness, Nuclear Madness, Paranoia Energy, Analogy Unclear,
Analogical Dialogue, Between Distance, Between Diameter, Between Doctor,
Doctor Energy, Red Blood Energy, Red Blood Cross, Photo-Electric,
Red Cross Blood, Red-Cross Trade, Live Red-Blood Data, Photography,
Spiral Energy, Nuclear Spiral, The New Energy, The New Messiah,
The New Lucifer, The New Jesus, The New Muhammad, The New Gospel,
The New Cross, A Doctor's Note, Write...unclear, A Doctor's Hand Code,
A Doctor's Tribe, A Doctor's Chemical, A Doctor's Love, A Doctor's Search,
Change Heaven and Earth, Change Electrons, Human Electron,
Human Cell Order, Human Life order, Order Human Life, Police Human Life,
Police Human Cell, Police Human Jail, Change Computer, Change The
Genesis,
The Jew Genesis, The Fire Genesis, The Adolf Genesis, The Gold Genesis,
The Death Genesis, The Same Genesis, The Noah Genesis, The Boat Genesis,
Oikoumene Fuck, Funerary Fuck, Funerary Home, The Skull Key,
Suffer Aids Fuck, Immune Energy, Immune Unclear, H.I.V. Immune Image,
Team Image Immune, My Computer, Christ Himself, Origin Christ,
Magnetic Christ, World Christ, First Christ, The First God head, The First
Brain,
The Magnetic Brain, The World Brain, The Chicken's Brain, Astrolatry,
The Laws of Mind, The Sky of Mind, The Laws of Pain, The Laws of Rape,
Discriminating, The Laws of David, Illumination, Astrologers, Judas Iscariot,
A Scale of Justice, A Mind of Justice, Key of Justice, Home of Justice,
Civilization, Environment, Oscillation, Gravitational, The Egyptians,
The Egyptian Ra, The Egyptian Idea, Egyptian R.N.A.+ D.N.A., Maltese
Cross,
Your Naked Image, Your Naked Eye, Your Eye Image, Your Shadow,
Electrical Charges, News Complex, News Photon, Nameless News,
News Dynamics, News Volume, Massive News, Police News Man,
Liar's News Page, News Doctrine, Church Doctrine, Sin's Doctrine,
News mens' Mode, News Agenda's Feed-Back, Newsmens' Demo,
News Life Agenda Act, News Men-Life Act, Editor's Sickel, Editor's Copy,
Editor's Double, Editor's Slave, Catholic Genesis, Catholic Start,
Temple Genesis, Babylon Genesis, Catholic 'Mind' Change,
Same Catholic Dogma, Moses Genesis, Qur'an Genesis, Desert Start,
Genesis Barrier, Pope's Genesis, Devil's Genesis, African's Genesis,
Earth's Genesis, Earth Egg Genesis, Earth Adam Genesis, Genesis Advocate,
Advocated Jury, The Chips are Up, The Laws are Up, Policeman begin Act,
Policeman Demo Act, Nature's Rise, Critical Point, Critical Cross,
Pope John Paul, Holy of Holies, Penis and Pinis, Spitting Image,

*150 = Codex Nasaraeus, Story of Life, Alphabetical Order, Communication,
Bio-Technology, Lie Technology, Reductionism, Data Technology,
Space Programme, Brain Programme, Cancer Programme, Programme Cut,
The Astral Body, The Astral Hero, Big-Brother Body, Pervert Branch,
Marxist Branch, Marxist Body, Blue Movie Hero, Blue Movie Girl,
Blue Movie Body, Hero Existence, Body Existence, Branch Existence,
Body Experience, Integrated Monad, Hero's Script, Body's Biology,
Biological Body, A Satellite Body, Digital Tele-Body, Digital T.V. Body,
Signalling Body, Digital Radar Body, Body Observer, Electronic Body,
God's D.N.A. Formula, Dust Formula, An Atom formula, Pyramid Dust,
The Dust Mirage, The Israel Blur, The Grave Dust, Politic's Monad,
Political Mirage, Angle of the Moon, Vertical Order, Missing Word,
Genetic-code Word, Object Word image, Eye Word Obect, Computer Team,
Computer Ten{*1+0}, Witch-Craft Team, Science Numbers, Ten Electrons,
Numbers Father, Numbers Science, Micro Numbers, Pythagora's Cabala,
A Pythagora's Idea, A Pythagorian Ra, Idea Development, Developments,
Egg Corpuscles, The Adam Garden of Eden, The Egg Garden of Man,
The D.N.A. Atom of Man, The D.N.A. Atom of Air, The Language of Man,
The Language of Om, The Language Logo, The Lords Logo, The Lord's

Atom,
Magnetism Atom, Magnetism Logo, The Sign Language, The Logo Language,
The Atom Quark, The Atoms Atom, The Danger Signs, Skeleton Sign,
Skeleton Atom, Skeleton Logo, Skeleton Phase, Immortal Lord, Immortal

Atom,
Immortal Logo, Atom Compound, Atom Interval, Invisible Danger, Invisible

Atom,
"Invisible...'I'...am God", Calcination Phase, A Live Calcination,
A Blood Calcination, Calcination Apogee, Side-by-Side Logo, Sing Side-by-

Side,
Atom M/C Squared, Logo M/C Squared, "A+O Logo Squared",
Atom Wave Offer, In-accessible Atom, Body and Bone Atom, Full Logo

Circle,
Full Atom Circle, Zodiacal Sign Map, Catholic Sign Map, Catholic Mafia

Sign,
Catholic Mob Sign, Temple Mob Logo, Catholic Bible Logo, Swatsika

Monad,
Swatsika Omen, Swatsika Time, Time Diffusion, The Dead Time Flow,
Monad Diffusion, Epoch Diffusion, Satellite Time, East Star Omen,
East Star Time, East German Monad, East German Time, Moon Body Time,
Regulated Birth, Regulated Moon, Moon & Sun Angle, Human Love Angle,
Human Chemical Angle, Human's Eye Angle, Satellite Rock, Physical Moon,
Physical Birth, Coloured Birth, Human Child Birth, Human Parents,
Human D.N.A. Cross, Adam's Death Cross, Adam Changes Parent,
Changes Parent D.N.A., Changes Parent Egg, Dodo's Egg Parent,
Change Dodo Parent, Change Egg's Parent, Change Babies Parent,
Babies Change Unclear, Change Babies New Life, Change Families Babies,
Jew Families Death, Africa Families Death, Same Families Death,
Families Death Balance, Cancel Families Death, Adolf Families Death,
Adolf Cross Jew, Adolf's Nuclear Idea, Same Jew Parent, Same Jewish Ideas,

Same Jew Ruler, Same Africa Ruler, Change Africa Ruler, Alpha Nuclear
Fire,
Escom's Fire Balance, Escom's Death Balance, Escom's Gold Balance,
The Key of Escom, The Omega of Escom, Electro-Magnetic, The Cycle of
Evil,
The Blood of Evil, Electricity Beam, Electric-City Head, Electric Moon Head,
Control of Life, Control of M/C2, Control of Bomb, Cyber Control,
Chicken Control, Grave Control, Serpent of Life, Fuse-Link of Life,
Fuse-Link of M/C2, Fuse-link of Bomb, Story of Eve, Cyber Story,
Three-Six & Nine, The Key of Heaven, Chicken Story, Chicken Control,
Story of Life, Story of Eve, Heavenly Science, Heavenly Star, Heavenly
Scope,
Heavenly Zodiac, Heavenly Muse, Heavenly Father, New Earth Light,
Earth Sin Past, Understanding, On-Line Service, Web-net Service,
Web net Mind Key, On-Line Buddhaism, Service On-Mind, Mafia-net
Service,
Mob-net Service, Agang-net Service, A Pagad Team Mind Lock,
"W.W.W. Service", Synthesize, Serpent of Arabia, Ark of Judgement,
Day of Judgement, Judgement of Mafia, Judgement of Mob, Rome
Judgement,
Kaffir Judgement, A Bush Judgement, A Sacred Judgement,
A Judgement Circle, A Nato Judgement, Homo-Judgement, Mars Current,
Venus on-line, King David on-line, Mind Key on-line, God's Binary Law,
God's OT/NT Law, Always...On-Line, Always...On-Mind, Critics...On Film,
Daily Judgement, Darrell...The Judge, Darrell...The Beast, Darrell & Real
Space,
Darrell & Real Brain, Darrell & Law Brain, Darrell & Child Brain, Darrell's
You,
Darrell's News, Darrell's Sins, Darrell's Church, Darrell's God Eye,
Darrell's A Word, Darrell's Atomic, Shadows You, From Criminals,
From Angel-of-Death, From Team-of-Death, Balance Angle of Form,
Change Angle of Earth, Seven Creation, Seven Biology, Biological Centre,
Cosmo Biology, Angle of Sphinx, Belt of Sphinx, Cobra of Sphinx, Holy
Sphinx,
Sphinx Word, Genetic in-breeding, Sex-Grammaton, Secret Name of God,
Anonymous I.D., Nondescript I.D., Biological Earth Age, Transcendental,
Name of Destiny, Seed of Knowledge, The Sun Ratio, The Whole Sun,
The Plant Chemical, The Godly Love, The Divine Love, The Diety Love,
"GOD IN THREE GODS", Biomedical Research, Biomedical in Chemical,
Animal's Mind-Key, Animal's Mind-Fuck, Animals Pain Key,
Pain a Animal's Mind, Drugs Lock Mind, Mind-lock Drugs, Home pain
Drugs,
Lock the Child mind, Fuck the Child Mind, The Mind Print, The Blue Print,

*151 = Jesus Christ, The Messiah God-Head, The Jesus God-Head, The Nuclear
Brain, The Brain Energy, Moves Matter, Holy Spirit, Pure Spirit, Spirit Word,
Verbal Spirit, "I am the Son of God", Four Spirit, God Mystery, Virtual Son,
Mercury Blood, Solomon Tree, Father and Son God, Schizophrenia,
Split Mind Eye, Split Mind Image, Split Naked Mind, God Solution, Data
Solution,

Mystery Data, Mega Mystery, Lie Solution, I.Q. Solution, Magnet Spirit,
Magnet Theory, Magnet Radiation, Pure Radiation, Word Radiation,
Verbal Radiation, Magnet Fission, Word Fission, Pure Fission, Pure
Geneology,
Magnet Asteroid, Verbal Asteroid, The Magnet Zodiac, The Science Vow,
Kill the Messiah, Cut the Unclear, Cut the Clear Image, Show the Mirage,
Blur the Show, Pyramid Centre, Pyramid Show, Compass Centre,
Voodoo Centre, The Grave Centre, Triangle Centre, A Bermuda Tri-angle,
A Bermuda Time Angle, Place of the Dead Body, Infinite Centre, Souls
Centre,
Pharaoh's Centre, A Biological State, A Biology Centre, Mummies Science,
Micro-Mummies, Zodiac Mummies, Sedated Mummies, God Men Mummies,
Editorial Science, Pharoah's Alphabet, News Media Science,
News Media Scope, Esoteric Gemini, Esoterical Brain, Split Distance,
Split Diameter, Split Madness, Split Human Head, Split The Self, Split Infra-
red,
Electric Split, Split Death Seal, Split Death and Hade, Split Death's Head,
Reform Scholar, Revenge the Self, Doctor Revenge, Body Boils Blood,
Body Blood Boils, Vengence call Blood, Man Vengence Blood,
Hari-Kari Doctor, Living and Dying, The Little Buddha, The Mind Genesis,
The Pain Start, The Dead Sea Scroll, The Dead Sea Mother,
The Dead Sea Nature, The Dead Sea Words, The Dead sea listen,
All The Dead Listen, All Listen Radio?, Big-Brother Radio, Radio
Telegraphic,
Telegraphic Monad, Tele-graphic Time, Telegraphic Omen, Radio & Tele
Signal,
T.V. & Radio Signal, Digital Radio & T.V., Radio & Radar Plasma,
Cosmic T.V. & Radio, Radio & T.V. Hour, Radio & T.V. Papacy,
T.V. & Radio Queen, Mars and Venus, Samson and Delilah, Political Play,
Political Voice, Story Play, British Empire, Controllers, Doctor's of Law,
Forbidden Fruit, Forbidden Energy, The Birth of Mind, Computer Mind,
The Dictionary, The Word Science, The Verbal Science, Revolution,
Christ...the King, The Omega Christ, Angel of New Born, Phoenix He-man-
egg,
A Phoenix egg-mind, Cosmic Memory, The Yoke Plasma, The Cosmic Past,
The Cosmic Light, Hierarchy Past, Master's Past, Gomorrah Past,
Nucleus Yoke, Nucleus Shell, Seal's Nucleus, Nucleus egg seal, Past Nucleus,
Light Nucleus, Shock Nucleus, Pregnant Yoke, Pregnant Semen,
Created Nucleus, Master's Shock, Master's Latin, Master's Index,
A inner-side of Life, News of Life Begin, Life Mode of News, Energy &
Matter,
Physiology, Moves and Stand, Ageless Wisdom, Logo's Wisdom,
Language Wisdom, Diabolical Wisdom, Ageless Monkey,
Ageless Book of Adam, Ageless Wife of Adam, Age of News-paper,
Age of Publishing, Hierographical Beam, Hierography beam, Africa Historian,
Adolf Historian, Jew Historian, Same Historian, Historian Change,
Historical Mode, Historical Feed-back, Historical Demo, A Historical Law,
Einstein Rule, Einstein's = E{M/C}2, Start a Rocket, Count Down Deal,
Perfect Start, Flying Start, Surface Start, Starting Mark, False Starting,
Hot Starting, Demo-Frequency, Frequency Feed-Back, Young People,

The Young Child, The Young Feet (**Ref: Radio Frequency *161),

*152 = Seventy Nine, The New Christ, The Science of Mind, The Star of David,
The Father of Mind, The Father of David, Genealogy of David,
The Origin of God, Genealogy of Food, Computer Key, A Computer Mind,
Number's Order, Number Nature, Number's Word, Configuration, Sefirotic
Tree,
Big-Brother Tree, Mad-Sex Change Cycle, Sex Change Big Son,
Sex Changing A Mind, Changing a Mind Cycle, Big-Brother Sex, Marxist
Tree,
The Aids Death Blood, The In-Sex Cycle, The Blood in Sex,
End the Blood Cycle, Patient's Blood, Patient's Tree, Chemist Doctor,
The Brain Doctor, The Spiral Cut, The Critical Cut, Hari-Kari The Brain,
Suffer the Cut, Cut the Doctor, Doctor the Cancer, Murder The Mind,
The Analogical Brain, The Brain Madness, The Brain Analogy,
The Brain Paranoia, The Electric Brain, The Brain Diameter, The Electric
Space,
Patient's Sex, The Hidden Doctor, No-Body Matter, See Body Matter,
Condom Food Cycle, Condom Sex Food, Israel Mind Sex, Jerusalem Sex,
Pervert Sex, Marxist Sex, Marxist Cycle, Marxist Crime, Marxist Blood,
Israel Sex Film, Mind Sex Movie, Blue Sex Movie, Blue-Blood Movie,
A Pope's Sex Life, Sex Scripts, Blood Scripts, Sex 'D.N.A.' Biology,
Sex and Biology, Biological Sex Idea, The Earth Alchemy, The Earth Water,
Water Biology, Bloods Biology, Evil Biological Idea, Natal Egg Biology,
A Biological 'Baby-Come', A Biological Baby Child, Biological Mankind,
Biological Wo-man, Biological Dual-man, Biological Copies, Soul Brother,
Biological Queer, Queer Biology, Ancient Biology, Mediaval Biology,
Crime Scripts, A Sacred Tree of Life, A Sacred Son of Life, Sacred Lord of
Life,
Sacred Atom of Life, Atom Cyber Circle, Green Bush of Life,
Green Apple of Eve, The Devil's Sex, The Devil's Tree, The Earth's Tree,
The Earth's Cycle, The Earth's Blood, Temptations, Lucifer Genesis,
God Sex Genesis, A Devil's Sex Life, Parent Genesis,
Divine Adam and Eve Egg, "Naked Adam...Eve...and Able Cain",
Cain kills Able for 'C', Doc Hippocrates, Hippocratic Basic, Hippocratic Hate,
Free Thoughts, Free Thought Idea, Basic Thoughts, Chicken-Thought,
Chicken Current, Cyber Current, Cyber Thought, Free Isotopes,
Conscious-Basic, Basic Conscious,   Conscious Binah, Concentrated Ark,
Life's Free mantra, "I Believe in One God", God's Free-Children,
God's Basic Sacrifice, God's One-Kingdom, God's One Number, Childrens'
Vow,
Childrens' Word, Free the Life of Life, The Basic Life-of-Life,
The Basic Life of Eve, Free The Agenda of Life, The Fair Agenda of life,
The Chickens' Monad, The Chicken's Doom, Save the Chiken Egg,
Save the Adam-Chicken, Save Chicken's Neck, Save Male-Cocks' End,
A Male Chicken's Cycle, A Sex-Male Chickens, A Male-sex Chicken,
Cock sex Chicken, World Life Cycle, Live World Cycle, World's Life Page,
The Genetic-Code Page, See the Genetic Race, See The Holy Bible,
Page the Holy Bible, Cock-World Cycle, Magnetic Cock Cycle,
Magnetic Life Cycle, First Life Sex, First Life Cycle, Chicken's Life Cycle,

The Holy Bible Ref., One Time barrier, Free Time Barrier, Free the dead
Barrier,
Monad Hate Barrier, Temple Mind-Key, Temple Food Key, Temple Home
Rape,
Temple's Queen, Temple's Papacy, Temple's Plasma, Cosmic Temple's,
Temple Cosmic Egg, Cosmic Sperm-egg, Cosmic Adam Sperm,
The Cosmic Seed Act, The Cosmic Birth, The Cosmic's Death,
The Cosmic's Gold, Changes The Sense, The Human Sense,
Basic Human Senses, One Human God-Eye, Free Human News, News
Theory,
Church Theory, Miracle Theory, A Word Theory, A Pure Theory,
A Police Theory, A Magnet Theory, A Holy Theory, New Phoenix Egg,
New Theory Idea, News Radiation, News Fission, Future News, News Future,
News Asteroid, News Mirror, The Star News, Tabloid News Call,
Tabloid News Man, Tabloid Air-News, Published Past, Past Prints,
Newspaper Image, Newspaper Eye, Temple & Tower, Born-again Chapter,
Adam and Eve's Record, Egg and Cock Armageddon, The First beast,
The Time Origin, The Original One, The Biological One, One Biological
Seed,
One Biological Bird, Free Bird Biology, The New Stars, The New Sciences,
The New Matter, Flower Children, Denominations, Denomination-Egg,
Homo-sexual-egg, Homo Sexual Adam, Homo Sexual Idea, Homo Chicken
Sex,
Rome Chicken Sex, Daily Chicken Sex, Daily Chicken Blood,
Dodo News Chicken, Dood News Chicken, Dodo News Grave,
Cyber Dodo News, Cyber Death News, Death Grave News, Rubbing Words,
Mother Goddess, Mother & Children, Mother's Love, Mother's Sun,
Mother's Chemical, Secular Chemicals, Doom's Day Cult, Ancient Mob Shit,
Ancient Mafia Shit, Ancient Latin Mafia, Ancient Latin Ark, Ancient Voodoo,
Ancient Brother, Ancient Souls, Ancient Pyramid, Ancient Symbol,
The Chicken Pyramid, The Ancient Chicken, The Ancient Cyber,
Ancient Ark Light, Ancient Bible Past, Ancient Baby Light, Ancient Day-
Light,
Dual-Man Baby Light,
*153 = Androgynous {+ & -}, New Coat of Arms, A Man and a Woman Balance,
A man and a Woman Alike, A Sex Change Woman, A Sex Change Queer,
A Judge's Sex Change, A Ancient Sex Change, An Ancient Change of I.D.,
An Ancient Change of Age, An Ancient Aryan Age, Diabolical Biology,
Biological Language, Biological Logos, Biology's Logo, The Holy Word,
The Word Order, The Pure Word, The Verbal Word, The Verbal Order,
The Police Order, The Police Vow, Police the Word, Police the Robber,
The Active Word, The Active Tune, Tune the Word, One Solid Word,
Free Solid Vow, Basic Solid Magnet, The Magnet Word, Atom's Biology,
The Sacrifice of God, Nuclear Bomb Force, The Nuclear Mad-Man,
The Unclear Head Man, Albert Einstein, Einstein's Vice, Einstein's Ten,
Basic Science of Mind, One Star of David, Basic Scope of Mind,
Einstein's Angle, Father Einstein, Einstein's Team, "N.A.S.A. Scientist,"
Eye Scientist, Frankenstein Back, Pa Frankenstein, The Lost Chemical,
Current Chemical, Sun Current, Voice Current, Chemical Thought,

The Twin Chemical, Human Knowledge, Birth Knowledge, Moon Knowledge,
Divided Moon Angle, The Count of God, The Number of God {**1 + 0},
Catch-22 Knowledge, Mathematical Monad, Arithmetic Omen,
The Ancient Voice, The Lost Note, Earth Minutes, Earth Magnetism,
Devil Skeleton, Pope Skeleton, Earth Skeleton, Earth Division, Christian Pope,
Christian Ship, Earth Grave Yard, African Grave Yard, African Dogmatism,
A Daily Dogmatism, Earth M/C Squared, African M/C Squared, Earth Suction,
Blood Cell Count, Live Life Sacrifice, Blood Life Sacrifice, Children Sex Life,
Children's News, Children and You, Theoretically, Earth Minutes, Pope's Minute,
The Live World, The Evil World, The Actor of Self, The Divine Actor,
The Godly Actor, The Diety Actor, The Genetic Actor, The Human Genetic,
The Genesis Sin, The New Genesis, Doctor Genesis, Pornography,
Reformation D.N.A., Adam Reformation, Egg in Formation,
End Adam Formation, End Idea Formation, New Computer, War Computer,
Computer War, The Human & Ape Fuck, Human + Ape R.N.A Clue,
Plant Genetic Code, Genetic Race Plant, Unidentified Name, Unidentified Seed,
Unidentified Aids, Family Planning, Ancient Planning, Planning Cain and Abel,
The Children of God, The Kingdom of God, The Paradise of God,
Natural Forces, Natural Family, Natural Times, Different Times, Different Forces,
Different Family, THE ILLUMINATI, Fisherman's Key, The Christ Mark,
The Initiation, Magic Vocabulary, Name Vocabulary, The Shrine of God,
The Zodiacal Logo, Nought and Eight,

*154 = The Revelation, A Riddle of the Beast, A Riddle of the Seer,
One Riddle of The Dead, One Riddle of Time, One Riddle of Doom,
A Riddle of the Judge, Cycle of the Earth, Blood of the Earth, Crime of the Earth,
Sex of the Earth, A Monad of the Earth, A Monad of the Pope,
A Omen of the Last, A Face of the Last Life, Cage of the Last Life,
The Bird's Cage of Life, The Jail-Bird's Cage of Life, The C.N.A.'s Politic,
The C.N.A.- Time Flow, The C.N.A. Satellite, The C.N.A. Human Body,
Big-Brother Circle, Marxist Circle, Mercury Reader, Mercury Rise, Daily Mercury,
Mercury's Life, Mercury's Agenda, Reporter's Cake, Reporter's Cabala {**Ancient
Tree of Life/**Ancient Cycle of Life}, History Dogma, Perpetual Dogma,
A Historian Dead-Data, Historical Dogma, Historical Liar, Mind Frequency,
Dead-Data Frequency, Rape Frequency, Pain Frequency, Harm Frequency,
Team Combination, Combination Ten {**1+0}, Angle Combination,
New Sound Angle, New Number Angle, Consonant Angle, Pre-Consonant,
Ten Consonant, Team Consonant, Robben Island Team, Number Nine + Ten,
Ten Commandment, Ten Pro-Verbs, Ten Logo Verbs,

The ten-dead- Atom D.N.A., Yin and Yang Mob, Yin and Yang Ark,
Mind Prisoner, Ancestor's Mind, First Lock & Key, Magnetic Lock & Key,
World Lock & Key, A Magnetic Mind Lock, Positive Cobra, Synthesized,
Pope's Motto, The Way To Hell, The Atom to E=[M/C] 2, The Way To Hell,
Nuclear Re-actor, Unclear Reactor, Clear Image in Actor, Not Real People,
Biological People, The Biological Chip, The Law Biology, The Ohm Biology,
Biological Ghost, The Earth Ghost, The Avatar Science, The Medusa Science,
Freemason Science, Freemason Star, Freemason's Angle, Freemason's Team,
Freemason's Vice, Satanism Science, Human Control, Birth Control,
Moon Control, Control's Death, Control's Change, Control's Africa,
Control's Gold, Balances Control, Changes Story, Human Story,
Human Gene-Marker, Human Land-Marker, Moon Land Marker, Star
Density,
Micro-Invariance, Science Invariance, Conjugated Chemical, Atlantis Star,
The Sea Returns, The Sea Turns In, Sea And Earth Science,
Sea...Earth...and Star, Definite Limits, Limited Measure, Limited Limits,
The Ending of Time, The Ending of the Dead, Ending of the Beast,
Ending of the Monad, Ending of the Omen, Pyramid of the Dead,
Voodoo of the Dead, Pyramid of Time, Tri-angle of Time, Timc-Angle of
Time,
Time Angle of Monad, Time Angle of Judge, Catch-22 Control,
A Courts Catch-22, A Court's Catch-Lead, A Numerical Catch-22,
Scientific Catch-22, Scientific Birth, Catch-22 Story, Death's Amnesty,
Murder's Past, Murder's 'Black-ball', African Murderer, Pope Murderer,
Earth Murderer, Free A.N.C. Murderer, Murderer Lived, Murderer 's Name,
Murderer's Aids, Mass Murderer, Alter Murderer, Disciple in Islam,
Taught in Islam, Moslem in Islam, Judaism in Islam, Forbidden In Islam,
Forbidden in Love, Forbidden in Voice, The Hidden in Love, Funeral in Islam,
Exist in Islam, The Mask in Islam, A Court Hide-away, A Moslem Hide-away,
Church Disguise, A Holy Disguise, News Disguise, Disguised Human,
A Wolf Disguise, Disguise a Past, Jews Disguised, To Conceal Woman,
Conceal Islamic Image, To Conceal Judges, To Conceal Queer,
To Conceal Dual-man, Woman Vision, "I am Who I am...under",
'Am I Who I am...under'?, Under-reverse?, Queen Reverse, Papacy Reverse,
Dual-man Vision, Nameless Jail Faces, Disguisable Hero, Disguisable Body,
Convict Nuns, Convicted Liars, Convicted Slave, Convicted Idols,
Master's Double, Master's Copy, Copy Life record, Double Tribute, Liars
Tribute,
Pregnant Dragon, Almighty Liars, Liars Promise, Double Promise,
Diabolical Mantras, Diabolical Statue, Language Statue, Copy of a Number,
Copy of Parent, A Copy of Children, Copy of Energy, Infinite Logos,
Finite in Logos, Disguisable Branch, Disguisable Girl?, Disguisable Body,
Nun's Brother, Diabolical Brother, Sumo Brother, Nameless Homo-face,
Islamic Vision, Islamic Doctrine, Islamic Empathy, Islam's Lost Face,
Islam's Daily Mob, Father's in Islam, Sciences in Islam, Christ in Islam,
God is with Us, God is With David, God is With Mind, God is With Buddha,
Picturesque, Digital Picture, Cosmic Picture, Queen Picture, Papacy Picture,
Picture Books, A News Picture, Ruin Picture, Picture Critic, Comic Pictures,
Digital-Electron, Electron Signal, Telegraph Signal, Cosmic Telegraph,
Cosmic Rhythm, Celestial Language, The Double Signal, The Double Plasma,

Copy the Pause, Copy The Rest, The Liars Vote, The Liars Ballot,
The Liars Pause, The Liars Rest, Modus Operandi, The Asian Crises,
Monstrous, Fourth Empire, Books of Thoth, The Second Coming,
The Robber Coming, Free Police Robber, Police Faces Robber,
Black & White Robber, Police Cemetery, Police Reforms, Police Micro-Chip,
Guilty Robber, Police Covenant, Esoteric Battle, Esoteric Vow, Esoterical
Monad,
Esoterical Judge, Esoterical Omen, The Esoterical-ma, European Island,
European Liars, European Slave, European Coolie, European Makula,
A Black & White Coolie, A Black & White Island, A Doctor's Pill-Bag,

*155 = Deuteronomy, Christianity, Christian Love, Christian Chemical, Christian
Voice,
Blasphemy Voice, Skeleton Chemical, Skeleton Voice, Skeleton Love,
Immortal Love, Skeleton Eyes, Skeleton Images, Skeleton Tribe, Skeleton
Note,
French Skeleton, Skeleton Bodies, A Skeleton Coffin, A Chicken Skeleton,
Body and Bone Chemical, A Skeleton look, A Skeleton Nose, Skeleton Cyber,
Magnetism Search, Compound Chemical, Invisible Chemical, Love Both
Sides,
Chemical Path Begins, Sun-Light Path, Sun Path Begins,
Chemical M/C Squared, Chemical A+O Squared, Sun M/C Squared,
Invisible Bodies, Vis-a-Vis Chemical, A Sun Face Squared,
Side-by-Side Chemical, Magnetism Chemical, Sun Magnetism,
Immortal Chemical, In-accessible Chemical, Sun Suction, Chemical Suction,
Offer & Wave Chemical, Chemical Before He Dies, Chemical Before Age-
Begin,
Image Before He Begins, Image Before Age Begins, Dead-Images before
Law,
A Chemical Born Before, Before a Chemical Atom, Before a Chemical Logo,
Before Piano-Logo, Calcination Chemical, Chemical Tree of Life,
Cycle of Bomb Chemical, Cycle of Sun Life, Cycle of Chemical Life,
Cycle of Chemical Bomb, Cycle of Chemical Agenda, The Roman Church,
The Roman News, The Rome News-bag, The News Room,
A News Room Agenda, The Mush-Room, A Mush-Room Bomb, The
Prophesy,
Millennium Aids, The Cosmo's Y.2.K., The Cosmo's Balance,
The Cosmo's Change, Cosmo R.N.A. & D.N.A. Change, Cosmo's Aids Death,
Aids Implosion, A Bomb Implosion, A Cell Implosion, "Aids...come like a
Thief",
The King and Queen, The King of Kings, The Word of King, Holy Name of
King,
Teth-grammaton, The Vow of King, Computer Brain, Ultra-Violet, Missing
Links,
Embryonic Arms, Sodium Chloride, Singularity, Conservation,
The Obscene Liars, The Obscene Minds, The Magic Hologram,
The Name Hologram, The Aids Hologram,

*156 = Nought and Six, The Egyptian God, The Circumference,

The Beginning and End, Numerical Order, The Public Order, The Crowd Order,
The Divine Order, The Godly Order, The Diety Order, The Plant Order,
The Genetic Order, Genetic Name Order, Genetic Seed Order,
Genetic Aids Order, The Genetic Word, Word Metaphor, Verbal Metaphor,
Holy Metaphor, Pure Metaphor, Police Metaphor, Active Metaphore,
A Solid Metaphor, A Mind's Metephor, Subjective Mind, Mother and Father,
Substitute, A Liars Metephor, A Liar's Society, The Holy Whole,
The Whole Word, The Holy Bible Name, Human Thought, My Thoughts,
Characteristics, Inquisition, Path to go to Ra, Righteous One, The Life of Darrell,
The Shadow of Life, Adam and Eve's Soul, Adam and Eve's Copies,
Adam and Eve's Alchemy, A Primal Symbol, A Biological Shadow,
The Justice Law, The Natural Law, The Unique Law, The Unique Ohm,
Unique People, The Different Lawn, The Undeniable Law,
The Child Mind of God, A Person's Logo, A Person's Atom,
The Begotten Image, The Begotten Eye, The Marijuana Image, The Eye Vision,
Vision the Image, The Electrical Image, The Electrical Eye, Electrical Language,
Electrical Atoms, Electrical logos, Synoptic-Eye, Synoptic Image,
God is a God of Love, God is a God of Chemical, Thessalonians,
"Let there be Light", Pierces the Veil, Pierces the Son, Pierces the Blood,
Pierces the Evil, Pierces the Cycle, Pierces the Ring, Flower-Power,
Secular-Power, Nature Power, Mother Power, Words Power, Magnets Power,
Pyramid of Khafre, Radio Activity, Atomic Nucleus, Super-Imposes, Polarization,
The Classic Catch-22, The Human Classic, The Classic Birth,

*157 = Star of Bethlehem, Astronomers, The Lunar Calendar, Star of Genesis,
Science of Genesis, Start of Science, Father of Genesis, Up-right Science,
Creative Energy, Creative Cross, Creative Messiah, Creative Jesus,
Creative Lucifer, The Creative Key, Computer Hacker, The Crucified Hacker,
News Society, Church Society, The Time Capsule, The Time's Science,
The Time's Calendar, The Calendar's Monad, The Calendar's Legend,
Scintillation {**To sparkle}, Luminosity, The Lunar Star, The Ancient Star,
The Ancient Science, The Ancient Father, Judgement Star, Fishermens' Key,
Fishermens' Home, Fisherman's Path, Fisherman's Bridge,
Fisherman's Lies, Fisherman's Clue, "Eli-Eli...Lama Sabachtani",
'God-God...Lama Sabachtani', The Pope Himself, The Devil Himself,
The Tree of Satan, The Blood of Satan, The Cycle of Satan, The Son of Satan,
The Cycle of Escom, The Escom Volt, The Escom People, The Life's Number,
The Number's Life, The Copper's Cell, The Electron Cell, The Life Electron,
Earth the World, Earth the Origin, The Magnetic Earth, Magnetic Biology,
Biological World, Biological Origin, World Biology, Biological First,
Money Biology, A Catholic Biology, The First Pope, The Devil Origin,
The Image of the Eye, The Image of Language, The Image of Logos,
Image of the Diabolical, Eye of the Language, X-Ray's of Atom, Atom's of X-Ray,

Logos of X-Ray, Language of X-Ray, The Image of the Ant, The Pope of
Rome,
Orthodox Jew, Orthodox Death, Orthodox Change, The Omen of the End,
The End of the Monad, The End of the Time, The End of the Epoch,
Synoptist,
The Image of the Eye, The Eye of the Eye, The Judge of the Beast,
The Judge of the Monad, A Hundred and Eleven, The Christ of God,
The God of Christ, The Data of Matter, The Data of Adam Kadmon,
The Data of the God Head, The Data of the Mega Head,

*158 = Darrell Gontier, North & South, Law of Magnetism, Field of Magnetism,
Ohm of Magnetism, Child of Magnetism, "I Split the Mind", Human
Magnetism,
Moon Magnetism, Birth Magnetism, Virgin Magnets, Virgin Nature, Virgin
Mother,
Mother Nature, Mother's Word, Mother's Vow, Loving Words, "I Split
Number",
Biological Number, Number Biology, Children Biology, "I Split Sound",
"I Split Perfect", "I Split Stone", "I Split Surface", Biological Stone,
The Living Earth, Power Source, Mind-Key Power, Computer Monad,
Computer Omen, Computer Epoch, Crucified the Beast, The Genesis Beast,
The Time Start, The Circulation, The Key of the Bible, The Clue of the Bible,
Cross of the Bible, Messiah of the Bible, Energy of the Bible,
A Sacrifice of the Bible, Parent of the Baby, Parent of Divine, Nuclear
Particle,
Energy Particle, Stuck Particle, Moves Particle, Repeats Energy,
Repeats Dialogue, Repeats New Life, Repeats New Cell, Repeats Parent,
Repeats Between, Nuclear Harness, Energy Harness, Abstract Energy,
The Father and Son, God Father + God Son, The Key of the Ark,
Cross of the Ark, Energy of the Day, Key of Knowledge, The Queen Sight,
Cosmic Knowledge, The Brains Plasma, The Cancers Plasma,
The Brains Signal, Medicine Knowledge, Genetic's Master, Records the Book,
Exotic Records, Armageddon Record, Life's Time-keys, Life's Magic Dead-
Keys,
Key of Satanism, Key of Freemason, Freemason Queen, The Public Queen,
Key of Society, Key of Judicial Code, Key of Judicial Race, Queen's Court,
Papacy's Court, Court's Signal, Court's Black-magic, Court sees Name,
Crime Court Name, Evil Court Name, Court's Action, Numerical Signal,
Numerical Books, The Pope Number, The Number Lived, Ancient Number's,
Ancient Picture, Judges' Rhythm, Queer Rhythm, Prison Parole, Symphonist,
Prison Evidence, Change D.N.A. of Crime Life, Cancel D.N.A. of Jail Blood,
Balance D.N.A. of Blood Cell, A Court Blood Cell, A Jail Court Veil,
A Nameless Warder, Jail's Police Omen, Jail's Police Judge, Name the
Numbers, Number the Names, Judge's Count, Judge's Sacrifice,
Judge's Children, The Bottom Line, The Biological Mind, The Mind Biology,
The Food Biology, The Biological Pain, The Biological Liar, The Bottom
Hole,
Bottom Number, The Forbidden Crime, The Forbidden Tree, The Forbidden
Sex,
The Aids Horror, Reverse the R.N.A., Reverse Mankind, The Forbidden Craft,

The Forbidden Trade, The Adam Kadmon Craft, The Christ Craft,
The Christ Ring, The Christ Blood, The Natal Matter, The Blood Matter,
The Mystery, The Solution, Aids Mystery, Aids Blood Matter, Aids Solution,
Name Solution, Spiritual Name, The Cosmic Brains, The Digital Brains,
A Transmitter, Quantum Wave, Outer and Inner, Hydro-dynamics, Robot-Vision,
Vision Stop, Blue-blood Stop, Policeman Stop, Di-electric Stop,
Shadow Complex, Nameless Readers, Massive Suicide, Adam and Eve's Ghost,
Pandora's Demons, A Computer Hacker, The Dead Calculation,
Middle Calculation, State of the Art, Centre of the Art, Centre of the Angle,
Centre of the Team, Centre of the Meat, The Pyramid Cobra, First Pyramid,
Magnetic Pyramid, Pyramid Origin, World Pyramid, The First Chicken,
The Chicken World, The Grave World, The First Grave, The Magnetic Coffin,
The World Coffin, The Chickens'-Chicken, The World Atlas, Magnetic Compass,
The Magnetic Divide, The First Sabbath, The First Womb, Pyramid's Grave,
Cyber Pyramids, Ra's Vocabulary, Advocate Truth, Truth Barrier,
Advocate Justice, A Chicken's Justice, The Cock's New-Life,
The Cock's New Eve, The Cock's the King, "I Think...Natural", 'Natural...I Doubt',
Unique Sperm, Unique Googol, Chicken's Voodoo, Chicken's Mantras,
Chicken's Formula, The Magnetic Mirage, The Feather Flight, Egg's Vocabulary,
Magnetic Missile, First Missile, Missile Origin, Rocket Missile, World Missile,
Medicine Capsules, Ruins the Brain, Pauses the Brain, Capsules' Signal,
Cosmic Capsules, The Brains' Forehead, The Brains' Mad Brain, Death Initiation,
Dodo Initiation, Death Chemistry, Gold Chemistry, Same Chemistry,
Jew Chemistry, Adolf Chemistry, Fire Chemistry, Chemistry Change,
Chemistry Balance, Egg's Chemistry, Same Vocabulary, Vocabulary Balance,
Balance the Truth, Balance the Justice, Temple Justice, Unidentified Death,
Unidentified Change, Unidentified Eggs, Africa Chemistry, Cancel Chemistry,
Alpha Chemistry, Chemistry Gland, Pituitary Egg, Pituitary D.N.A.,
Chemicals Reaction, Sun's Reaction, Sun's Egg Corona, Earth Pendulum,
African Pendulum, Pope Pendulum, Devil Pendulum, Liar's Thought,
Liar's Current, Current Liars, Current Manager, Slave Current,
Buddha Current, Food Current, The Inner Links, Pure D.N.A. + R.N.A. Body,
The Magnets Body, The Words Body, The Virgin Body, The Virgin Girl,
Links the Word, Links the Magnet, The Pure Alphabet, The Holy Alphabet,
The Verbal Alphabet, The Verbal Centre, The Pure Centre, The Magnet Centre,
News Story, News Control, Church Control, Control A Word, A Police Control,
News Gene-marker, News Land-Marker, News Echo-Marker,
Broad News Sheet, Human Mind News, Moon-Hole News, News Serpent,
News Agenda Marker, Ancient News Agenda, News Fuse-Link, Present News,
Orderly News, A Freemason Church, Orderly Church, A Numerical News,

A Nile News Paper, News Paper Key, Home News Paper, News Paper Clue,
A Moslem's News, A Moslem's Church, Mosque Language, Mosque Logos,
Ageless Mosque, Life and Death Text, Balances Text Agenda,
Changes Life-Message, Religion Message, Religion Text, Worded Religion,
A Language Unity, Regulate Text, The Black-Race Message,
The Black-race People, See the Text Code, See the Hand-Text,
Message Under Code, Message Under-hand, Under Hand Text,
Papacy Hand Message, Queen Text Code, Text Memory, The Child Memory,
The Law Memory, New Memory Code, New Religion Code, War-Race
Religion,
Wealth Religion, Taxes Religion, Change Cash Religion, Gold Cash Religion,
Balance Cash Religion, Change Land Religion, Desert Time Scale,
Desert Mind Monad, Mystic Text, Worded Virus, Text Sequence,
Judicial Sequence, The Law Sequence, The Ohm Sequence,
The Field Sequence, His Name Sequence, The Child Sequence,
The Chip Sequence, Queue Sequence, Bandits Sequence, Gangsta Sequence,
People Sequence, Jungle Sequence, Animals Sequence, Darwin Sequence,
Graphs Sequence, Complete Text, Study Text, Tribune Text, Animals
Anatomy,
Tombs Anatomy, Volt Anatomy, Text Incubus, Released Incubus,
Released Sequence, Released Virus, Released a Fungus, The Christ Son,
The Christ Blood, Christ...the Son, Serpent's Tail, Two-edge Sword,
Jumps Words, Returns Logo-age, Returns Signal, Two-edge Words,
The Identical Son, The Identical Tree, The Identical Blood, The Blood Matter,
The Crime Court, Aids Blood Matter, The Christ Chord, The Court Cycle,
Negative North, Negative Electric, Electric Circuit, Lawful Circuit, North
Circuit,
Lawful Wisdom, Lawful Monkey, Monkey Analogy, Analogical Monkey,
Wisdom Analogy, Analogical Wisdom, Critical Monkey, Monkey Madness,
Human Monkey Head, See Body Deficiency, Black Body Deficiency,
Monkey Doctor, Narcotic Doctor, The Identical Crime, The Identical Cycle,
The Identical Ring, Real Time Diameter, Real Distance Time,
The Real Dead Distance, Real Time Analogy, Real Critical Time,
Perceive the Self, Psychic Reform, South Sun-beam, Negative Chemical Edge,
Electric Author, Concrete Distance, Infra-red Deficiency, Doctor Deficiency,
Immune Deficiency, A Families Wisdom, A Families Deficiency,
A Parent Deficiency, A Monkey Parent, Psychic Analogy, Bermudha
Triangle,
Bermuda Time Angle, The Dead Bermudha Angle, Children of Israel,
Sacrifice of Israel, Count of Israel, Number of Israel, Count of Dust,
Children of Dust, Children of Peter, Sacrifice of Peter, Kingdom of Peter,
Peter...of Paradise, Mystic Eclipse, Jehovah Mystic, Worded Mystic,
Primal Mystic, Voices Reaction, Sound Reaction, Number Reaction,
Living Reaction, The Mind Reaction, Perfect Reaction, Empiric Reaction,
A First Reaction, A Magnetic Reaction, A World Reaction, A Chicken's
Reaction,
A Original Reaction, Economic Problem, A Computer Hacker, The Brain
Host,
Master's Brain D.N.A., Four Crosses, Crosses Word, Verbal Crosses,
Verbal Energy-act, Verbal Clear Image Act, Parent Birth Code,

Clear Birth code Image, A Clear Child Image of God, Organic Growth,
Beginning Matter, Mind-key Matter, Mind-lock Matter, Mind Clue Matter,
Power of Word, Matter of Word, Glory of Word, Word of Christ,
Word of Disciple, Taught of Word, Word of Mouth, Under the Diety,
The Diety Under, The Cosmic Diety, The Cosmic Plant, The Cosmic Record,
Copy for a Slave, Double for a Copy, Double Line Copy, Double Mind Copy,
Pint for a Pint, Cracking-a-Mirror, Cracking a Theory, Cracking Numbers,
Cracking the Double, Cracking the Copy, Cracking a Future, Cracking
Rhythm,
Ancient Rhythm, Mankind Rhythm, Alchemy change of Life,
Alchemy Balance of Life, Begin a Alchemy of Life, Technology Leap,
One Technology, Free Technology, Fair Technology, A Magic Technology,
A Aids Technology, A Name Technology, Basic Technology, Cosmic
Knowledge,
Cosmic Background, The Holy Head of God, The Missing Image,
Free Holy Back of God, Queen's Council, Queen's Court,

*159 = Word for Word, Vow for Vow, Pure for Pure, Holy for Holy, Pray for Peace-
Day,
Pray for Peace baby, Pray For Word, For Verbal Word, For Verbal Order,
For Verbal Police, Verbal-Vice Police, Second for Second, The Speed-of-
Light,
The Holy Octave, The Pure Octave, The Magnet Octave, The Word Octave,
Guardian of the Ark, Guardian of the Bible, The Divine Record,
The Godly Record, The Diety Record, Court's Record, The Public Record,
Society Record, The Whole Record, The Record Record, The Whole Limit,
A Digital Binary-code, A Cosmic Binary Code, A Cosmic Binary Race,
A Cosmic Knowledge, The Weeks Ratio, The Brain's Ratio, The Whole
Brains,
'L & R' Side of Brain Code, 'L & R' Mode of Temple, 'L & R' Mode of the
Balance,
Left and Right Image, Left and Right Eye, Eye Technology, Photograph
Image,
Eye Photograph, Biological Energy, Nuclear Biology, The Mirror Image,
The Naked Mirror, Magic-Eye Mirror, Change the Image of Life,
Cancel the Image of Life, Balance the Image of Life, Change the Mind Cycle,
Change the Film Cycle, Change the Food Cycle, Change the Vision,
Cancel the Vision, Cancel the Food Blood, Change the Food Trade,
Cancel Blue-Blood Seed, Cancel Blue-Blood R.N.A., Change Blue-Blood
Aids,
Cancel Dead Blue Blood D.N.A., Cancel Dead's Vision, Ultimate Science,
Ultimate Star, Magnetism Science, New Testament, New Statement,
New Newspaper, New Church Paper, New Torture, Self-Torture, War Torture,
New Human Word, Self...Borne in Mind, Sin...Borne in Mind,
New Social Science, Social-war Science, Self-Publishing, New Film Stars,
War Film Stars, New Mind Micros, Self Communicate, Communicated
Change,
Self-Visualise, Hierographic Radar, T.V. Hierographic, Divine Destiny,
Changing Destiny, Changing the Brains, Balancing Knowledge, Numerical
Diety,

The News Centre, The News Alphabet, Finish The News, The Cosmo News,
The Cosmo Church, The Atomic Alphabet, Roman Alpha and Omega,
Roman God...Himself, Roman God Origin, Hide Origin News, World News
Dog,
First News Dog, Magnetic News Dog, Twenty-Six, The Roman Alphabet,
Bill Gate's World, Bill Gate's Origin, Skeleton Science, A Human Skeleton,
Liars Star War, Mind's Analysis, Mind's Time Machine, Mind's Telescope,
Mind's Boundary, Liars Holograph, The Roman Centre, The Roman State,
The Music Centre, The Earth Messiah, The Earth Energy, The Pope Cross,
Liar's Hospital, Mind's Inflation, A Primary Science, Twist of The Dead,
Twist of Time, Twist of Legend, Twist of Doom, Time of Darkness,
Theory of the Dead, Glitter of the Dead, Glitter of the Monad,
Honour of the Dead, The Honour of Ma, The Mirror Image, Straightness,
Straight Human, Straight Birth, Vicarius Birth, Human Geography,
Moon Geography, Satellite Body, Satellite Hero, A Satellite Path,
Bridge a Satellite, God's a Satellite, Birth Principle, Moon Gravity,
Moon Space-Warp, Human Brain Warp, Human Space Warp,
Birth Brain Science, Cuts Umbilic Code, Cuts Knowlege, Godly Knowledge,
Earth Theology, African Theology, Mass Repellent, African Doctrines,
Collective Run, Mathematical Chicken, Genetic Engineers,
Genetic-Egg Engineer, Genetic Knowledge, Cyber Arithmetic, Darrell is You,
Adam and Eve is You, The Devil Lucifer, Solomon's Seal, The Nature of God,
The Words of God, The Mother of God, The Egoic Lotus, The Natural Angle,
The Natural Ten, The Natural Vice, The Egoic Mind Monad,The Egoic
Person,
The Team Justice, Magnetic Mind of God, Christian Science, Christian Star,
A Christian Birth, Christian Father, Synodic Month, The Face of the Moon,
Cycle of the Moon, Cycle of the Human, Sex of the Human, Blood of the
Human,
The Human Child Seed, The Human-Bone Aids, The Medical Aid Centre,
Aids Medical Aid Centre, Medical's Head Doctor, Medical's Mad Doctor,
Mad Medical Doctors, Mental Doctors, Doctor's State, Esoteric State,
Solar Doctors, Token Doctors, Show Doctors, Mental Likeness,
The Life Relation, Cell-Aids Likeness, R.N.A.-Cell Likeness,
Beyond D.N.A. Reform, The Life Covenant, Maximum Perigee,
Doctor's Alphabet, The Covenant Agenda, Current Vow, Doctors' Centre,
Guilty Centre, Guilty State, Surgeon's Home, Surgeon's Key, Surgeon's Lock,
A Surgeon's Food, A Surgeon's Rape. A Surgeon's Pain, A Surgeon's harm,
A Surgeon's Mind, Combination Cut, Cancer Combination, Brain
Combination,
Homo-Sapian Brain, Homo Cut Sapian, Deals The Life of Life, Cemetery
Centre,
White Cemetery, Human being Centre, Death and Hade's Centre,
Death and Hade's Aids Agenda, Death and Hell Aids Cell,

*160 = The Forbidden Apple, The Forbidden Bush, The Forbidden Drug,
Immuno/Immune, The forbidden Circle, The Life of Lucifer, Life Seed of Lucifer,
The Parent of Eve, The Energy of Life, Chicken Bird Parent, Air Travellers,
Eden Travellers, Standard Life Time, Standard Life Legend,
Standard Cock-Monad, Zero Speed Time, Dust Speed Omen,

Birth,
Three in One Monad, Three in One Time, The Monad Rebirth, The Time in

Moon-Light Epoch, Human & Beast Semen, Human & Beast Yoke,
Human & Beast Past, Moon Body Birth, Human Body Birth, East Star Birth,
God's Human Science, God's Human Micro, Birth Fussion, Moon Diffusion,
Human Satellite, Marxist Past, Marxist Light, Big-Brother Wolf, Electronic

Light,
Electronic Past, Blue-Movie Past, Death's Existence, Death Perverts,
Prick Pervert, Human Pervert, Hypnotic Drug, Hypnotic Bush, Philosophers,
False Prophets, Book Prophets, Prophets Charm, Prophets Saw,
Computer Logo, Computer Lord, Computer Danger, Computer Atom,
A Computer Cycle, Witch-craft Atom, One Crucified Cycle, One Crucified

Son,
Contemplated Life, Contemplated M/C2, Human Sperm Life, Brother-hood

Life,
Brother-hood Agenda, Voodoo Cross, Voodoo Energy, Pyramid Energy,
Pharaoh's New Life, Pharaoh's Energy, Pharoah's Messiah, Symbol Energy,
Nuclear Symbol, Compass Energy, Nuclear Formula, The Grave Energy,
The Nuclear Mirage, Blur the Clear-image, Blur the Naked Angle,
A Matrix Energy, A Biological Energy, Infinite Energy, Souls Messiah,
The Infinite Key, The Infinite Omega, One Infinite Mind, Quantum Cyber,
Chicken Quantum, Fanatical Propaganda, Regulated Crime, Regulated Blood,
Regulated Cycle, News Current, Current News, News Letters, The News

Octave,
Artistic News, The News Times, The News Monads, The Dead Earth News,
African News Legend, Atom News Graph, News Graph Logo, News Logo

Chart,
Sacred Logo News, The Wedding News, The Church Wedding,
Curse the News, A News Deliverer, Scroll-a-Letter, Poets Biology,
Electric-Biology, Doctor & Patient, Immune Patient, Biological Reform,
The Biological Self, The Biological War, The New Biology, Biological

Doctor,
Doctor Biology, Critical Patient, Patient Suffer, Biological Analogy,
Analogical Biology, Matrix Analogy, Matrix Diameter, Angel of the Soul,
Original in Form, Biological in Form, Biology in Earth, Propagandists,
Kings and Queens, A Twist of Time, Numbers of the Dead, Rhythm of the

Dead,
Rhythm of Time, Devil's Religion, Africans Religion, African Worship,
Devil Worship, Pope Worship, Earth Worship, Kiss the Earth Back,
Government Code, Red Government, A Government Lie,

*161 = The Noble Name of God, Holy Tree of Life, Pure Tree of Life, Holy Cycle of
Life, Pure Cycle of Life, Magnet Cycle of Life, Magnet Blood of Life,
Pure Blood of Life, Blood Order of Life, Cycle Order of Life, Pure Sex of

Life,
Life of Magnet Sex, Life of Word Cycle, Life of Sequences,
Agenda of Oikoumene, Agenda of Holy Vehm, Atlas-Geometry,
Geometrical Atlas, Geometrical Cyber, Funerary Grave, Geometrical Grave,
Chicken Descendants, Chicken Worship, The Chicken Skull,
Pure Chicken Blood, Cyber Funerary, Funerals Centre, Funerals Alphabet,

R.I.P. Logo Text, Book Logo Text, A Books Logo Atom, Atoms Language Area,

All Logo Languages, Cosmo's Funeral, Token Funerals, Holy Vehm of Life (**Initiation of a *Freemason (*96)), Police Life of Crime, Police File of Crime,

File Order of Crime, Numbers of Crime, Judicial Numbers, Text Numbers, Counts People, Identify the Law, Judicial Horror, Volt Electron, Animals Sacrifices, People Sacrifices, Judicial Sacrifices, Judicial's Children, Bishop's Sacrifice, Blue-Blood Children, Children Blood Line, A Chicken's Blood Line, His Neck's Sacrifice, The Oath's Token, The Oath's Centre, Court's Token, Court's Centre, Court's Orifice, Chambers base Centre, Red Bishop Centre, Red Knight Centre, Red Suit Centre, Jokeless Centre, Ho-Ho-Ho-Ha-Ha-Ha Token, Begotten Number, Paradise Vision, Begotten Children, Loving Vision, Bound for Freedom, Ancient Hierarchy, Judges Hierarchy, Queer Hierarchy, Woman Hierarchy, Splitting Image, Dynamically New, New Science of Mind, New Science of Food, Old I.T. System, Old Black System, Black Mafia Geography, Black-land System, Black cash System, A Black-Baby System, A Black Mob System, A Black Mafia System, Church System, News System, Miracle System, Rigor Mortis, Equilibration, President's Men, President's Agenda, President's Cock, Playboy Centre, Playboy Token, Fat Whore Centre, Red Whore Centre, Whore Race Centre, Text-Code Centre, Text Code Alphabet, Binary-Code Alphabet, Binary Code Centre, Red-Tape Code Alphabet, Pandora's Children, Pandora's Front, Ghost Numbers, Text Numbers, Reverse Text, Pentagon Text,

Text Rhythm, Copy the Message, Double the Essay, The Liars Message, Telegraph Text, Telegraph Message, On-line Telegraph, On-mind Telegraph, Telegraph On-film, Celeritas Volt, Circulate Text, Circulate People, Circulate On-line, Circulate On-film, Picture On-film, Picture On-mind, Picture On-line, Judicial Picture, Secular Records, Mother's Record, Mother's Saint, Armageddon Sword, Outer Limits, A Register of Death, A Register of Gold, A Register of Balance, A Register of Africa, Lap-top key-Board, The Monad Mind Key, Radio Frequency,

*162 = Sita Rama Kishna, The Root of David, The Root of Buddha, The Root of Mind,

The Death of Adam and Eve, The Holy Ghost, Adam and Eve's Children, Life and Death Children, Life and death Sacrifice, The Black Race Children, Children Anatomy, Study Children, Complete Number, The Magnet Eclipse, The Holy Drugs, The Root of Pain, Circuit-Breakers, Inflammable Energy, Electrical Energy, Begotten Energy, Marijuana Energy, Nuclear Volts, Unfaithful Oath, Messianic Stop, Scientist Oath, Hippocratic Oath, Hippocratic Cut, A Hippocratic Mark, Hippocratic Mask, The Creation Oath, The Biology Oath, The Biological Oath, The Biological Cut, VIVISECTOMY,

Magnetism News, Skeleton News, News Minutes, Grave Yard News, Church Grave Yard, Cycle of News Agenda, Market the News, Christian News,

Christian Church, Vis-a-Vis News, News Division, Blasphemy News,

Church Blasphemy, Dogmatism News, Ultimate News, The Magnet Eclipse,
The Magnet Romance, The Magnet Text, The Magnet People, The Holy Text,
The Text Word, The Worded Word, The Magnet Worded, Secret Sacrifices,
Secret Numbers, Secret Electron, Secret Rhythm, Secret Picture, Stop the
Copy,
Stop the Double, Stop the Third, The Brain Biology, The Cancer Biology,
The Biological Brain, Biology Matter, Biological Adam Kadmon, Biological
Christ,
The God-head Biology, "I Split Matter", "I Split the Brain",
"I Split Adam Kadmon", The Bottom God Head, Circular Matter, Matrix
Matter,
The Brain Matrix, The God-head Script, Disciple Script, "I Split Identical",
God's Biological Life, Forbidden Biology, Court Sentence, The Devil Court,
The Pope Court, The African Court, Court Biology, Biological Court,
Circular Court, Biological Law Key, Child Dream Biology, Funeral Script,
Funeral Matrix, Biological Funeral, The Riddle Exist, The Devil Exist,
The Devil's Exit, Churches Funeral, Kingdom For Ever, Paradise For Ever,
Living For Ever, Children For Ever, Ford Foundation, Book Foundation,
Block Foundation, Identical Twins, Identical Biology, The Faces of Energy,
The Faces of Nuclear, The Un-clear of Faces, Un-clear Faces of Name,
The Faces of Jesus, The Faces of Messiah, The Faces of the Omega,
Faces of the God Son, The Faces of Lucifer, The Cross of Faces, My Son is
Evil,   My Son is Live, My Time is Alive, My Omen is Alive, My Atom is Legend,
My Logo is radio, The Dead is My Lord, Time is My Logo, Time is my
Speed,
Speed is my Monad, The Devil is Alive, The Earth is Alive, The Pope is
Alive,
The Devilish Joke, The Pope is Lord, The Pope is a Veil, The Pope's Science,
The Pope's Zodiac, The Two Popes, A Splitting Image, A Loving Vision,
The Count Down,

*163 = The Elixir of Life, The Door in Heaven, The Pope in Heaven, The Promised
Land, New South Africa, African Computer, Devil Computer, Earth Computer,
African Witch-craft, African Obituary (**Relating to the Death of a Person,,,a
register of Death), African Book of the Dead, African Illusion, African
Sorceries,
African Strength, African Gymnastic, African Insanity, African Pictures,
The African Genesis, African Aids Start, African Body Centre,
White African Body, Earth, Hell and Heaven, A Rome & Greek Centre,
A Rome & Greek Alphabet, A Rome & Greek Token,
C.N.A. Basic Greek Alphabet, Same Evil Print, Live Death Print,
Centrifugal Force, Corroboration, Lord's Pentagram, Atom's Pentagram,
Logo's Pentagram, Language Pentagram, Diabolical Heirarchy,
Master's Language, Planet's Master, Logo's Nucleus, Atom's Nucleus,
Diabolical Nucleus, Pregnant Nuns, Ancient Serpent, Woman Serpent,
Dual-man Control, Judges Control, Controls Time, Controls Doom,
Controls Beast, Controls the Dead, Inspirations, Prostitute, The Devil's Slave,
The Temple Slave, The Temple Dogma, The African's Slave, Missing
Children,

Missing Number, The Computers, Beyond the Cosmo, Beyond the Centre,
The Door in Jesu, South African T.V., South African Radar, Translatory,
Singularities,

*164 = The Alpha and the Omega (A+O), Roman Numerals, Mercury News,
Satellite News, Politic's News, Church Politics, News Fussion,
Enlightened News, Chemical Logo News, Chemical Atom News,
News Chemical Danger, Blown-up News, The Naked Eye News,
The Editor's Key, The Temple Keys, News Apocrypha, Roman
Numbering(*0+1),
News Life Editor, Church Life Editor, Temple & Church Life,
A Temple & Church Bell, A Temple & Church Echo, Magnetic Church Echo,
"Original News Head", Secular Biology, Hymns Biology, Words Biology,
Biological Words, Magnets Biology, Biological Magnets, The Earth's Magnet,
The Pope's Word, The Pope's Vow, The Pope's Tune, Melodic Minor One,
First Church Land, Church Cash Money, Biological Nature, Nature &
Biology,
Biological Mother, The Birth Parent, The Human Parent, My Biological Mom,
My Biological Dream, My Biology Key, Death & Dream Biology, Biological
Virgin,
Biological Stomach, The Mortal Earth, Bacillus Biology, The Key to Heaven,
The Human Messiah, The Human Jesus, The Human God Son,
God's Creative Child, God's Creative Law, God's Creative Field,
God's Creative OHM, God's Creative Chip, Micro-chip Robot, Stop Micro
Chip,
Micro-chip D.N.A. Reader, "The C.N.A.'s Micro Chip", Micro-chip Post,
Micro Chip Suicide, Esoteric Suicide, Reader's Harmony,
The C.N.A.'s Resonance, The Human Cross, His Sacrificial Death,
Unclear to Escom (**Electrical Supply Commission=*Nuclear Power of
South
Africa), THE CRUCIFIXION, The Key to Satan, The Human Energy,
The Human Nuclear, The Birth Unclear, The Moon Energy, The Moon
Moves,
The Sun Stands, The Stars Play, Rotates Earth-Ma, The Earth Mother,
"Abba Mother-Nature", White Blood Cells, Blood's Life Centre,
Live Alphabet Life, Live Alphabet Agenda, Island of Patmos, Island of Pluto,
Liars of Human Race, Dogmas of Human Race, Copy of Human Race,
Double Race of Human, Copy Code of Human, Genesis Copy Code,
Genesis Double Race, "Adam, Eve, Cain, and Abel's Eden", Human-Body
News,
Human Hero News, Life's Sex Centre, Life's Crime Centre, Life's Tree Centre,
Life's White Son, Eve's White Son, Eve's Human Past, Life's Solar Pole,
Life's Standard Agenda, Life's Resistance, Eve's First Fuck,
Life's Standard Cock, Chicken-Cock's Word, "Cock-a-doo-loo-doo-back",
Life's Mutation, Three-in-one-Life, Past in one Life, Life's Dying Sun,
Eve's Dying Love, Life's Historian, Life's Prediction, Life's Inquiry,
Life's Ten-Horns, Nuclear Bomb Science' Unclear Albert Cell,
Nuclear Micro-Cell, A Unclear Micro-Echo, A Distant Star-Head,
Electrical Micro-Head, Begotten Micro-Head, Begotten Science Head,
Mad Electrical Science, Doctors Stop, Doctors Demons, Doctors Shadow,

A Doctors Ghost, Tuth's a Doctor, Pandora's a Doctor,
A Animal's D.N.A. Doctor, A Umbilic's Analogy?, One's Childhood Seed,
The Holy Googol (**Symbol of "Infinity(*106)"...symbolised with the Figure

lying on its side.), S.A.B.C. & The A.N.C. Messages, S.A.B.C. Top-Sport,
All Top-Sport, A Top-Sport Act, A Homo-Sport Act, A Rome Sport Act,
A Kaffir Sport Act, Sea-Kaffir Sport, Sport Madness, Critical Sport,
Sport Analogy, Analogical Sport, Greatest People, Greatest Animals,
Greatest Jockey, Greatest Bishop, Greatest Knight, The Greatest law,
The Greatest Chip, Greatest Mr.Rich, Greatest Echo Balance,
Greatest Echo Change, Greatest Land Change, Greatest Jungle,
Coincidental Laws?, Computer Hacking, Divide the Embryo,
Divide the One Brain, Witch-Craft Hacking, Chicken Witch-Craft,
The Crucified Chicken, Computer Run, Computer Blur, Computer Mirage,
Computer Cyber, Witch-Craft Grave, Voodoo Genesis, Voodoo Start,
Pyramid Start, Pharoah's Genesis, Slaves Pyramid, Liar's Pyramids,
Ra's Mind Formula, Egg's Originator, Adam's Mirror Image, Hollywood
Image,
Pandora's Eye-Camera, The Holy Bible Key,

*165 = Vicarius Filii Dei (** "One" of the Roman Catholic Pope's Many
Titles/Mottos... meaning, inter-alia, 'A SUBSTITUTE FOR THE SON OF GOD'),
Stood-in For Him, Peter-act-Christ, 'Primal-Primus', Bishop Society,
The Roman Popes, Knight Society, Barons Society, Primal Society,
Jungle Society, Animals Society, People Society, Darwin Society,
America's Society, Judicial Society, The Law Society, The S.A.P. Society,
The S.O.B. Society, The Child Society, Nazi's Society, (**This list is endless; from
the 'One' thread of Social fabric, "One" could unwind the Geneology of
Existence. However, It is best left alone for this moment in Time, as there is a Special
*Tree-of-Knowledge for our so-called Scientific Experts to endeavour its climb at
their own detriment. There will be *A BLACK-PAGE STOP, *See a Page STOP, to
prevent Your own Venture into the "FORBIDDEN ZONE OF THE BRAINS
MEMORY". Anybody, who goes beyond that "Black-Page" will find their *RETURN
(*96), totally non-negotiable.

That is *Guaranteed(*96), *To You(*96)...,*My Father(*96).

Continuation of: *165

Micro-soft ware, Blind man - Begin seeing, On-Line Knowledge,
On-mind Knowledge, Text Knowledge, Essay Knowledge,
Judicial Knowledge, Tree of Knowledge, Cycle of Knowledge,
Cycle of Free-mason, Ring of Freemason, Tree of Freemason,
Freemasonry God, Freemason Bishop, Freemason Knight, The Roman Popes,
Black Nobles' Red Tape, Prints Text, Published Text, Published OT+NT,
Published Zero A.D., Released News Image, Freemasonry Lie, Retro Virus,
Freemasonry Data, Freemason Goat-God, Freemason Book-God,
The Brains Beholder, The Brain's Volt, Electrified Veins, Electrified Volt,
Electrified Graphs, "Volt=I x R =Volt", The Brain's Binary, Electrical Matter,
Ancient Current, Ancient Thought, Ancient Judgement, Judges Judgement,

Mankind Judgement, The Dead Up-right Adam, Cain and Abel Up-right,
Cain and Abel Judgement, A White Judgement, A Token Judgement,
A Letters Alphabet, A Alphabet-Current, A Thought Centre,
The Dead Conscious, The Monad Creation, The Creation Legend,
Biological Letter (A+O), The Dead Scientist, Conscious Monad,
Pharoah's Life Time, Pharoah Judge's Life, Pharoah Judge's Rabbi,
Israel Rabbi Text, Israel Life Text, Mose's Covenant?, The Old Temple Bible,
Temple Doctors, Catholic Doctors, Catholic Cemetery, The Catholic Church,
The Catholic News, The News Editor, Babylon's Doctor, Babylon Cemetery,
Doctors Sperm, Human-being Sperm, Computer Chemical, Computer Voice,
Parallel's Ghost, Umbilic Knowledge, The Child Knowledge,
The Bone Knowledge, Message in Number, Numerical Text, Message in
Sound,
Worded in Number, Worded in Voices, Message Return, Message To You,
From Brain in Body, From Alien Space-Man, Space-Ship Life Mode,
Space-ship Agenda Mode, Space-ship Bomb Mode, Earth Space
(M/C)2Mode,
The God-Head's Message, The Three Sixes, The Triple Six, Supreme Logos,
Supreme Language, A Language knowledge, A Language Code Worded,
A Race-Language Text, Sacred Body Text, The Law for human, Horatio
Nelson,
Brother Nelson, Brother William, Your Brother, Brother's Word, Pyramid
Scroll,
Pharoah's Ganglion, Shooting Star, Serpent of Doom, Serpent of Time,
Control of Time, Control of the Dead, Hours of the Day, Hours of the Ark,
Mind-Key of the Bible, Self-Realisation, The God Head Vision, Mirror
Energy,
Reconstructed, irror Photo, Nuclear Theory, Nuclear Radiation, Photo
Radiation,
Nuclear Fission, Nuclear Formulae, Unclear Objective, Genealogy Cross,
Parent Genealogy, Future Messiah, Messiah Theory, The Omega Theory,
The Key Theory, Between Darkness, Between Naked Light,
Go-Between the OHM, The Prison Key, "Im Time...Doing Time",
'Im the Dead...Doing Time', Mandela's a Long Time, The Mandela's Record,
Madiba's Timed Release, October Project, Genesis Project, Start Nothing,
Different Embryo, Different Genesis, In-breeding Genesis, Genesis
Languages,
Unique Genesis, Justice Acquired, Within the Logo, Within the Garden,
Within Aids Pill, The Monkey Pill, The Monkey Logo, The Monkey Lord,
The Monkey Garden, Monkey AIDS Logo, The Dowism Logo,
"A Six & A Nine of Sex", A Six & A Nine of Blood, Blood of Society,
Tree of Society, Crime of Society, Trade of Economics, Trade code of Wealth,
Cycle of 'One Dollar', Trade of Euro-Rand, Rand Life = Red half Cent,
Knowledge of Crime, The Devil is Pope, The Pope is Pope, Resurrection,
Electrical Power, Mind Blood Power, Blue Blood Power, Begotten Power,
Marijuana Power, A Mathematical Science, A Mathematical Star,
A Mathematical Zodiac, Mathematical Copy, Mathematical Double,
"A + 1 and a '0+O' Zero /Omega", Arithmetical Body, Arithmetical Hero,
Arithmetical Greek, Archetypal Latin, The Hidden Latin Life,
The Hidden Latin Agenda, Omni Latin Science, Light Shock of (M/C)2,

Life,
Shock of Light Cell, Binary Mind Light, Black Hole & Light Hole, Past Christ

Christ's Text, Jehovah Mind Light, On-Line-Mind Past, Judicial Blue Light,
Wolves & Foxes, Alsatians Pedigree, Half-tail Pedigree Race,
Red Tail Foxes Race, Written Past, Light Written, Lode Stone Light,
Star Wave Light, Top Science Poet, Latin & Rome Science, News Observer,
The Contoller, News Intergrid, The Tabloid Camera-man, The Tabloid
Freelance,
The Blind Man Sight, The Sight Beholder, Disciples Text, News back to
Earth,
Erasmus On-line, Digital Satellite, Human Digital Body, Digital Moon Body,
Digital Moon Hero, Niel Armstrong, David Wolf on Mir, Space ship Miller,
Earth Space People, Moon Team On-Line, Birth Vice People, Doctors for
Life,
Jail For Doctors, Agenda For Doctors, The Begotten God-Head,
The Begotten Brain, Begotten Christ, Electrical Micros, Immanuel the God
Head,
Begotten Adam Kadmon, "I Split Myself", 'I Split the Time', "I Split The
Monad",
Divine Principle, Godly Principle, The Faces of Adam Kadmon,
The Faces of Christ, A Science Constant, A Constant Star, The Medusa's Fork,
The Avatar's Tomb, Future Messiah, The Future King,
The Old Age & The New Age, United Sacrifices, Nations United,
The Child Parent Deal, Mom and Dad in Paradise, The Child in Paradise,
America's Playboy, An Atom Bomb...was God, An Atom Cell...was God,

*166 = Tetragrammaton, Israel Cyber Logo, The Doctor Science, The Science Doctor,
The Diameter Science, The Critical Science, The Madness Science,
The Paranoia Science, Naked Infra-red Light, The Eternal Star, The North
Star,

Northern Sun, The Eternal Scope, The Eternal Micro, The Analogical Science,
Aids Micro Analogy, Analogical Aids Science, Analogical Name Science,
Analogical Surname, Surname Analogy, The NOBODY Science,
Prisoner's Name, Prisoners AIDS, The Prisoners, Just a Number Deal,
"Just a Number Died", A Number just died, Jesus...just died,
The Death of Jesus, The Alpha of Jesus, The Cancel of Gematria,
The Cancellation Act, Yesterday Hidden, Cut Yesterday, Umbilical Cord Cut,
Kill Yesterday, Kill the Sacred Ten, Cut the Sacred Angel, Kill The Biblical
Angel,
Name Horoscopes, Aids Horoscopes, R.N.A. & D.N.A. Horoscope,
Your Earth Image, The Perpetual Adam, Earth History, Pope History,
African Prisoner, Biological Beginning, Earth Prisoner, Earth Frequency,
Earth Ancestors, Ancestors Lived, African Ancestors, A African Historian,
African Continent, The A.N.C. Robben Island, The C.N.A. Genetic Coding,
African History, The C.N.A. Combination, The C.N.A. Satanic Craft,
The C.N.A. Satanic Cycle, Rome's Proverb, Newspaper Logo, Publishing
Logo,
Communicate Logo, Mathematician Logo, Visualise Logo, Film Stars Logo,
William Clinton, A Husband For Rent, A Texas Playboy, Hollywood
Feedback,

Hollywood M/C2, Light Vibration, Potentiality, Gontierism's Head,
To Serve His God, Solveig Walking, Past Vibration, Life Information,
The Skeleton Life, The Skeleton Cell, New Technology, The Government,
Magic-Government, Government Aids, Govern the Earth, Government Name,
Keepers of the Name, Keepers of the Aids, Keeper of the Gates,
Keeper of the Earth, Keeper of the Devil, Keeper of the Pope,
Keeper of the African, One African Zulu, Symbolic Language,
The Alphabet Logos, The Alphabet Language, The White Planet,
God's Revelation, Bi-directional Path, Bi-directional Bridge, The poor People,
Faithful and True, Israel's Faithful, Monkey Wisdom, Psychic Author,
Book Author of Adam, Negative South, Monkey Circuit, Creative Monkey,
Gestapo Germany, Psychic Wisdom, "I ching the Dowism", The Sacred
Wisdom,
The Circle Wisdom, God's Revelation, The Zen Vision, The Symbol of God,
The Time Symbol, The Pyramid Legend, The Pyramid Omen, The Christ
Light,
The Christ Past, The Balance of Energy, The Cross of Death,
The Cross of Africa, Solar System, Alphabet System, System Centre,
Cosmo System, Centre in-accessible, Magnetism Centre. Suction Centre,
Brain of Skeleton, Ultimate Centre, Centre of Life-cycle, Centre of Blood-cell,
White Skeleton, White Body and Bone, Skeleton Centre,
Skeleton Alphabet (A+O), Centre M/C Squared, Electron Energy,
Moves Electron, Nuclear Numbers (1+0), Nuclear Electron, Yellow Parent,
Coloured Parent, Coloured Cross, A Diplomatic Law, A Diplomatic Child,
Coloured Blood Data, Coloured 'Rh' Blood, The Dead White-Race-code,
White Monad Race Code, Red Chemical Reaction, Chemical Race Reaction,
Code Sixty Nine, Code Ninety Six, Code Sixty Five, Chemical Gas Reaction,
Pituitary Code, Mind Code Current, Current Food Code, Freemasonry Race,
A Freemasonry Lie, A Freemasonry Flag, The Base Wheel of Life,
The Cyber Code of Life, The Cock & Hen of Chicken, Messiah's Sacrifice,
Parent and Children, The Image of Christ, The Eye of Christ,
The Image of A Master, All Upon a Cross,

*167 = The Magic Skeleton, The Lock and The Key, The Key and The Dream,
Lucifer and The Omega, Jesus and Lucifer, Nuclears Energy,
"(-) Cross and (+) Cross", The Holy Messiah, Coloured Parent,
The Holy Parent, The Pure parent, The Parent Vow, Coloured Unclear,
Clear Coloured Image, The Jewish Word, The Gematria Word, The Jewish
Vow,
The English Word, The Holy Cross, The Cross Word, The Jigsaw Alphabet,
The Alphabet Jigsaw, News Puzzle, A Word Puzzle, A Police Puzzle,
A Magnet Puzzle, A Mathematical Word, A Magnet Arithmetic,
An Arithmetic Body, News Chronicles, News Time Liars, Church Chronicles,
Wars Chronicles, Collective News, A Collective Word, A Collective Magnet,
Musical News Beat, Genesis News Beat, Beethoven's Riddle,
Human News Logo, New Language Birth, Human-War Logos,
News Dogma Monads, Journal Master, Vocabulary Monad, Paparazzi's Faces,
A Paparazzi 's Name, A Paparazzi's Magic, Paparazzi's Basic,
Journalism Image, Naked Journalism, Book Journalise, A T.V. Journalise,
Journalise a War, News Paper Circle, Circle Paper News, Nato Paper News,

Bush Paper News, The Dead Vocabulary, Sacred Past News,
America's Past War, Jungle Past War, Jungle War Shock, War Shock People,
New Volt Shock, New Labour Shock, The Truth Monad, The Justice Judge,
Judge the Truth, Judge the Justice, Journalist OM, Air Journalist,
News Paper's Echo, Journalist Call, A Journalist Code, A Journalist Hand,
Newspaper Graph, Newspaper Chart, Hierographic Chart, Hierographic Tomb,

Publishing Chart, A Publishing Logo, A Publishing Atom, Publishing Chamber,
Torture Chamber, Testament-Chamber, Stamement Void,
Communicate Chamber, Communicate Void, Drug Statement,
Ma and Pa Testament, Sever Red-Tape Page, Sever Red-War Page,
Sever New Race Page, Sever New Bind Code, Sever War Race Code,
Untie New Race Page, Unite New Black Race, Eclipse Black War Code,
Eclipse Black War Race, Eclipse Black War Dance, Stamp the Black Feet,
Toy-Toyi Change, Toy-Toyi Africa, Toy-Toyi Death, Pandora's Death Box,
Holy Human Circle, Holy Human Vein, Holy Human Flesh, Hollywood Africa,
Pandora's Words, Pandora's Diurnal, Journalistic A+O, Journalise Book,
Pandora's Nature, Pandora's Sword, Pandora's Camera Balance,
Electrical Nature, Begotten Nature, Begotten Words, Electrical Mother,
Centralised Birth, Mother Guldvog, The Editor's Brain, Mother's Text,
Editor's Print, The Brain's Editor, Freemason Editor, Freemason Temple,
Freemason News Bag, Postman Stamp, Glomail Post Man, Glomail Air Post,
Alpha and Omega Verse, Alpha and Omega Text, Printing Order, Holy Printing,
Magnet Printing, Pure Printing, Printing Word, Mafia Printing Mob,
Symbolic Text, Symbolic Message, Symbolic Stamp, Cyber Post Office,
Atlas Post Office, Womb Post Office, Womb Brain Post, Stop Chicken Kill,
Control Stop, Stop Amnesty, Dimension Centre, Dimension of Space,
Dimension of Brain, Psychiatrist, TimeTravelling, Turn the Clock Back,
Spiritual Self, Adam and Eve's Travel, Computer's Feed-back,
"Im A Computer Aids", The Crucified Past, The Genesis Light,
The Genesis Poet, The Genesis Paper, The Genesis Yoke, Witch-Craft Member,
Sorceries Light, Sorceries Past, I'm One Computer, Cyber Frequency,
Machine Frequency, Cyber History, History Machine, Chicken History,
Chicken Birth and Death, A Classic Catch '22' Block, A Catch-22 Classic Book,
A Hieroglyph Book, A False Hieroglyph, A Hieroglyph Mark (**any difficult
Character to Read/*any difficult Character-image read.), Brain-Hieroglyph,
Comparative Cancer, Super Brain-Space, Super Space Brain,
God's Words March, The Holy Bible Cut, The Holy Baby Cut,
The Holy Baby brain, Umbilical Biology, Chemistry Doom, The Dead Chemistry,
Time Chemistry, Illuminati Monad, The Blind Monad See Back,
Snakes and Sword, The Blind beast can Read, Can Read Revelation,
South African Agenda, African Monkey Life, African Monkey Cell,
The Doctor of Death, The Doctor of Africa, The Doctor's Mind,

The Doctor's Rape, The Doctor's Pain, The Mind's Analogy, The Liars
Analogy,
The Analogical Liars, The Critical Mind, Immunes the Pain?,
Immunes the Mind?, The Rape of the Mind, The Rape of Children,
Hierographically, The mind of Children, Nuclear Weapons,
Nuclear's Photo, State of being Hidden, John the Baptist, Inkulunkulu,
The Supreme Being, The Blessing of God, The Balance of madness,
Balance of the Critical, Thermodynamics, Protestants, Satan's Harvest,
Biological Earth Date, Original Earth Date, The Earth's Record,

*168 = Bi-directional Time, Bi-directional Monad, The Bi-directional Ma,
God Father & Daughter, Colour Harness, In-breeding Mind Key,
In-breeding Mind King, William and Harry, Mother Grundy, Words
Hologram,
Secular Hologram, Words Unity, Word Sequence, Mystic Words, Mystic
Nature,
Anonymous Echo, Anonymous Dagne, Virtual Child Echo,
Dead-sea's echo Scroll, Dead-sea's Land Scroll, A Dead-Sea's Bible Scroll,
A Nondescript Bible, Abstracted the Self, New abstracted Seed,
Branch Abstraction, Body Abstraction, Hands Abstraction, Greek Abstraction,
Pipe Abstraction, The Fourth Beast, The Covenant-box, The Covenant Key,
Messiah Covenant, Nature Study, The Key of Egypt, The King of Egypt,
The King Pattern, Children of the King, Home of the Children,
Mom of the Children, The Queen Children, The Papacy Children,
Hierarchy Children, Hierarchical Children, Hierarchy Paradise,
The Key of the Nile, The king of the Nile, The Key of the Mind,
The Key of the Buddha, The Home of the Mind, Dark Hole of the Mind,
Dead Mine-Hole Children, Parent of Children, Unclear Pattern,
Unclear Resonance, Nuclear Resonance, Nuclear Pattern,
A Sacrifice Resonance, A Children Resonance, Cross Resonance,
Parent Resonance, A Children Cemetery, Nuclear Friction, Maximum Energy,
The Black Magic Sacrifice, The Chips are Down, Inter-active Tele,
Inter-active T.V., Inter-active Radar, Self inter-active, The C.N.A. News-
paper,
Daily Newspaper, Synthesizer, Free Information, Information Leap,
Contemplated Mind, Human Computer, Computer Birth, Human Witch-craft,
The Human Genesis, The Moon Genesis, The A.N.C. Torture,
The A.N.C. Statement, Kaffir Testament, Rome Torture, Homo Torture,
Two New Planet, New Star Planet, New Science Language,
New Science Logos, Diabolical New Star, New Star Quark, New Star Signs,
News Star Logo, A dead Albert Einstein, Science face Einstein,
Einstein's Chemical, Einstein's Voice, Sound of Energy, Relative Master,
Electron Master, Computer Actor, Number's Master, Master Numbers,
The Key of Joseph, The Dream of Joseph, The Dream of Number,
Ancient Key of Mind, Ancient Key of David, Light is my Body, The Burning
Circle,
The Burning Bush, Bush Scientist, Conscious Snake, Bi-directional Time,
Bi-directional Beast, Bi-directional Monad, Time Twisting, Oscillating Time,
Oscillations, Nano-Technology, The Birds and the Bees, Brain Technology,
This is my Body, Immuno-deficiency

*169 = Lord of Judgement, Year of Judgement, Logo of Judgement,
        Model of Judgement, Up-right Darrell, Cross of Jesus, Parables of Jesus,
        True Stories, Photo of Jesus, Fish Life of Jesus, New Life of Jesus,
        Dialogue of Jesus, Gospel of Jesus, Preacher of Jesus, Ruler of Jesus,
        The Lock of Jesus, Dialogue of Gematria, Gospel of Gematria, Cross of
Nuclear,
        Cross of Parent, The Key of I.V.X.L.C.D., A Number of Jesus,
        A Kingdom of Jesus, A Sound Of Energy, Sound Metaphor, Sound
Knowledge,
        Audios base Sound, Beethoven Sound, Musical Head Tempo,
        The Musician Monad, Musician Logo-echo, Music Beat Master,
        Melodic-minor-Ten, The Deaf and Dumb melodic, Musician's Melodic,
        Bi-melodic Direction, Instinct Melodic, Geometrical Melodic, Geometrical
News,
        The North Melodic, Interior News, Descendants Melodic, Computer Science,
        Computer Micro, Witch-craft Science, Computer's Ten (1+0), Computer's
Vice,
        Computer Teams, Crucified the God-Life, The God-Life Embryo,
        Genesis Formulae, Genesis Theory, Genesis Genealogy, Genesis Fish-Logo,
        Micro-seed Genesis, A Micro-cell Genesis, A Micro Life Start, Embryo
Genesis,
        Calculate the Star, Calculate the Science, Calculate the Calendar,
        Doom's Day Count, Doom's Day Children, Doom's Day Number,
        Doom's Day Sacrifice, Doom's Mob Sacrifice, Monad's Mafia Sacrifice,
        The Jone's Sacrifice, America's Race Sacrifice, Nazi's Race Sacrifice,
        Nazi's Gas sacrifice, Hitler Control, A Computer Actor,
        The Avatar Image Balance, The Avatar Image Change,
        The 'A+O' Changes Avatar, The Common Factor, The Genetic Number (1+0),
        The Godly Number, The Diety Number, The Divine Number, The Missing
Link,
        The Missing Body, The Missing Hero, The Missing Girl, Missing Mother,
        Mother Missing, Umbilic-bag Missing, Aborted Existence, Aborted Observer,
        Critical Abortion, See Body Cemetery, The Missing Branch, World Control,
        Money Control, Monetary Science, The Biological Circle, Christ's Number,
        Christ's Sacrifice, The Virgin Mary, The Mother Mary, The Human Mother,
        The Birth Mother, The Nature Birth, Human-seed Nature, The Virgin Birth,
        The Nirvana Birth, Communications, Micro-Computer, The Veil of Silence,
        The Blood of Silence, The Trade of Silence, Space Time Travel,
        The Change of Matter, Messianic Christ, The Balance of Celeritas,

*170 = Genetic Engineering, World Wide Web Code, The Dead Sea Scrolls,
        All the Dead Scrolls, All the Dead Magic Alphabet, All the Dead Prophet,
        Human Mutation, Birth Mutation, Gemini Mutation, Seventy-four,
        The Numerical Key, Numerical Energy, Numerical Cross, Primus Energy,
        Number Crunching, Children Control, Sound Control, Voices Control,
        Chemicals Control, Letter of Text, The Omen of Text, Letter of the Law,
        Turn Back the Time, Turn back the Monad, The Chaos Theory,
        God walked with Man, To Serve and Obey, Joseph of Arimathea,
        Doctor's Master, The Enlightened One, The Holy Christ, The Pure Disciple,

The Disciple Vow, The Electric Train, The Eye of Horus, The Great Pyramid,
Pyramid Particle, Angular Rhombus, The Eye of King David, Lord God Almighty,
Geography of Time, Lecturer of Time, Lecture of the Dead, Space Time Warp,
The Message of The Dead, The Verse of the Dead, Monad of Inner-self,
Dimension of Time, Equation of Time, "MELODIC MINOR SCALE",
Essence of Nature, Essence of Words, Shadow of Words,

*171 = Molecular Sperm, Pyramid Biology, The Biological Grave, Biological Brother,
Voodoo Biology, Symbol Biology, A Biological Biology, A Biological Sentence,
A Biological Script, A Circular Biology, A Biological Matrix, Compass Biology,
A Biological Presence, Biological Time Angle, Biological Formula,
God's Biological Home, God's Biological Key, God's Biological Mom,
Triangle Biology, The Biological dead Ten (1+0), Infinite Biology,
The Biological Atlas, Harmonised Centre, The Chicken Biology,
The Biological Chicken, Harmonised Alphabet, Harmonised Music,
A Melodic Minor Scale, A Melodic Minor Mind, Indirect Viewing,
Armageddon Mystic, Saints Mystic, Godly 'egg' Mystic, Saints Anatomy,
Life and Death Records, The Seal of Baptism, The baptism of Hell,
Shadow of the Beast, Shadow of the Time, Shadow of the Monad,
The Dead Seed of Adam and Eve, The Biological machine, The Biological Axis,
The Biological Cyber, Talking in Parables, Talking in English, Words & Numbers,
Rosetta Stone, Rosetta Number, The Lost World, The Twin World,
The Ancient World, The Ancient Chicken-egg, The Lost Origin,
Diplomatic People, The Diplomatic Law, Satiety is Reached,
The Seal of the Beast, The Beast of Hades Name, The Seal of The Monad,
The Name Seal of The Dead, Numerical Analogy, Analogical in Number,
Power of the Mind, Chemical Mind Power, Synoptic Chart, Synoptic Circle,
Revelation Chart, Bi-directional Circle, Human History, Birth History,
Moon History, Eternal Knowledge, Creation Symbol, The Earth Symbol,
Bottom Symbol, The Seal of The Rock, The Seal of the Judge,
The Seal of the Omen, The Legend of Adam and Eve, The Image of the Lord,
The Image of the Logo, The Image of the Atom, The Eye of The Atom,
Language of the Logo, Language of the Lord, Logos of the Logo,
Baby's Umbilical Cord, Baby's Umbilical Mind, An Atomic Nucleus,
A Dead News Nucleus (**If You should want to know...what nobody knows, read
what everybody reads...two weeks Later), A Reflection of New,
A Reflection of Self, A Godly Reflection, A Thousand Years,

*172 = The Illumined Mind, The Illumined Buddha, The Eight-fold Path,
The Eight-fold Zen, Intermediate Way, The Nakedness of God, The Lost Voices,
The Lost Children, The Lost Number, Count the Lost, The Lost Notes,

Numerical Analogue, A Numerical Analogy, Self Realization, The Lost
Kingdom,
New 'I.T.' System, New Page System, See New System, The Twin Sacrifice,
The Cain and Abel Sacrifice, The Mankind Sacrifice, The Dual-man
Kingdom,
The Eden Death Sacrifice, The Holy Words, The Holy Nature, The Pure
Nature,
The Four Nature (**N.E.W.S.), The Fouir Words, The Sixty Nine, The Ninety
Six,
The Sixty Five, The Chemical Reaction, The Love Reaction, Stop the People,
Stop the Message, Stop the Text, Stop the Labour, Stop the Husband,
Stop the Mom and Dad, The Curri-Culum, The Education Monad,
Intermediate Logo, The Holy Nirvana, The Pure Nirvana, The Beginning of
Hell,
The Living and the Dead, The Pyramid of Life, The Compass of Life,
The Triangle of Life, The Ten Monad of Life (1+0), The Key of Christ,
Cross of Matter, The Omega of Christ, Power of Nuclear, Cross of Christ,
Point of Matter, Alpha and Omega Nuclear (A+O), The English Alphabet,
The Jewish Alphabet, The Gematria Alphabet, The White Cross,
The Centre Cross, Nuclear God...Himself, The Solar Energy, The Solar
Messiah,
The Cosmic Christ, The Cosmic Adam Kadmon, The Keys of Science,
The Key to the Bible, Parent to the baby, The Science of Word,
The Mindkey Science, Gematria of Judaism, Cross of King Juda, Virtual
People,
Religion Wisdom, Cross of the Godhead, The Godhead of Nuclear,
Computer News, Church Computer, News Witch-craft, Roman Witch Craft,
Affirmative Action,

*173 = Opposite Two, Beauty and the Beast, Opposite Star, Opposite a Moon,
The Key of Genesis, Genesis of Parent, The Key of Genesis, Opposite Angles,
Sunday Tribune, The Time's Cross, The Monad's Cross, Electronic People,
Michel De Nostredame, Weight and Measure, Nuclear Physics, Start of
Nuclear,
The Nature of Mind, The Nirvana of Buddha, The Family Jewels,
Magnetic System, World System, School System, Money System, First
System,
Power to You, News Eye Matter, Naked News Matter, Print Naked News,
A Computer News, Historian Word, Historian Vow, News Dichotomy (** A
division of two parts...to cut...red-tape), News Propagandas, Linguistically,
News Mathematics, News Telepathy, Radar News Stop, Stop Tele News,
The Alpha-Omega News (A+O), News Rotation, Holographic News,
Unknown News, Our Church Science, Our Church Father, Our News Science,
Our News Scope, Micro-chemical News, West & East News, Left-Wing
Matter,
The Dead News Token, The Dead News Centre, The Dead Alphabet News,
Monad News Centre, News Time Centre, A Greek Alphabet News (A+O),
Ten Commandments (1+0), Dance of the Electron, Dance of the Numbers,
Computer Graphic, Electronic Text, Electronic Stamp, The Electronic Field,

Analogue to Digital, Story Analogue,

*174 = Numbers & Measure, Spectroscopy, Chemical Compounds, Finite Illusion,
Mathematical Language, Mathematical Logos (1+0), Stoning of Satan,
New World Order, New School Order, New Magnetic Order, New Magnetic
Law,
New Money Order, Our Planet Earth, Sun & Earth Atoms,
The Egg with no Name, The D.N.A. with no Name, West Meets East,
Electric Current, Critical Current, Diameter Current, Analogical Current,
Analogical Thought, Thought Analogy, Thought Reform, Current Reform,
Poets' Thought, Thought Write, The Monad Writes, Doctor Logo Chart,
Doctor Pill Chart, North Current, The Sacrifice of the Dead,
The Count of the Dead, The Children of the Dead, The Kingdom of Doom,
The Kingdom of the Dead, Kingdom of the Beast, The Number of Time,
Multiplication, The Atom's Number, The Logo Numbers, The Lord's Sacrifice,
The Man in the Moon, The Air in the Human, The Air in the Auto,
The Man in the Auto, The Great Sphinx, Pyramid of Khufu, Your Holy Image,
Your Pure Image, Your Word Image, The Magnet's Action,
The Image of the Earth, The Philosopher, The Eye of the Earth,
The Image of the Devil, God in Three People, God In Volt-Light,
The Light Formula (**V=IxR), Logo Mystery, Logo Solution, Speed Mystery,
Danger Mystery, Crash Mystery, A Crime Mystery, A Crime Solution,
A Blood Mystery, The Iron Formula, Genetic's Divergence,
Genetic Egg Divergence, Genetic Adam Divergence, Symphonious,
Adam...Eve...Cain and Abel Birth, Human Adam...Eve...Cain and Abel,
The false Prophet, The False Alphabet Name,

*175 = Seventy-seven, The Circumference, Holy Trinity, Word Trinity, Inquisitions,
Protest Action, Rouse to Action, Make Love not War, Consciousness,
The Sixth Sense, The World Line Web, The World Mind Web,
The World Mafia Film, The World Film Web, The Origin Bible Film,
Hollywood Hero, Hollywood Body, Iron Curtain, The First Mind Web,
The Magnetic Mind Web, The magnetic Stop, The World Stop, Stop The
Origin,
The Money Stop, The School Stop, Curri-culum Law, Living Principle,
Number Principle, The Christ Centre, The Cosmo Christ, The Cross of Time,
The Cross of the Dead, The Energy of the Dead, A Political Group,
Subjective View, Subjective Dogmas, Subjective Minds, A Story Character,
A Character Control,

*176 = The Identical Twin, The Identical Cain and Abel, The Christ Twin,
The Adam Kadmon Twin, The Holy Child of God, A Living Principle,
The Secret Number, The Secret Kingdom, The Secret Children,
The Children Secret, The Children Stop, Shadow the Children,
The Robot Children, The Blood of Jesus, The Cycle of Jesus,
Blood of the Cross, Blood of the Messiah, Trade of Nuclear Seed, Purity of
Body,
Water Purity, A certain Quality, The Sex of Energy, The Tree of Energy,
The Cycle of Nuclear, Numbers and Alphabet, Orthodox Jews, Orthodox
Birth,

Genetic Mutation, The Pope's Origin, The Earth's Origin, The Creative Word,
The Creative Magnet, The Creative Vow, Metallic Magnetism, Metallic Word
Key,

Photographic Mind, Begotten Mind Tree, Marijuana Mind Sex,
The World Wide Web, The Magnetic Wide Web, The Temple Origin,
The Money Temple, Working Mother, Working Nature, Story Words,
Nature Story, New Information, War Information, Self Information,
Computer Hackers, Universal Laws, Universal Sky, Computer Jargon,
Computer Alphabet (1+0), Cosmo Computer, Computer Centre,
White Computer, A Computer Zero,

*177 = North and South, Alphabet of the Science, Alphabet of the Tens,
State of the Arts, Token of the Arts, Centre of the Angles, The Tree Wise-
men,

The Devil's Number, The Devil's Children, The Pope's Children,
The African's Children, The Pope's Kingdom, South African T.V.,
South African Tele, South African radar, South African War, New South
African,

New African Monkey, New African Wisdom, South African Lady,
South African Boy, The Disciples Blood, The Disciples Son, The Disciples
Sex,

The Live Powers, The Bloods Power, The Water Power, Power the Water,
The Evil Powers, The Trade Knowledge, Aids Blood Knowledge,
The Forbidden Trees, The Forbidden Blood D.N.A., The Forbidden Adam
Tree,

The Forbidden Egg Cycle, The Forbidden Egg Tree, The Forbidden Egg Craft,
Phoenix Pyramid, Phoenix Voodoo, Chicken's Egg Voodoo,
Chicken's Ra Voodoo, Magnetic Egg Pyramid, Battery Chicken Aids,
A Battery Chicken Cock, Terrestrial Cock, Battery Chicken Cell,
A Battery Chicken Jail, "uKlulunkulu", Pituitary Gland, Pituitary Eggs,
Pituitary Balance, Pituitary Change, Chemical Reaction Balance,
Chemical Reaction Change, Chemical Eggs Reaction, Sun's Reaction,
Sun's D.N.A. Reaction, Ra's Sun Reaction, Electron Reaction, Electron
Biology,

Biological Electron, A Henwood Electron, A Human Code Electron,
Micro-code Electron, Micro-code Horror, Reverse Science Code,
Beam Beyond darkness, Beam Beyond the Micro, Beam Beyond The Star,
Beam beyond the Night, The Mark of the Omen, The Mark of the Beast,
The Mark of the Time, The Book of The Legend, The Book of the Dead Seed,
Mental Potential, Mind over Matter, Mind over Power, Power over Mind,
God and Satan Power, Star War Power, Star War matter, Mediaval
Meditation,

The Mediaval Christ, The Alchemy Matter, The Alchemy Christ,
The Chemist Alchemy, The Chemist D.N.A. Tree, The Chemist Mad Logo,
The Chemist Head Pill, The Chemist Mad Pill, Chemist R.N.A. & D.N.A. Pill,
The Diabolical Master, The Language Master, Shadow Reflection,
Terrestrial Life, Terrestrial Cell, Terrestrial Eve, Terrestrial Bomb,
Egyptian Sun God, Tribute to Caesar, Tribute to the Dead, Tribute to Doom,
Tribute to Time,

*178 = Corpus Christi, Compass Electron, Pyramid 's Kingdom, The Creation Word,

The Biology Word, The Biological Word, The Word Biology,
The Magnet Biology, The Biological Magnet, The Biological Order,
The Pure Biology, The Police Biology, Coloured Biology, A Coloured Colour,
Editorial Biology, Regulated Biology, Physical Biology, Biological
Propaganda,
Biological News Media, Biological News Life, The Prophet of God,
The Third Insight, The Alpha and Omega of God, The Alphabet Name of God,
The Written Law, Written Text, Written Message, Written Essay, Written
Verse,
Lode Stone Text, The Hidden Life Text, The Hidden Life Message,
Omni-Science Text, Binary mind Text, Umbilic Cord Text,
The Umbilic Child Mind, The Umbilical Brains, Umbilical Knowledge,
Saints Knowledge, Umbilical Prints, Life Taught Message, Eve Taught the
Child,
Stability of Mind, Stability of Food, Stability of Pain, Stability of Rape,
Stability of Dogma, Shadow and the Light, Shadows the Past, Past the
Shadows,
The Adam and Eve-egg Past, The Adam and Eve Egg-Yoke,
Adam's New Garden of Eden, Adam's New Garden of Man,
Cancel New Atom of man, Cancel New Logo of man, New Alpha Logo of
Man,
New Fire Atom of Air, New Change of Air Clone, New Change of Man
Clone,
New Clone of Mankind, Dolly Lamb Text, Diabolical Lamb Meat mafia,
Ark of the Covenant, Covenant of the Mafia, Micro-chip of the Mafia,
Spiritual Cyber, Spiritual Sheep, Sheep Mystery, Chicken Mystery,
Machine Mystery, Mirage Mystery, Grave Mystery, Grave Solution,
Chicken Solution, Womb Mystery, Atlas Solution, Coffin Mystery,
A Earth Mystery, A Pope Mystery, A African Mystery, A Devil Solution,
A Solution Lived, A Earth Solution, The Chronological-Age,
The Chronological I.D., Chronological Body, Chronological Name I.D.,
Chronological Name Age, Ark of the Covenant, Day of the Covenant,
Covenant of the Bible, Covenant of the Baby, Covenant of the Mafia,
Doctors of the Day, Doctors of the Bible, Doctors of the Baby,
Doctors of Aids-bug, Doctors of Baby Seed, Two Body Parts, Two Parent
Body,
Parent Father Body, Nuclear Science Branch, Nuclear Micro Body,
Nuclear Science Hero, The Camera Star Hero, The Home Star Hero,
The Camera Star Body, The Camera Girl Star, Photo Body Star,
Photo Body Science, Photo Body Micro, Scope Body Photo, Body Controller,
Hero Controller, Steven Spielberg, Pictorial Terms, A Human Body Energy,
A Human Body Photo, The Jerusalem Key, Big Brother Energy,
Big Jewish Brother, Classical Physics, Spiritual Life Beam, The Earth's
Energy,
The Earth's Messiah, The Pope's Cross, The African's Parent,
The African's Messiah, The Race Against Time, The Race Against The Dead,
The Race Against Doom, Race Against the Beast, Learning the Alphabet,

Learning Alphabet Magic, The Faces of the Moon, The Dark of the Moon,
Genetically Modified, Historian Alphabet, Modified Human Past,
Modified Human Semen, Modified Human Yoke, Modified Birth Yoke,
White Mutation, Alphabet Mutation, Mutation Centre, Zero Speed Centre,
Zero Logo Centre, Magnetic Lock Centre, Magnetic Key Token,
The Coincidental Law, Coincidental Text, Coincidental People,
Coincidental War Code,

*179 = The Pure Chicken R.N.A., The Holy Pyramid, The Pyramid Vow,
The Pyramid Magnet, Divine Laws of David, Divine Laws of Mind,
Divine Laws of Buddha, Diety Laws of Food, Plant Laws of Food,
Genetic Laws of Mind, Genetic Laws of Pain, The Divine Wisdom,
The Monkey's Brain, The Chinese Dowism, Knowledge & Wisdom,
Numerical Wisdom, Wisdom in Number, Wisdom in Sound, Wisdom in
Voices,
The Tree of Christ, The Son of Christ, The Blood of Christ,
Electronic Commerce, Electronic Doctor, Electronic Paranoia,
Electronic Madness, Electronic Reform, Electronic Death Seal,
Begin Electronic Change, Electronic Sun Beam, Computer's Atom,
Computer's Logo, Computer Language, The Living Number, The Living
Children,
The Living Sacrifice, Count the Living, Count The Children,
The Children Sacrifice, The Living Sound, The Kingdom Sound,
The Children Sound, The Magnet Formula, The First Bottle, The Magnetic
Bottle,
The Pure Fraction, The Word Fraction, Human Robot Form,
Human Earth Robot, Human Earth stop, Hypnotic Drugs, Hypnotic Message,
Hypnotic Text, Hypnotic Verse, President Message, President's Tomb,
President's Chamber, President Red-Tape, Presidential Monad,
Presidential Omen, America's President, The Holy Brother, The Voodoo Vow,
The Pure Voodoo, The Pyramid Order, The Brother Order, The Pure Symbol,
The Holy Symbol, The Word Symbol, Editorial Symbol, Editorial Voodoo,
The Forbidden Apples, The Forbidden Message, The Forbidden Text,
The Forbidden Verse, The New Jerusalem, Ayatollah Khomeini,
The New Big Brother, The Big Brother War, The 'BIG-BOY' Brother,
Coloured Brother, Coloured Voodoo, Doctor's Patient, Critical Patients,
Nobody's Patient, Patient Analogy, Analogical Patient, Patient's Suffer,
Patient's Madness, Patient's Paranoia, Patient's Death Begin,
Deaf and Dumb patients, Patient's Immune, Biological D.N.A. Analogy,
Analogical Idea Biology, Electro-Magnetism, Phases of the Moon,
Analogue Satellite, Master Satellite, Moon's Satellite, Human's Satellite,
Exotic Satellite, Magazine Satellite, Brain-cell Satellite, Cancer Cell Satellite,
Human Body Brain Cell,

*180 = The Earth's Master, The African's Master, The African's Alchemy,
The Pope's Master, Signs of the Zodiac, Language of the Zodiac,
Language of the Star, Language of the Micro, Language of the Father,
Language of the Night, Language of the Science, Language of the Tens (1+0),
Language of the Angels, Red Blood Cell Count, Red Blood Cell Sacrifice,
Afrikaans Children Race, Logo of the Christ, Born of the Christ,

Born of the God Head Seed, Born of the God Head Name, Atom of the Christ,
Days of the Christ, Nun of the Christ, Sister of Jehovah, Sister of the Child,
Sign of the Christ, Speed of the Christ, The Logo of the Brain,
The Speed of the Brain, The Atom of the Brain, The Green of the Brain,
"I AM GOD OF THE CHRIST", 'I AM THE GOD OF CHRIST',
"I AM THE GOD OF THE GOD HEAD", Adam and Eve's Genealogy,
Adam and Eve's Future, Adam and Eve's Darkness, The Future Past,
The Future Light, The Light & Darkness, The Last Supper, The World's Light,
Veil of Illusion, Cycle of Illusion, The Light's Origin, Linear Dimensions,
Mind's Dimensions, Holes Dimensions, Mind's Revelation, The mind's Vision,
Children's Vision, Darrell's Theory, Darrell's Future, Darrell's Honour,
Darrell's Change of Life, Darrell's Balance of Life, Darrell's Cyber Balance,
Darrell's Dodo Chicken, Darrell's Phoenix, Darrell's Formulae, Darrell's
Objective,
Darrell's Genealogy, Darrell's Tattoo, Darrell's Prison, Darrell's Democratic
Idea,
Darrell's Name Science, Darrell's Aids Science, Darrell's Emotion,
Darrell's Radiation, Darrell's Fission,

*181 = Yot-Huh-Waw-Huh (**Y.H.V.H.), Zeus and the Muse, Zeus and the Star,
Zeus and the Zodiac, Moses and the Father, Commandments of God,
The Vis-a-Vis of God, Information of God, The Holy Key of God,
The Word Key of God, Gematria Word Of God, Gematria Data of Word,
Nuclear Data of Word, Energy Data of Word, Moves Data of Word,
Jewish Monad Vow, The Dead Jewish Vow, Reformation Monad,
The Dead Reformation, The Skeleton Monad, The Skeleton Legend,
The Skeleton Beast, The Skeleton Omen, The Medical Skeleton,
Medical Pollution, The Dead Patient Atom, Blood Symbol Monad,
Medical Blood Symbol, Medical Trade Symbol, Live Medical Voodoo,
Evil Medical Brother, The Birth of Adam and Eve, The Deaths of Adam and
Eve,
Medical Aids Skeleton, The Red-Cross Monad, The Tree of Life Monad,
The Tree of Life Legend, "Im A Computer Monad", 'Im A Computer Judge',
Computer Robot, Computer-Culum, A Judicial Computer, Secret Computer,
Computer Secret, The Mind of Justice, The Scale of Justice,
The Theory of Law, Black & White Justice, Armageddon Judgement,
Up-Right Primate, Current Records, The Dead Logo of Israel,
Doom Logo of Israel, Doom Atom of Israel, Time Logo of Israel,
Motion and Inertia, The Morning Star, The Angles Theory,
Genetic code Genealogy, The Naked Democratic Ape,
Democratic Ape Language, Democratic Ape's Logo, Sphinx & Phoenix,
Apes Democratic Garden, Holy Bible Theory, Holy Bible Genealogy,
Baby Word Genealogy, A Human Cell Theory, The Moon Glitter,
The Human Genealogy, The Birth Genealogy, The Moon Asteroid,
Genetic Surname Code, The Missing Father, The Missing Star,
A Computer Text, A Computer Binary, The C.N.A.'s Computer,
Basic Computer Chip, The C.N.A.'s Witch Craft, Rome's Computer,
One Computer Chip, One Computer Child, One Computer Law,
A Digital Computer C.D., The Missing Science, The Missing Micro,
Shadow of the Moon, Shadow of the Human, The Stop of Birth,

The Culum of Birth, The Stop of Human, "STOP THE START",
Stop The Genesis, The Adam and Eve Genesis, The Theory of Child,
The Child of Darkness, Knight of Darkness, Glitter of Bi-Star, Knight of
Honour,
The Law of Honour, The Honour of Law,

*182 = "I and My Father are One", 'I and My Science are One, Born Again Christian,
Light of the World, Past of the First, Past of The Origin, The Origin of Light,
Yoke of the Reborn, Will of the First, Will of the World, The Origin of the 'I
am',
The Key of Justice, The Lock of Justice, The Joke of Justice, Cross of Justice,
The Sacrifice of Satan, The Count of Satan, The Kingdom of Heaven,
The Children of Satan, The Beginning of Time, The Beginning of The Dead,
The Beginning of Doom, Legend of the Beginning, Monad of the Beginning,
Quantum Mechanics, The Christ Himself, Adolf Hitler Himself, President
Himself,
Saint John Himself, God of Israel Himself, Eye of the Mirror, Image of the
Mirror,
Image of the Darkness, Eye of the Darkness, Light the Darkness,
Image of the Theory, Eye of the Phoenix, Vengence Unlimited, Lights
Reflection,
Exists with God, Pyramid Knowledge, Voodoo & Satanism, National Courts,
Brother Freemason, Voodoo Society, Numerical Symbol, Numerical -
Formula,
Infinite Knowledge, The Pyramid Diety, The Godly Pyramid, The Divine
Pyramid,
The Desert-sea Mirage, The Desert area Mirage, The Desert Sea Grave,
The Godly Statue, Pharoah's Knowledge, Triangle Knowledge,
Formula Knowledge, Fraction Knowledge, Fraction in Number,
Fraction in Sound, Fraction in Voices, See the Kingdom of God,
Science of the Bridging, Bridging of the Science, Bridging of the Micro,
Bridging of the father, Future Theory, Futuristic Law, Captain Prinsloo,
My Father...My Son, My Father...My Blood, Alpha Bravo...Alpha Crime,
Universal Church, Universal News, Revelation Church, South African
Legend,
South African Doom, South African Monad,

*183 = Vine of the Sword, Sword of the Vine, Words of the Sacred, Vows of the
Sacred, Words of Wisdom, Sword of Dowism, Nature of Psychic, Nirvana of Psychic,
Big-Brother's Police, Big-Brother's Word, Big-Brother's Tune,
Big-Brother's Order, Active Big-Brothers, A Active Big-Brother Head,
A Active C.N.A. Big-Brother, A Script Control, A Patient Control, Voodoo
Control,
Compass Control, The Atlas Control, The Control Leader, A Biological
Control,
A Biological Story, Statue Control, "I Split a Control", A Matrix Control,
A Supreme Biology, The Orderly Cyber, The Forbidden Sound,
The Forbidden Sacrifice, The Forbidden Children, The Forbidden Voices,
The Secret Name of God, Self Imposed Limits, Shadow the Name of God,
Holy Circumference, Police Circumference, Word Circumference,

Magnet Circumference, Four Circumference, Pure Circumference,
Circumference Order, Love at First Bite, Chemical at Magnetic Field,
Hollywood Chemical, A Hollywood Cyber, A Hollywood Grave,
Pandora's Chemical Box, Pandora's Chemical Camera, Electrical Sun Camera,
Begotten Chemical Camera, Pandora's Chemical Home,
America's Children Home, America's Paradise Dream,
The American Dream Path, The American's Dream Lie,
The American's Camera Lie, The American's Camera-data,
The American Voodoo, The American Pyramid, The American Brother,
Slow to Develop, World Witch-Craft, Hitler Witch-Craft, Witch-Craft Origin,
A Brother Geronimo, World Computer, Magnetic Computer, Computer
Origin,
Money Computer, Virus of the Mind, School Computer, God's Creative Laws,
God's Creative Dead Key, Selfless Souls, Warless Souls,
The Day of Judgement, The Ark of Judgement, The Bible of Judgement,
Abstract Judgement, A Current Law of God, The Living Christ, The Living
Matter,
The Living God Head Name, The Christ Sacrifice, The Christ Children,
The Christ Paradise, The Christ Kingdom, The Christ Number,
The Adam Kadmon Sacrifice, The Living Power, The Number Power,
The Serpent of Life, The Serpent of Eve, The Story of Life, The Control of
Life,
The Agenda of Control, The Media of Control, King Solomon's Cabala,
King Solomon's Cake, Three-body Problem, Light body Problem,
Sound Vibration, Number Three Shaft, The Light of the Mind,
The Light of Children, Children of the Light, Children of the Past,
Life and Death of Children, The Attack of Children, The Children of Black
Race,
Code of the Black Children, Missing White man, Missing Parents,
Missing Lost Race, Alphabetical Editorial, Missing Sacred Book,
Alphabetical News Media, Alphabetical News Agenda, Alphabetical
Propaganda,
Electric Magnetic Field, World Illusion, Magnetic Illusion, Hitler Illusion,
A Desert Illusion, A Temple Illusion, The Dead Sea Illusion,
The Dead Sea Pictures, The Light of the Film, Life and Death of the Mind,
Religion of the Mind, Memory of the Mind, Memory of Children,
Children of the Wolf, Silence of the One Lamb, Silence of the Free Air,
Silence of the One Man, Silence of the Free Call, Call of the Free Soul,

*184 = The Forbidden Fruit, The Forbidden Energy, The Holy Spirit, The Jesus
Christ,
Jesus Christ Name, The Energy & Matter, Name Energy Matter,
Nuclear Energy Name, The Pure Spirit, The Word Theory, The Police Theory,
The Robber Theory, The Magnet Theory, Baptism of Wisdom,
The Beast of Wisdom, The Monad of Wisdom, The Omen of Wisdom,
The Time of Wisdom, Divine Revelation, Godly Revelation, Diety Revelation,
The Godly Vision, The Divine Vision, The Brains Vision, Begotten
Knowledge,
Marijuana Knowledge, Live mind Knowledge, Primal Race Vision,
Jungle Race Vision, People and Animals Code, Darwin's Binary race,

Letters come Alive, Darrell's Plant Life, Darrell's Diety Life, Child Birth Theory,
Child Birth Genealogy, Shooting Star, Moon Field Theory, white...Yellow & Red,
My Magnetic Bottle, Captain Lief Guldvog, Guldvog Knowledge,
Norway Mind Cycle,

*185 = Molecular Biology, Star war Biology, God and Satan Biology,
Biological Science War, Hospital Biology, Biological Hospital,
Biological Boundary, Biological Analysis, Biological Time Machine,
Pure Mind Biology, Immortal God Science, Invisible Particle, Invisible Harness,
Particle Identikit, Skeleton Data Science, Skeleton Harness,
Skeleton God Father, Harness Both Sides, "Come Alive With Us",
Dr Nkosazana Zuma, News Technology, New D.N.A. Technology,
The Skeleton's D.N.A. Cell, Skeleton's Aids Agenda, The C.N.A. Information,
News Electron Cell, Narcotic Nkosazana, Nkosazana Deficiency,
A Vis-a-Vis Monkey, A Monkey Skeleton, A Red Cross Life Fuse,
Mommy's Birthday, His Master's Chemical, His Master's Voice,
His Master's Love, His Master's Search, To Serve His Gods,
The Computer King, The Computer Key, The Computer Nerd,
One Computer Mind, Basic Computer Mind, Counts the Word,
Gravitational Field, The Magnet Electron, The Magnet Rhythm,
The Word Rhythm, The Word's Number, The Children's Word,
The Police Sacrifices, The Magnets Number, The Pure Electron,
The Police Horror, Reverse Police Name, Police Reverse Name, Holy Mystery,
Word Mystery, Magnet Mystery, Police Mystery, Verbal Mystery, Verbal Solution,
Word Solution, Magnet Solution, Police Solution, Solution Order, Solution Vow,
Active Solution, Computer Energy, Computer Nuclear, A Computer Number,
God's Testimony, The Magnet Rhythm, The Birth of Jesus, The Birth of Energy,
The Birth of Nuclear, Parent of the Birth, Parent of the Human,
Energy of the Moon, The Key of the Moon, The King of the Human,
The Birth of The Omega, The Birth of Messiah, The Sefirotic Tree(**Related to
the Cabala's Tree of Life), The Sefirotic Son, The Sefirotic Blood,
Dead Poet's Society, Dead Poet's Prints, Released by Dead Poets,
Text by Dead's Poet, Specially Gifted Men, Specially Gifted Life,
Spiritual Teacher, Mystery Teacher, Reflection of A Light,
A Reflection of the End, Bottomless Pit, Bottomless Path, Bottomless Bridge,
A Bottomless Brain, Matrix Brain Light, Biological Brain Light,
Eye of Pandora's Camera, Image of Pandora's Box, Image of Hollywood,
Eye of Hollywood, Electro-Magnetic Image, Image of Nelson Mandela,
Image of the Book of Life, Images of Big Picture, Image of Judgement Day,
Images of Pearly Gates, Virtual Image of God, Hollywood Light,
Hollywood Shock, The Law Department, Legal Practitioner, Hade's Practitioner,

Practitioner Feed-back, Practitioner Dies, Saint Lucifer Cycle, Saint Lucifer Tree,

Saint Lucifer Trade, The Doom's Day Cult,

*186 = Electro-Magnetic Field, Genesis Magnetic Field, Genesis Magnetic Law,
Genesis First Law, Genesis Generation, Selfish Generation, Slave's Generation,
Rastafarian Genesis, Genesis First Child, Genesis Sequences,
Genesis Descendants, Geometrical Start, Genesis Geometry,
Calculate Anno Domini, Genesis Holy Vehm, The Skull Embryo,
The Doctor's Copy, The Doctor's Double, Doctor's Aids Dogmas,
The Riddle of the Beast, The Riddle of the Time, The Riddle of the Monad,
The Riddle of Aids Legend, The Riddle of the Omen, The Omen of The Earth,
The Riddle of the Judge, Monad of the Name Riddle, An Established Soul,
An Established Alchemy, Digital Photograph, Digital Energy Circle,
Cosmic Photograph, Photograph Signal, NATO Nuclear Plasma,
Unclear NATO Signal, The Omen of the Pope, Digital Technology,
Papacy Technology, Black Magic Technology, Black Aids Technology,
Medicine Technology, Plasma Technology, Cosmic Technology,
Signal Technology, A News Technology, Atomic Mystery, Atomic Solution,
News Mystery, Atomic Inversion, News Inversion, Books Technology,
News Time Travel, Holographical News, The News Order Agenda,
The News Life Order, The Atomic Word Cell, The Atomic Bomb Order,
Black & White Picture, Reverse Black & White, The Atomic Celeritas,
The Atomic Rhythm, The News Telegraph, Copy the Likeness,
Double the likeness, Celeritas Relation, Micro-chip Electron,
Micro-chip Numbers (1+0), Esoteric Telegraph, Esoteric Bush-War,
Doctors Pentagon, Identify Doctors, Doctors Picture, Doctors Horror,
A Doctors Genealogy, A Doctors Objective, The Liars Cemetery,
A Doctor's Future, The Minds Resonance, Mind's Telegraph Image,
Potential Energy, Nuclear Potential, Messiah Potential, The Potential Key,
Computer Genius, Computer Doctor, Critical Computer, Witch-craft Doctor,
Computer...No...Body, Electric Computer, Lawful Computer, Lawful Witch-craft,
Computer Analogy, Analogical Computer, Analogical Witch Craft,
Computer Madness, Computer Reform, In Computer Form, Devil in Computer,
Lived in Computer, Death and Hade Computer, The Fisherman's Key,
The Fisherman's Clue, The Fisherman's Omega, The Identity of God,
The Chronicles of God, The Arithmetic of God, God of the Mathematical,
Collective Name of God, The Musical beat of God, The Century of God,
The Initiates of God, Mount of Olives, Wisdom of Primate, The law of Coincident,
Talk to Your Bank, Words Rotate Air, New Human Planets, New Moon Planets,
New Human Languages,

*187 = Symbol of the Beast, Symbol of the Time, The Symbol of the Dead,
Symbol of the Omen, The Pyramid of the Dead, Skeleton for the Dead,

Interval for the Dead, Immortal Pyramid, Invisible Pyramid, Pharoah's Identikit,

Pharoah's Grave Yard, Voodoo Chicken Blood, Inaccessible Pyramid,

Symbol of Re-birth, "I am the Alpha and the Omega (AW)",

Pyramid of Human End, "I am the Fire and the Box",

'I am the Death and the Dream', Look and Learn Method,

Look and Learn Alphabet, Look and Learn Token, The Knowledge of a Child,

The Fourth Empire, Man's Testimony, The Pope's Motto, The Tree of Creation,

The Cycle of Creation, The Primal Creation, The Primal Biology,

The Biological Jungle, The Biological Animals, The Biological People,

The Darwin Biology, The Primal Matrix, The Black-hole Bottom, Television Actor,

Computer Actors, Moon's Pictures, Optical Illusion, Optical Pictures,

Exotic Optical Image, The Reflection of God, The Human's Embryo,

A Partless D.N.A. Birth, Computer Analogue, Computer Master,

Computer Scholar, Two New Planets, Two War Planets, Star-War Planets,

Micro-War Languages, The Chemical Science War, The New Chemical Science,

Star War Time Scale, Monad Mind...Time Machine,

The dead Mind the dead Machine, Natural Parousia, Unique Parousia,

Star War Justice, New Justice Science, Self Justice Science, Radio-Astronomy,

Universal Forces, Ancient Revelation, The Blind Judges Can See,

Synoptic Forces, Bi-directional Forces, Equilateral Forces, Pressure Forces,

The Monad's Vision, Judgement Vision, Current Vision, Vision Thought,

Hydrogen Formulae, Hydrogen Theory, The Brain's Theory,

The Brain's Radiation, The Brain's Fission, The Brain's Objective,

The Brain's Genealogy, The Genetic Formulae, The Genetic Theory,

The Genetic Fission, The Genetic Objective, The Divine Honour,

The Godly Honour, The Diety Honour, The Godly Formula, The Plant Theory,

The Plant Genealogy, The Public Genealogy, The Democratic Public,

Democratic Society, Objective Mind Light, Freemason Prison,

Zonderwater Africa, Judicial Prison Race, Future Knowledge, Numerical Future,

Numerical Formulae, Theory in Number, Theory in Sound, Theory in Voices,

Primus Spirit, Primus Theory, Knowledge of Adam and Eve, The Brain's Prison,

Brain's Technology, Divine Technology, Space-Time and Matter,

Brain times the Brain, Sub Atomic Particle, New News Particle,

War News Particle, Quantum Physic, Computer Hackering,

Hackering the Crucified, Hackering the Embryo, Genetic Technology,

Daily News Papers, Current Vision, Current Volume, Complex Thought,

Mind Sex Current (-/+), Current Food Trade, Current Sex Rape,

Current Crime Dogma, Up-right Crime Dogma, Current Crime Film,

Programing the Child, The Mafia Child Program, Higher and Lower Mind,

Hackering the Mistake, Hackering Words Life, Hackering Alpha and Omega I.D.,

Hackering Alpha & Omega Life, Hackering Murder Agenda,

Hackering Cell Murder, Hackering Jail Murder, Secular master Cell,
Secular Jail Master, Bacillus Cell Split, Murder Cell Contact, Jail Murder
Contact,
Missing Story, A Life and Death Amnesty, A Jails Amnesty Balance,
Cancel a Jails Amnesty, The Human Control, The Birth Control,

*188 = Angular Momentum, The Balance of Destiny, The Change of Destiny,
The Death of A Son of God, The Change of Atlantis, The Change of Uniform,
Uniform Nakedness, Pentagon Uniform, Telegraph Knowledge,
Rhythm In Number, Numerical Rhythm, Messianic Destiny,
Messianic Mind Light, A Messianic Son of God, Orderly Theory,
Live Story Book, Numerology Book, Book Psychology, Prophet Mark of God,
Judge of Character Mark, Chronological age Mark, Millennium Freedom,
Constantia School, The Year of Creation, The Lord of Creation,
The Logo of Creation, The Atom of Biology, Biological Human Body,
Computer's Science, The Year of the Rabbit, The Year of the Earth,
The Biology of the Year, The Biology of the Logo, The Biology of the Atom,
The Biology of the Garden, The Biology of the Lord, The Birth of Christ,
God the Holy Ghost, God the Holy Text, The Common Factors,
Mathematical Factors, Mathematical Records, Mathematical Soldier,
Mathematical Tongue, Mathematical Life Span, Mathematical Genetics,
Mathematical Armageddon, Neurotic Deficiency, The Concrete World,
The Real World Time, The Real World Monad, The Real Magnetic Monad,
The Missing Links, The Missing Centre, The Missing Alphabet,
Newspaper Editor, God is a Living Word, God is a Living Magnet,
Magnet Energy is God, Pure Energy is God, Pure Energy Chemical,
Chemical Word Energy, Pure Sun Energy, Synthetic Music, Synthetic
Alphabet,
Communication Balance, Begin a Communication, A Communication Mode,
A Codex Nasaraeus Mode, A Alphabetical Mode Order,
A Alphabetical Word Feed-Back, Jesus Christ Mode, Holy Spirit Mode,
Traditional Music, Traditional Alphabet, Traditional centre,
The Holy Bible Alphabet, The Genetic Code Alphabet, The White Genetic
Code,
The White Genetic race, Christ's Numbers, Perpetual Energy, Addington
Hospital
The Perpetual Dream, The Perpetual Key, The Perpetual Defeat,
*189 = Where Satan Dwells, The Key of Death and Hades, The Key of Death and
Hell, Cross of Death and Hell, Parent of Human Hell, The Key of Black & White,
Homo-Sapien Cross, Inside Hollywood, Hollywood Vow, The Coming of
Jesus,
The News of Jesus, The Righteous One, Lost Circumference,
The Beginning and the End, The Creative Number, The Secular Power,
The Words Power, The Nature Power, The Christ nature,
The Key to The Time, The Key to the Beast, Twisting of Time,
Twisting of the Dead, Twisting of the Legend, Twisting of the Judge,
Universal logos, Universal language, Corpuscle of Light, White Technology,
Alphabet Technology, Central News Agency, The Skeleton Dead Key (AW),
Cosmo Technology, The Monetary Fund, Awaken the Skeleton,
Higher and Lower Self, The World of Meaning, Technology Today,

Technology Centre, Funerary Ritual, Altered Mind States,
Mind's Electrical Charge, Mind's Mysticism, Mind's Mystic Key,
Lord Shiva of the Dance, Logo of the Mind's Code, Thin Blue Line Micro,
Thin Blue Star Line, Micro Development, Science Development,
Micro Corpuscles, Angles Parallel-o-gram, Intuition Science,

*190 = The Star of Bethlehem, The Star of Genesis, The Father of Genesis,
The Night of Genesis, Start of the Star, Start of the Micro, The Best Computer,
Computer Words, Computer Nature, Secular Witch Craft, Members of the
News,
Members of the Church, Doctor of the News, The Numerical News,
A Gontierism Order, Mind of Gontierism, Hollywood News, Pandora's News
Box,
Pandora's News Camera, Micro Controller, Science Controller,
A Human Controller, Parallel Universe, Christ's Human Mode, Historian
Print,
Standard Cell Print, Magnetic Key Print, Solar Pole Print, The Brain Mutation,
Generated Computer, Super Computer, Computer Cyber Data,
Mortal Computer, Your Computer, My Computer Dream, My Computer Key,
My Delirious Mind, My Mind Potential, Editorial Control, My Mind
Telepathy,
My Pain Telepathy, My Mind's Mathematic, Editorial Story, Words and
Numbers,
Creation Symbols (AW), The Omen Seal Number, The Dead Seal The
Number,
The Omen Seal Number (666), Holographic Mind Balance,
The East and West Data, The Unknown Path, The East & West Path,
Synoptic Charts, Synoptic Circles, Synoptic Text, Synoptic Verse,
Revelation Text, The Begotten Text, The Begotten Verse,
The Bi-directional Snakes, The Holy Serpent, The Serpent Vow, The Pure
Story,
The Holy Story, The Fishermen's Key, Computer's Tune, Computer Order,
Colloid Chemistry, Robot Vocabulary, ILLUMINATI EYE IMAGE,
Film of Hollywood, Film of Nelson Mandela, Nelson Mandela News,
A Twisting of Legend,

*191 = The Secret Doctrine, The Tabloid Bulletin, The Tabloid Hierarchy,
Freemason Hierarchy, Hierarchy Knowledge, Courts Hierarchy,
Linking of Each Group, Master of Each Group, Master of Each Character,
Master Character Balance, Change Character Master, Micro-chip Control,
Micro-chip Story, Black & White Story, A Editorial Story, A Editorial
Control,
A Human Law Control, A Physical Control, A Propaganda Story,
A Story Lived and Died, A Sacred Book Story, The Old Bible Story,
The C.N.A. Book Story, Relation Story, Esoteric Control, Doctor's Story,
Doctor's Control, Cemetery Control, Controls Death and Hade,
Human-being Control, Story Resonance, Reforms Story, Reforms Control,
Informs Control, Nile Paper Hierarchy, Mind Light Nucleus,
Geometric Knowledge, Freemason's Master, Divine Life Knowledge,
Number-22 Knowledge, The Number-22 Ratio, The Catch-22 Division,

The Catch-22 Skeleton, The Vis-a-Vis catch-22, The Human Skeleton,
A Freemason's Doctor, A Freemason's Diameter, A Freemason's Madness,
A Freemason's Paranoia, Nobody's a Freemason, The Analogical Law of God,
No Justice Analogy, Black Justice Analogy, See Analogical Justice,
Natural Black Analogy, See Different Analogy, See Different Diameter,
See A Unique Energy, One Serving Whole, Intense Suffering,
The African Century, The Earth's Chronicles, The Collective Names,
The Collective Earth, Mathematical Biology, Biological Acceleration,
Matrix Infinity, The Musical African Beat, The African Genesis Eden,
Time's Biological Table, Ancient Biological Mind, Earth Chemical Reaction,
Earth & Sun Reaction, Earth & Sun Biology, Biological Arithmetic,
Birthdays Biology, Birthdays begin all end, Birthdays Feed-back Cycle,
The Whole Process, Soul Unfoldment, Old-age vivi-section,
Cancer Vivi-section. Cut Vivi-section, Brain Vivi-section, Anti-Vivi-section,
Week Vivi-section, Kill Biological Sense, Cut Biological Signal,
Brain Plasma Biology, Brain Signal Biology, Biological Brain Medicine,
Biological Digital Brain, Biological Brain-Pause, Brain matrix Signal,
Biological Brain Signal, Bottom Brain Plasma, Bottom Space Plasma,
Anti-Space Home-Signal, Hollywood Signal, Pandora's Home Signal,
Pandora's Camera Signal, Holy Ghost Signal, Holy Text Signal,
Holy Message Signal, Pure Text Plasma, Audios Digital Tune,
The Christmas Tree, The Christmas Cycle, Holy Crucifixion,
The Ancient Numbers, The Twin Numbers, Current Numbers, Current
Electron,
Current Picture, Picture Thought, Judgement Numbers, The Two-edge Sword,
The Two-edge Words, The Two-edge Nature, The Secular Nature,
The Words Nature, The Mother's Vow, The Serpent's Tail, Self's the Serpent,
The News Serpent, Control the News, Red-Tape Prophesy,
The Ten Sacred Text, The Umbilic Unity, Umbilical Cord text,
Umbilical mind Message, Umbilical Language Key, Mom's Armegeddon Son,
Comes like a Biblical Thief, Comes Like Current, The Millennium Law,
The Millennium Child, The Key of Knowledge, The Key of Society,
The Joke of Society, The King of Playboy, The Home of Economics,
The Key of satanism, The Omega of satanism, Black-magic Repulsion,
Cosmic Repulsion, Television News, Heads of Government,
National Parks Board, Digital repulsion, Lap Top Computer,

*192 = Magnetic Inter-play, Inter-magnetic Chemical, Ancient World Chemical,
The Brains Faculties, Numerical Knowledge, Primus Knowledge,
Satanism Knowledge, Voodoo Arithmetic, Pyramid Century, Collective
Symbol,
Collective Formula, Collective Souls, The Grave's Time Scale,
Mind the Grave's Omen, For His Own Release, Release His own Team,
World of Thought, Computer Graphics, Editorial Thought, Editorial
Judgement,
Origin of Thought, Dance of the Electrons, Christ's Disciples,
The Church of Christ, Christ's Knowledge, The God Eye of Christ,
The Christ Image of God, The God Image of the God-Head, Faithful Witness,
The New Testament, The New Statement, The Self-Torture, The War Torture,

Torture the New, The News Prophet, The New Publishing, The New Newspaper,

The Twist of Time, The Twist of the Dead, The Coming of Christ,
Personal Formulae, Personal Theory, The Knowledge of Sin,
The Knowledge of Self, The Knowledge of Nine, The Brains of the Fish,
The Genetic of the Self, The Genetic of the New, Philosophical Taoism,
Philosophical Buddahism, Philosophical Mind Key, Symbol of Creation,
Symbol of Biology, Unorthodox Jew, God in Three Person,
The Coming of the God-Head, Uniform Knowledge, Spherical Skeleton,
Skeleton Change of Life, Skeleton Balance of Life, Dodo Chicken Skeleton,
The War Newspaper, The New Film Stars, The Lady Film Stars,
The New mathematician. Conscious Energy, Nuclear Scientist,
Messianic Star War, English Scientist, A Number Scientist,

*193 = The False Prophets, The Books Prophet, Compound Numbers,
The Philosophers, The Prophet's Book, The Prophet's Mark,
The Language Numbers, The Logos Rhythm, The Numbers Language,
Multiplications, The Number of Times, The Judges of Number,
The Reverse of Time, The Reverse of the Dead, The Reverse of Doom,
Reverse of the Monad, The Omen of Horror, The Beast of Horror,
The Legend of Horror, The judge of Horror, Destiny Control,
Modern Technology, Mechanical Technology, Dynamic Technology,
The Law Technology, Judicial Technology, The Face of the Future,
Cycle of the Future, Cycle of the Theory, Virtual Reality, On mind Technology,
Technology on-Line, "W.W.W"-Technology, Binary Technology,
The Bone Technology, Worded Technology, Infra-structure,
The African Renaissance, God of the Universe, The Man without a face,
Blue blood Cell Count, Begotten Life Number, Inverted Knowledge,
The Government Code, The Government Race,

*194 = Labore et Constantia, Honour of the Lord, Honour of the Logo,
Theory of the Logo, Theory of the Atom, Reconstruction, "I am Your Partner",
Spirit of the Lord, Fission of the Logo, Fission of the Atom,
Electric Magnetic Force, Critical Magnetic Force, Critical World Time,
Mystic Symbols, Mystic's Formula, Mystic's Pyramid, Pharoah's Mystic,
Genetic Diversity, Plant Diversity, Genetic Development, Divine Development,
Divine Crucifixion, Genetic Corpuscles, The Divine Garden of Eden,
The Plant Garden of Eden, The Genetic P`ill of Man, The Genetic Atom of Man,
The Genetic Logo Atom, The Genetic God Himself, The Godly God Himself,
Hydrogen Smoke bond, Plant hydrogen bond, Genetic Hydrogen Bond,
Whole Hydrogen Bond, Created in the Image of God, Living Principles,
The Holy Voice of God, The Pure Voice of God, The Chemical word of God,
The Pure Love of God, "I Think...therefore...I am", Revelation Shrine,
The begotten Kingdom, The Begotten Number, The Number Vision,
The Sacrifice Vision, The Children Vision, The Empiric Vision, Lateral Inversion,

The Outer limits, The Splitting Image, Splitting The Image, Splitting the Eye,
Splitting Atoms, Splitting Logos, Language Splitting, Yellow Sub-marine,
A Skeleton Celeritas, A Messianic Skeleton, A Skeleton Picture,
A Skeleton Pentagon, Religious Time-Bomb, The President's Men,
The President's Life, The President's Agenda, The President's Cell,
The President's Jail, A Theory of Service, A Honour of Service,
Magnetic Star Dust, World Star Dust, Magnetic Dust Micro,
General George Meiring, Human Medicine Doctor, Science Doctor of Mind,
Science Doctor of Pain, Doctor of pain micro, The New Star of David,
The New Science of Mind,

*195 = The Hippocratic Oath ("Again ye have heard that it hath been said by them
of old time, Thou shalt not forswear thyself, but shalt perform unto the
Lord thine oaths: But I say unto You, 'Swear not at all; neither by heaven;
for it is God's throne: Nor by the earth; for it is his footstool: neither by
Jerusalem; for it is the city of the great King. Neither shalt thou swear by
thy head, because thou canst not make one hair white or black. But let
your communication be, Yea; yea; Nay, nay; for whatsoever is more than
these cometh of evil"...St. Matt. 5:33-37), The Identical twins,
Christ Lives in Man, The Secret Numbers, The Secret Sacrifices,
Darrell and his Shadow, South African Police, Synoptic Cross, Synoptic
Gospel,
Synoptic Dialogue, Revelation Dialogue, The Begotten dialogue,
The Synoptic Key, Left Path & Right Path, The Black Cross of Death,
See the Cross of Death, See the Liars Cross, See the Liars Nuclear,
See the Mind's Energy, Lies of Hollywood, The Hollywood Fox,
The great Illusion, Computer Harness, The Crucified Harness,
Crucified the God Father, The Genesis God Father, Contemplative Mind,
Contemplative Buddah, The ultimate miracle, The ultimate News,
Numbers and Alphabets, Begotten Word of God, The Trinity of God,
The Genetic coding of God, The Crucifying Omen, The anointed name of
God,
The Armageddon name of God, The Primate name of God,
The Omega Revelation, The Begotten Son God, The Begotten Messiah,
The Begotten Jesus, The Begotten Lucifer, The Immanuel Cross,
The Inflammable Nuclear, The inflammable energy, The Electrical Cross,
The Electrical Energy, The messiah Hormone, The Parent Hormone,
Christ Conscious, Christ's Current, Christ Thoughts, Computer's Jargon,
The Ford foundation, Darrell's Arithmetic, It is for Judgement, Darrell's
Century,
Darrell's Identity, Darrell's Chronicles, Darrell's Musical beat,

*196 = The Lord's Pentagram, The Pyramid of Light, The end of the Pyramid,
The end of the time Angle, The compass of the end, The true Judgement,
The Watt Current, The True Current, The Israel Judgement,
Rabbi Israel Star War, The end of the infinite, My own soul mate,
My earth soul mate, Triumph of Darrell, The Pope's numbers,
The Pope's Sacrifices, Paths that lead to God, Bridges that lead to God,
Ships of the Desert, Temple of the Desert, Personal Knowledge,
Synthetic Sound, The Hierarchy Language, The Hierarchy Logos,

The Nuns Hierarchy, The Diabolical Hierarchy, The planet Hierarchy,
A Temple of all the Gods, Origin of all the Gods, Digital Information,
The Skeleton Signal, The Skeleton plasma, The Cosmic Skeleton,
The Cosmic Magnetism, Cosmic gravity cell, Mind...body and spirit,
Body's Mind Spirit, The Reverse stages, Reverses the Earth,
The African Witch-craft, Witch-craft Biology,

*197 = The Pope meets Mandela, Turning the Clock back?, Turning back the brain,
Compendium of the Bible, Remain anonymous, Anonymous Vow,
Anonymous Police, Anonymous Robber, Anonymous Order,
Freedom of the Press, Judgement of Christ, Judgement of Character,
Character of Thought, Divine magnet Energy, Agent of repulsion,
Active Saint Lucifer, Rose Croix chapter, Omen of Gontierism,
The Human law Chapter, Omen of Gontierism, Pandora's language key,
Technique of sound, Technique of Living, Techniques of chemical,
Symbolic Thought, The Holy Bible count, The chronological ages,
The everlasting ages, The Septuagint ages, A synthetic sound, Synthetic songs,
The explosive Law, The Island of Patmos, The everlasting Life,
The Adam Structure, The Egg Structure, The D.N.A. Structure,
"R.N.A. & D.N.A. Structure", Seed & Egg Structure, Seed & Egg Cell-
Mutation,
Everlasting Alphabet, Everlasting Centre, Everlasting Cosmo,
The Prophets of God, Science of the Presence, Genetic Information,
The Skeleton Saint, Magnetism Knowledge, Immortal Knowledge,
Invisible Knowledge, The Invisible Sight, Pictured Side-by Side,
The Brains Compound, Offer oscillate Wave, In-accessible Binary-code,
The Brains M/C Squared, The Brain's Nuclear-deal, Numerical Body and
Bone,
The Brain's a Time Machine, Human-cell-meat People, Human meat labour
Life,
Human Team jail Labour, Grave Yard Society, Chicken Blood Society,
Mechanical Machinery (M/C)2, Chicken Satanism Craft, Inter-web Cyber Cycle,
Live Blood Suction, Live Sex Suction, Play-boy Identikit, President Clinton,
Modern Machinery (M/C)2

*198 = The Tree of Knowledge, The Tree of the Cannabis, The Tree of Freemason,
A Genetic-Information, The Tree of Satanism, The Editorial World,
The Holy Brothers, The Words Symbol, The Magnet Pyramids,
The Verbal D.N.A. Formula, The Key of Solomon, Gematria of Solomon,
The Key of Apocrypha, The Key of Politics, The Key of the Demons,
The Serpent of Time, Serpent of The Doom, The Control of Time,
The Control of the Dead, Story of the Time, The Story of the Dead,
The Icon of Politics, Magnetic Repelltion, Mirror Reflection, World
Repelltion,
The Resurrection, The News Observer, The Computer Voice, The Shooting
Star,
The Self Realisation, The New Realisation, The Digital Human Body,
The Human Body Signal, The Human Body Plasma, The Digital Satellite,
The Digital Moon-Body, The Divine Principle, The Godly Principle,

The Principle Plant, The Hours of the Day, The Hours of the Bible,
The Electrical Power, The Begotten Power, The Future Energy,
The Future Unclear, The Living Numbers, Nought is Creation,
The Principle Ratio, The Principle Diety, Nought is Biological,
Creation is Biological, The Earth is Biological, The Whole Principle,
The Skeleton Zero, The Skeleton Dust, The Whole Dimension,
"I am the Holy Image of God", Talking in Tongues, Synchronisity,
Hydrogen & Nitrogen, Virtual Hierarchy, A Virtual Third Image,
A Virtual Aryan Image, Adolf Hitler's Message, Adolf Hitler's Nazis,
Adolf Hitler's People, Adolf Hitler's Ghost, Virtual Process, Moon's Prophesy,
Moon's Umbilical Cord, Human's Umbilical Cord, Birth's Umbilical Cord,
Human's Umbilical Mind, Phases of the Moon, Tomorrow's War,
Human Transport, Auto Transport, Human Relativity, A Relativity Past,
A Relativity Light, Aids Retro Virus, Cutting edge of Medicine,
Cutting edge of Black magic, The October Project, Solveig Walking Again,

*199 = The Words of the Amen, The Nature of the Name, The Name of the Mother,
The Seed of the Nature, The Seed of the Virgin, The Name of the Virgin,
Nuclear Mystery, Jesus Mystery, Messiah Mystery, Occult Mystery,
Lucifer Mystery, The Omega Mystery, Parent Mystery, A Children mystery,
God Son Mystery, Cross Mystery, The Omega Solution, The Key Solution,
Nuclear Solution, Jesus...the only God, Ancient Mysteries, Masters of
Wisdom,
Masters of Dowism, Mode of Relativity, Science Relativity, Micro Relativity,
Lord's Crucifixion, Atoms Combustion, Logos Combustion, Hydrogen
Particles,
Language Combustion, Language Development, Logos Development,
West and East languages, Language Diversity, The Garden of Eden's Logo,
Hydrogen Atom Bond, Hydrogen Logo Bond, Published Logo Bond,
The Alpha and Omega Logos, The Alpha and Omega Language,
Decipher the Alpha and Omega, The Alpha and Omega Signs (AW),
The Alpha and Omega Quark, Hollywood Heroes, Virtual Society,
Hollywood Hero-act, Hollywood Girl Act, Pandora's Computer, Computer
Vision,
The `Crucified Vision, The Genesis Vision, Computer's Text,
Computer's Digital C.D., Washington's Circle, Washington's America,
Washington People, Washington Text, The Washington Law,
A Washington House, A Washington Logos, Television People,
Television V.I.P. Deal, Digital Television C.D., Digital C.D. Illusions,
The Story Text, The Red-tape Story, The Death Land Story,
Control the Death Echo, Change the Echo Control, Balance the Echo Control,
God's Language Symbol, God's Ageless Symbol, God's Ageless Pyramid,
Future Generation, Developed Computer, The Inner Ghost Being,
The Holy Ghost Being, Begin the Pure Text, Information Today,
Alphabet Information, Information Centre, The Skeleton Alphabet,
The White Skeleton, The Cosmo Skeleton, The Skeleton Token,
Complementary Angle (><), Complementary Ten (1+0),
Fanatical Propaganda Team, Computer Logo Ten (1+0), Ten Ones and Zeroes,
Propagandist's Dogma, Free and Dynamic Press?, Basics Heavenly Bodies,

Original History, History Biology, Historical Biology, Birth and Death Biology,
False Prophet's Team, Book Prophet's Vice, Veils of Illusion, Sight Distinction,
Allah's Press Text,

*200 = The Words of the Allah, Mosques Theory, The Words of the Free,
The Nature of the Free, The Basic Chemical Nature, The Basic Chemical Words,
The Basic Islam Words, Moslem's Big Brother, Red-Tape by Big Brother,
Big Brother's Print, The Holy Bible Print, The Genetic Code Print,
The Divine Character Code, The Diety Character Race, Souls in Prison,
Brother in Prison, Time-angle in Prison, The Dead Team in Prison,
The Dead Meat in Prison, The Dead Ten In Prison, Doom Team in Prison,
Back Prison Numbers, The Faces of the Virgin, The Face of Christ's Image,
The Naked Face of Society, The Naked Face of Freemason,
Lode Stone Theory, Written Theory, Omni-Science Theory, The Prison Master,
Logo Word Fission, Sun-shine Theory, The Making of the Science,
The Making of the Star, The Making of the Micro, The Judge of Judgement,
The Time of Judgement, The Omen of Judgement, The Beast of Judgement,
The Judgement of the Dead, Number Judah and Israel, Count Judah and Israel,
Sacrifice Saint Peter, Saint Peter's Chemical, Zeus and the Muses,
The State of being Hidden, Catch-Twenty-Two, Catch The Triple Six,
Catch the Three Sixes, Catch Neil Armstrong, Catch David Wolf on Mir,
Catch Miller by the Feet, Alien Man catch Space Ship,
The Alien's Chemical Cyber, The Alien's Chemical Legacy,
Alien Man Catch Moon Team, America's Moon Team Catch,
America's Moon Team Image, Pictured Naked on Film, The Theory of Satan,
Computer Virus, Computer's Secret, Darrell's Computer, The Computer Light,
The Computer Yoke, The Computer Past, A Begotten Computer,
Micro Soft's Genetic, A Computer Vision, A Computer Policeman,
The Mount of Olive, The Original Earth Date, The Biological Earth Date,
The Biological Records,

*201 = Born again Christians, The Theory of Light, Theory of the Past,
Darkness of the Past, Desk Top Computer, Prints God's Word,
Published God's Word, Released by God's Order, Proclaimed God's Word,
Dr. Hendrik Verwoerd, South African Judges, South African's Monad,
South African's Seer,

*202 = Letters Come to Life, Magnetism System, Skeleton System, Viv-a-Vis System,
Skeleton Skeleton, Skeleton Identikit, Skeleton Grave Yard,
Origin of The Species, Chicken Skeleton Yard, Christian Skeleton,
Christian Dogmatism, Red Cross Skeleton, Ultimate Tree of Life,
Ultimate Trade of Life, Ultimate Blood of Life, The Market System,
The Diabolical System, Full Circle Division, Skeleton Lock and Key,
New Science of Service, War Science of Service, Service of War Scope,
Service of Star War, Service of God and Satan, Thirty Nine Step,

Thirty New Step, Veil of Government, Cycle of Goverment, Sex of Goverment,

Blood of Government, Crime of Government, Tree of Government,

Government of Evil, Veil of Symbology, Text Symbology, Worded Symbology,

Collective Society, Collective Knowledge, Collective faculties, World's Computer,

Magnetic Computers, Mathematical Knowledge, The Mathematical Brains,

The Brain's Arithmetic, The Forbidden Numbers (1+0), The Cross of Jesus,

Nuclear Chemical Energy, The Applicable Numbers, The C.N.A. Nuclear Print,

Total Solar Eclipse, Alphabet Language Text, Eclipse Alphabet Logos,

Unite Alphabet Atoms, Nuclear War Missile, Inflammable Air Missile,

New Pyramid Energy, Egyptians Pyramid, Egyptians Missile,

Egyptians' Pharoahs, Ra's Egyptian Soul, Ra's Egyptian Mantra,

The Last Born of the Dead, The Last Logo of the Dead, The Last Atom of Time,

The Pope logo of the Dead, The Devil logo of the Dead,

The Logo of the Dead Lived, The Lord of the Dead Lived,

"I am God of the Up-right", 'I am God of the Judgement', The Lord of Judgement,

The Logo of Judgement, Human Body Judgement, The Year of Judgement,

An Equal Development, Catholic Development, Catholic Crucifixion,

An Optical Illusion, Diabolic Passion Play, Diabolic Editorial Play,

The Christ's Sacrifice, The Published Sacrifice, The Christ's Kingdom,

The Christ's Children, The Heavenly Christ, The Heavenly Power,

The Heavenly Glory, The New Life of Messiah, The New Life of Jesus,

The New Life of Lucifer, The New Life of the Omega, Only Begotten Son,

Only Begotten Tree, The Parables of Jesus, Doctrines of Jesus,

Eternal Life of Jesus, Eternal Life of Lucifer, Eternal Life of Energy,

Atonement of Lucifer, The Key of the God Son, Theological Hierarchy,

Master's Theology, Nuclear Physicist, English Physicist, A Number Physicist,

Physicist Dialogue, A Sound Physicist, Photo Physicist, Atomic Plant Mistake,

Mandela's Government, Ghost Government, Digital C.D. Government,

Mafia Team Government, Web-Net Government, Government Text,

Mechanical Government, Modern Government, Government Spacing,

Government Space Area, A Government Space Act, "All A Book Government",

The Government Law, Judicial Government, Bishop Government,

Knight Government, Check-Mate Government, Nazi's Government,

Ancient Text Evidence, Text Number Order, People Number Order,

Nazi's Sacrifice Order, Count Text Order, Judicial Count Order,

Judicial Police Sacrifice, The C.N.A. Government Head,

The A.N.C. Government Head, Kaffir-Head Government,

Mad Kaffir Government, Rome Government Head, Nazi's Prisoners,

A Catholic Church Bishop,

*203 = King David and Solomon, The Holy Spirits, The Magnets Theory,

The Life of God the Father, The Reflection of Self, Reversed Engineering,

The Genetic Engineering, Artificial Intelligence, Engineering the Brains,
A Total Solar Eclipse, A Total Solar Romance, King Solomon's Mind,
Begotten Intelligence, Gontier Intelligence, Guldvog Intelligence,
Blue Blood Intelligence, Marijuana Intelligence, Electrical Intelligence,
Umbilic D.N.A. Intelligence, Mom and Dad's Intelligence, Policeman
Intelligence,
On Mind Information, On Line Information, Binary Information,
The Law Information, The Skeleton Name Law, The Magic Skeleton Bone,
The Skeleton Ghost, The Snakes Skeleton, The Web-Net Skeleton,
The Skeleton's Cobweb, The World Wide Web Code,
The Magnetic Web-Key Code, The Magnetic Web-Lock Code,
The First Catholic Race, Original Catholic Omen, Original Catholic Monad,
The Realisation of God, Gravity System, Christian Authors,

*204 = The Anti-Christ Circle, Doctor's of Religion, Doctor's of the Light,
Doctor's of the Past, The Old Bible of Religion, The Sacred Anti-Christ,
The Sacred Christ Brain, The Sacred Revelation, The Biblical Revelation,
The Revelation Chart, Violent Earth Quake, Resonance of the Past,
Adolf Hitler's Skull, Adolf Hitler's Human Head, Adolf Hitler's Paranoia,
Adolf Hitler's Hari-Kari?, Adolf Hitler's Death Seal,
"A Adolf Hitler Head...NoBody"?, Adolf Hitler's Madness,
Pandora's Death and Head Key, Pandora's Death & Hades Box,
Hollywood Analogy, Analogical Hollywood, Resonance of the Light,
Sex-body of Religion, Blood-body of Religion, Blood-body of Life and Death,
Live-body of the Light, Live-body of the Past, Blood-body of Mystic,
Live-body of Osiris, Live Branch of Memory, Tree-branch of Anatomy,
Live-body of Anatomy, Virus of Doctors, A Fungus of Doctors,
Doctors of a Doctrine, Doctrines of a Doctor, Sequence of Doctors,
Sequence of D.N.A. Doctor, D.N.A. Sequence of Doctor,
Insect's D.N.A. of Doctor, Mind Parasite Doctor, Doctor Parasite Mind,
Genetic Lie of Doctors, Genetic Code of Head-Doctor,
Head Doctor of Genetic Race, Parasites of Doctor, The Attack of Doctors,
The Yoke of Doctors, Semen Aids of Doctors, Medical Aids Dad of Doctors,
The Dead Aids of Mercury, Freddy Mercury H.I.V., Monad of Mercury Aids,
Aids Doom of Mercury, Aids Omen of Human Body,
Aids of Medical Human body, Medical Aids of Human-body, Passive
Resistance,
New Pill Resistance, A Genetic Code Resistance, A Resistance of the Bone,
A Divine Code Resistance, Formulae Resistance, Resistance of Death Agenda,
A Resistance of Drugs, Self Preservation, Resistance of Suicide,
The Micro Resistance, The Science Resistance, A Resistance of Volt,
A Resistance of the Ohm, A Resistance of People, A Resistance of Animals,
Anarchy of Resistance, A Resistance of the Law, Resistance of a Ghost,
Stop of Resistance, Standard Cell of a H.I.V. Bug,
Standard Cell of a Digital C.D., Standard Cell of A Volt,
A Life Standard of People, Battery Resistance, Battery Chickens Home,
Slowing Light Speed, Current Light Speed, Johnson Space Centre,
Johnson Brain Centre, Johnson Cancer Centre, Current Light Atom,
Computer Brain Logo, A Nuclear Reactor Logo, A Nuclear Reactor Pill,
Compound Pill Chemical, Compound Logo Chemical, Physician's Aids Trade,

Physician's Medicines, Vocational Training, A Computer Training,
Group Integrity, Disciple Integrity, Christ Integrity, Christ Enlightment,
The Intelligent Brain, Known Symbolism, Identical Symbolism, Court
Symbolism,
The Synoptic Chart, The Synoptic Circle, The Bi-directional Chart,
The Bi-directional Circle, The Bi-directional Bush, The Intergrated Circle,
The Equilateral Circle, The Bi-directional Snake, The Rosetta Stone,
The Rosetta Number, Children's Door-Keeper, The Genetic Decoding of God,

*205 = Hand Written Text, Code Message Written, Hand Written OT/NT,
Written By Jehovah, One with all Souls, Fair with all Souls,
Free with all Time Angle, Manifested Omni-Science, Omni-Science
Knowledge,
A Sacred Science Knowledge, The C.N.A. Published Science,
The C.N.A. Society Science, The C.N.A. Micro Prints,
The Brain's a Sacred Science, Word Psychology, Pure Psychology,
Natural Conscious, Natural Scientist, Unique Scientist, Different Scientist,
Conscious Mind of God, Conscious Mind Monad, Time Scale Conscious,
Conscious Mind Seer, Mad-People Scientist, Conscious Mad People,
Mad People Concentrate, Mad Scientist People, Language Scientists,
Lotus Conscious, Justice Scientist, A Statue Scientist, A Voodoo Scientist,
A Pyramid Scientist, A Conscious Pharoah D.N.A., A Conscious 'Ra' Pharoah,
A Conscious Compass, North & South Monad, West and East Energy,
West and East Moves, The West and East Lock, Parallel-o-Gram Ruler,
Parallel-o-Gram Point, Nuclear Development, Photo Development,
The Omega Crucifixion, Messiah Crucifixion, Stuck-Parallel-o-Gram,
Between Parallel-o-Gram, Escom's Development, The New-Light Energy,
Critical Light Energy, Unclear Light Analogy, Electric Light Analogy,
Infra-red Light Energy, Sun-beam Light Energy, Spiral Light Energy,
Escom's Light Reform, Escom's Death & Hades Past, Your Mirror Image,
Technology Highway, The Key to Society, The Key to Knowledge,
Written Knowledge, Lode-Stone Knowledge, Children's Law Court,
S.A.P. Children's Court, The Key to Satanism, The Lock to Satanism,
Creation Seed of Mankind, The Biology of Mankind, The Earth Seed of
Mankind,
Biological Name of Mankind, Biological Aids of Mankind,
Biological Aids of Woman, Biological Aids of Dual-man,
Biological Aids of Queer, Biological Aids of Judges, The Logo Law of
Judges,
Law Records of Judges, Armageddon Law of Mankind,
Primate Law of Cain and Abel, Human Judges Armageddon,
Ancient Human Primate, The Cross of Christ, The Parent of Christ,
The Energy of Christ, Chemical Nuclear Matter, Chemical Energy & Matter,
The Cross of Power, The Cross of Glory, The Cross of Adam Kadmon,
The Dialogue of Christ, The Parables of Christ, The Gospel of Christ,
The Disciple of Jesus, The Gematria of the God Head,
The Dream of Adolf Hitler, The Mystery of God, The Alphabet Word of God,
The Holy Centre of God, The Magnet Centre of God, The Pure Centre of God,
Cross of Sun-Light, Captured in Black & White, Captured in Micro-chip,
Vision in Micro-Field, A Vision in Micro-image, Complex in Micro-Ohm,

Complex in Likeness, Likeness in Vision, End Likeness Vision, Vision in Relation,
Blue-Blood in Human Being, Mind Cycle in Human Being,
Mind Cycle in Human Mode, Food Trade in Human Feed-back,
Mind Cycle in Human Demo, Vivi-Section Science, Conjugate Micro-Wave,
Computer Micro-Chip, The History Science, The History Father,
Past & Future Science, The Yin-and-Yang Science, The Yin-and-Yang Micro,
Magnetic North Star, First Diameter Science, Magnetic Paranoia Science,
World Sedated Madness, Vibration of Nuclear, Cross of the Germans,
A Swatsika Body and Bone, A Swatsika's Hands Law,
A Human Body's Hand and Feet, Gospel of Saint John, Energy of Mirrors,
Jesus Christ is God, The Origin of Words, Rhythm of Numbers,
The Editorial Words, The Origin of Nature, Six and Nine Rhythm,
Nine and Six Numbers, The Circulation of Data, The Circulation of God,
The Lord of Principle, The Principle of Logo, The Dowism Religion,
The Wisdom Religion, A Bi-directional Circuit, A Bi-directional Wisdom,
Hydrogen & Oxygen, Window's 98, William's Windows, Department of Labour,
Combination of the Law, Combination of the Ohm, Combination of Text,
Genetic Coding of People, Genetic of African People, Record of African Labour,
Record of African Wealth, Record of African Death Land,
Record of African Gold Land, Robben Island Genetic Race,
Robben Island Brethren, Missing Human Micro, Africa's Missing Father,
Africa's Missing Angles,

*206 = Head of John The Baptist, Anti-Vivisectomy, Brain-Vivisectomy,
Cancer-Vivisectomy, Vivisectomy Cut, Abusive Animal Research,
Abusive Drug Research, Ganglion Drug Research, Bacillus Drug Research,
Mortal Drug Research, Speaking in Tongues, The Ten Commandments (10),
The Invisible World, The First Skeleton, The Said Ten...Side-by-Side,
The Holy Resistance, The Word Resistance, Editorial Resistance,
The Pure Resistance, The Magnet Resistance, The Historian Word,
The Standard WORD Agenda, Editorial Mutation, Coloured Historian,
A Yellow History, Reverse History, Copy the History, The Black & White Mother,
Human Coloured Past, White Coloured Blood, White Coloured Sex,
White Coloured Tree, Historian Editorial, Pentagon History, The Slave History,
The Liars History, The Historical Liars, The Historical Dogmas,
The Coolie History, The Makula History, The Historical Koran,
"The Aryan History", The A.W.B. Historical Name, Hollywood Stars,
Holy Ghost Stars, Pure Ghost Stars, The Great Invocation, Television Actors,
Mysticism Actors, Pandora's Camera Actors, Hierographical Actors,
Pythagorean Actors, Promised Land Actors, The Holy Figure of God,
The Ancient Word of God, The Holy Fishes of God, Quantum Physics,
Anthropic Principle, Religious Theory, Religious Prejudice, Trinity Prejudice,
Trinity Theory, Combination Theory, The Life Span Theory,
The Fission Image of God, The Mirror Image of God, Positive Theory,
The Divine Purpose, The Godly Purpose, Universal Churches,

Bi-directional Churches,

*207 = The Sacrifice of the Beast, The Omen of the Sacrifice,
The Monad of the Kingdom, The Legend of the Kingdom,
The Time of the Sacrifice, The Children of the Doom, Nervous Break-down,
The Unforgivable Sin, The Unforgivable War, The Everlasting War,
The Everlasting Self, The Everlasting Fish, Christian Murder Code,
Christian Race Murder, The Number of The Beast,
The Kingdom of the Monad, The New World Order, The New Magnetic
Order,
The New World Police, The New Triple Six, The New Three Sixes,
The New Septuagint, The New Chronology, The Self Controller,
The War Controller, The New Controller, The New Catholic Church,
The Catholic Church Fish, The Catholic Church War, The Sound of The
Beast,
The Sound of The Monad, The Identity of the Beast, The Identity of the
Monad,
Chronicles of the Time, Chronicles of the Beast, Name Number of the Beast,
Count Name of the Beast, Computer Knowledge, Witch-Craft Knowledge,
The Genesis Society, Genesis Aids Society, Roman Catholic Doctor,
Roman Catholic Skull, Electronic Counting, Big-Brother Mob Sacrifice,
Big-Brother Mafia Sacrifice, Sacrifice Big-Baby Brother, Perverts Harness,
A Perverts Deficiency, Human-Body Blue-Movie, The Human-Body in-Sex,
Electronic Satellite, Politics Big-Brother, Marxist Politics, Satellite Observer,
Electronic Moon Body, Electronic Human Hero, Apocrypha Observer,
Jerusalem's Politic, Marxist Swatsika, Editorial Holocaust, Holographic
Hierarchy,
Jewish Government, English Government, The Arab's Government,
Communist Party, Actor of Hollywood, Actor of Nelson Mandela,
Phenomenal Existence, The News After the Date, The Day after the News,
Nuclear Government, Unclear Government, The Government Lock,
The Government Joke, Donkey Government, Government Dialogue,
Stuck Government, Government Ruler, Hade's Government Seal,
Government Parables, Government Drug-Act, Government Photo,
Occult Government, Government War Agenda, Government War Bomb,
New Government Life, New Government Agenda, New Government Bomb,
A Living Government, A Government Front, A Perfect Government,
A Children Government, Parent Government, Families Government,
Jesus Government, Messiah Government, The Omega Government,
The King Government, Proud Government, One Government Mind,
One Holy resistance,

*208 = Mode of Communication, Resourceful State, Resourceful Centre,
Human Physiology, Moon Physiology, Ring Around the Sun,
The Keys of Death and Hades, The Keys of Relation, Keys of the Esoteric,
The Keys of the News, The Keys of the Church, The Word of the Church,
The Keys of the Old Bible, The Locks of Doctors, The Vow of Doctors,
The Keys of Harmony, The News Before the Date, The News Before the Day,
Escaping the System, Escaping Information, The Nuclear Skeleton,
Nuclear Information, News Room Voodoo, News Room Missile,

Mush-Room Missile, Prophesy Symbol, Prophesy Formula,
A Biological Prophesy, Millennium Biology, Infinite Implosion,
The Sacred Ten Formula (10), Genetic Manipulation, A Planetary Alignment,
The Holy Trinity, The Creative Numbers, The Musical 'Minor' Beat,
Beethoven Musical Fair, Beethoven's Musical Face, Beethoven's Editorial,
Beethoven's Chemical Ten (10), The Creative Rhythm, Life's Creative Energy,
Life's Creative Cross, Nuclear's Real-Time Bomb, Nuclear's Deficiency
Bomb,
Editorial Deficiency Agenda, The Psychic Numbers, The Author's Number,
The Author's Count, The Author's Kingdom, The Living Authors,
Our God is With Us, Our God is With Mind, Delusion of Grandeur,
Delusion of Marijuana, Delusion of Mind Cycle, Delusion of Immanuel,
Delusion of Vision, Delusion of Life & Light, Delusion of Past Life,
Current of Past Life, Thought of Past Life, Judgement of Nameless,
Current of Di-electric, Complex of Thought, Current Key of God,
Current Key of Data, Lode-Stone Current, Written Thought,
The Hidden Life Current, The Hidden M/C2 Current, Binary Mind Current,
Binary Mind Thought, Binary Mind Logo Chart, On-Line Mind Current,
On-Line Mind Judgement, On-Line Film Judgement, Current Film On-Reel,
Christ Life Ascension, Star-Wave Current, Digital C.D. Mind Thought,
Rasoldavel Logo Chart, Omni-Science Current, The C.N.A. Current Science,
Mosques Current, Artistic Mosques, The Mosque's Octave, Mosque's Letters,
Mosques & Minarets, Incoming Technology, The Ancient Mosques,
The Islamic Mosques, Mustapha's Mosque, Al- Qur'an Technology,
Moon-Code Technology, Human-Race Technology, Repeats Technology,
Repeats God's Words, Repeats the Live Book, Repeats the Formulae,
Newspaper Formulae, Publishing Formulae, Muslim Communicated,
The Muslim Vision, The Muslim's Text, Communicated Languages,
The Reflection of Time, The Reflection of the Dead, Reflection of the Monad,
Reflection of the Legend, Illuminati Vision, Unidentified Vision,
Begotten Initiation, Zodiacal Logo Vision, Blue Blood Chemistry,
Begotten Chemistry, Darrell and Dagne Reitnog, The Mad People's Text,
The Mad People's Message, Text Chemical Reaction,
"OT/NT Chemical Reaction", Drug's Chemical Reaction,
Veins Chemical Reaction, The Chemical Ohm Reaction,
The Chemical Bone Reaction, The Chemical Bone Biology,
The Biological Chemical Bone, The Biological Chemical Law,
"I Believe Biological Voice", Biological Voice Message, The Brains
Imagination,
The Delirious Brains, The Brain's Dichotomy, The East and West Brain,
The East and West Space, Cut the West and East, The Brain's Rotation,
Earth-Space Rotation, The Brain's Telepathy, The Brain's Mathematics,
The Alpha and the Omega Brain, The Alpha and Omega Space,
The Public Door Keeper, The Brain's Holographic, The Brain's Door-Keeper,
The Public Earth Keeper, African Society Keeper, Published Propagandas,
Prints Propagandas, Released By Propagandas, Red-Tape By Unknown,
Human Energy Matter,

*209 = Parallel Universes, Process of Detachment, Master's of Editorial,
Hierarchy of Human Law, Process of Propaganda, Masters of Propaganda,

Conquer of Hierarchy, Errors of Hierarchy, News Media of Hierarchy,
News Agenda of Hierarchy, Irrational Numbers, Irrational Picture,
Irrational Electron, In-going Information, The Skeleton Skull,
The Skeleton Doctor, The No-Body...Skeleton, The Eternal Skeleton,
The Electric Skeleton, The Skeleton Reform, The Grave Yard Skull,
The Immune Skeleton, The Skeleton Death Seal, The Skeleton's Past,
The Skeleton's Yoke, The Magnetism Analogy, The Magnetism Spiral,
The Invisible Nobody, The Invisible Doctor, The Invisible Diameter,
Nuclear Protection, Protection Unclear, The Unclear Facts of Life,
The Covenant-box Key, Parent Immorality, The Nuclear of Atom Bomb,
The Energy of Atom Bomb, Atom cell name of Parent, The Mind Key of
Parent,
Mad Scientist Children, Mad Scientist Front, A Mad Rocket Scientist,
Scientist Genealogy, Scientist Theory, Scientist Balance of Life,
Scientist Change of Life, Scientist Formulae, Fission Scientist,
The Micro Scientist, The Scientist Science, Democratic Scientist,
Asteroid Scientist, Conscious Theory, "I Believe in God Honour,"
'I Believe in Objective God,' "I Believe in The God Father",
Brain Energy Fission, Future Brain Energy, Future Space Energy,
Honour the Creation, Honour The Earth Seed, Honour the Pope Name,
Honour the Devil Name, Lucifer's the Child of God, Messiah's The Child of
God,
Lucifer's Laws of Mind, The Omega's Laws of Mind, Egyptians Editorial,
Editorial Chemical valence, Editorial Polarity, The Editorial Book of Adam,
Editorial Text Monad, The Dead Editorial Text, The First and the Last,
The Origin and the Earth, Pyramids Existence, The Magnetic Existence,
The Static Existence, The Marxist World, The Marxist Money,
A Marxist Big-Brother, Marxist Brothers, Marxist Bureacracies,
A New Electronic Signal, A Electronic War Signal, Electronic Book Plasma,
Electronic Nano-Meter, Electronic Brain Meter, Electronic Space Meter,
Hierograph's Script, A Big Brother Observer, Electronic Radio Science,
"F.M. Micro Controller", Parallel 'F.M.' Universe, The Stars of Bethlehem,
The Christ of Bethlehem, The Christ of Genesis,
The Adam Kadmon of Genesis, The Crucified God Himself,
The Genesis God Himself, Life's Christmas Son, Life's Christmas Tree,
Life's Christmas Cycle, Eve's Christmas Tree, Electronic Radio Phone,
Chemical Logo Acceleration, Chemical Speed Acceleration,
Cosmic-Head Repulsion, Heads of Government Head,
Heads of A.N.C. Government, Mode of A.N.C. Government,
Television News Head, Films of Nelson Mandela, Films of Hollywood,
Films of Pandora's Box, Comrade of Nelson Mandela, Island of Nelson
Mandela,
Slave of Nelson Mandela, Dogmas of Nelson Mandela, Colloid D.N.A.
Chemistry,
A Modern Face Technology, A Mechanical Face Technology,
A Mandela's Face Technology, Twisting Vision, Nameless Twisting,
Twisting Photon, Complex Twisting, Electrical Twisting, Bi-directional
Vision,
Twisting the Ohms, Twisting The Laws, Twisting Policeman, Twisting Police
Call,

Twisting Thieves, The Crucified Criminals, Criminals Witch-Craft,
Criminals Genetic Crime, Criminals Genetic Blood, Criminals Record Cycle,
Criminals Crime Record, Police Criminals Cells, Police's Criminals Jail,
Criminals Obituary, Criminals Book of the Dead, Criminals Book of Time,
Criminals Mark of Time, Criminals March of Time, Criminals Language
Book,
Criminals Decipher Book, Who's Who...Criminals?, Bandit Twenty-Six?,
Gangster's "26" Number, A '26' Gangster Prison, Gangster Prison Code,
Prison Gangster Cain, Prison Gangster "27", Prisoner's Master,
Prisoner Hierarchy, Prisoners Jail-Brain, Prisoner's Jail-Space,
Prisoner's Cell-Space, Government Safety, Government Salary,
Split Government, Exotic Government, The Fishermen's Keys,
Sun Speed Acceleration, Collective Sun Atom, Collective Chemical Logo,
A Radio Satellite Science, A Radio Satellite Star, A Radio Micro Satellite,
Live Human Body Science, Evil Human Body Science,
Human Body Blood Science, Collective Human Body, Politic's Time Tables,
Electronic Time Warp, A Ring Around the Sun, The Third Born of The Dead,
The Dogmas Born of Legend, The Koran Logo Language,
Decipher the Koran Logo, The Third Born of Time, Numbers and the
Alphabet,
Numbers and the Cosmo, Telegraphs the Alphabet, The Alphabet's Rhythm,
Thunder and Lightning, A Incoming Technology, Newspaper Electron,
Newspaper Celeritas, The Newspaper Copy, Newspaper Telegraph,
Newspaper T.V. Graph, Newspaper Radar Graph, Statement Radar Graph,
Graph New Statement, Circle New Statement, Nato War Statement,
Nato Bus Testament, Taxi-War Historian, Taxi-War Agenda Beginning,
Taxi-War Prediction, A Unknown Taxi-War, Hade's Hoot Frequency,
Hoot feed-back Frequency, Hoot-Hex Frequency, Hoot Frequency Dies,
Driver's Frequency, Hooter-Demo War-Lord, Same Hooter Key Logo,
Africa Zulu War Lord, Africa Zulu Bus Lord, Africa Zulu Combi Lord,
Taxi-War Standard Agenda, Black & White Taxi-Bus, Taxi-War Mutation,
Petro-Net Taxi-Bus, Petro-Garage Taxi War, Petro-Team Taxi War,
New Petro-Net Taxi, New Petro-Net Chemical, Petro-Net Chemical War,
Nuclear Team Chemical War, Nuclear Team Love War,
Auto-Net Back Taxi War, Auto-Garage's Relation, Toyota Back Taxi War,
Toyota Back New Taxi, Motorvia Taxi War, Motorvia New Taxi,
Motorvia Taxi bus, Motorvia Employee, Motorvia's Economic,
Motorvia Wealth Race, Motorvia & Samcor Race, Motorvia & Auto-Net,
Motorvia & Auto Garage, Motorvia & Hoopers, Motorvia & Barons Code,
Motorvia Labour-Code, Motorvia Lifo-Job-Code, Henry Ford Model 'T' Code,
Henry Ford Society, Henry Ford & Fairmont, Henry Ford & The Dead Model,
Henry Ford & The Dead Logo, Henry Ford's Economic, The Volkswagen
Omen,
Basic Volkswagen's Code,

*210 = The Christmas Trees, Determination of Self, Race to Save the Planet,
Race to Save the Logos, The Way of the Cross, The Way of the Parent,
The Way of the Messiah, The Logo of the Gospel, Records of the Gospel,
Records of the Messiah, Records of the Parent, Records of the Jury,
The Jury of Armageddon, The Lord of the Cross, The Atom of the Nuclear,

The Atom of the Energy, The Garden of the Messiah,
The Garden of Eternal Life, The Logo of Eternal Life, The Logo of the
English,
The Logo of the Cross, The Way of God the Son, The Logo of God the Son,
Visions of the Lord, Visions of the Logo, Visions of the Atom,
Visions of the Garden, Solomon's Vision, Apocrypha's Vision, Integrated
Visions,
The Naked Eye's Vision, Satellites Vision, A Inner-Self Visions,
Time's Flow Vision, Ancient Past Vision, Ancient Light Vision,
Chemical Logo Visions, Ancient Di-Electric Light, Judges Complex Past,
Judges Nameless Past, Judges Past Doctrine, Eclipses Judge's Past,
Eclipses Ancient Past, Unites Ancient Past, Language of the Begotten,
Logos of the Policeman, The Man with Hell's Name, The World's Last
Chance,
The Second Born of the Dead, The Vow Born of the Dead,
The Vow Born of Time, The Word Born of Time, Editorial Logo of the Dead,
Divinity of Christ, Divinity of the God Head, Divinity of Adam Kadmon,
Christ Image of Christ, The Dead Centre of Matter, The Dead Centre of
Christ,
Christ Pyramid Omen, The Dead Christ Pyramid, Christ Epoch Formula,
Christ's the Dead Pharoah, Christ Image of the God Head, Victory of Christ,
Mathematics of Christ, Mathematics of Sciences,
Alpha and Omega Mathematics, The Polarities of Life, The Polarities of Cell,
The Left and Right of Life, Corpus Christi Life, Corpus Christi Cell,
Genetically Modified Cell, Genetically Modified Life, Computer's Blood Cell,
The Life of the Phoenix, A Beginning and the End of Life, Compass
Polarities,
Tri-Angle Polarities, Time-Angle Polarities, The Pituitary Gland,
The Pituitary Eggs, The Pituitary Balance, The Pituitary Death,
Change the Pituitary, Change the Chemical Reaction,
The Same Chemical Reaction, Balance the Chemical Reaction,
Balance the Sun Reaction, Re-change Under the Sun,
Change Under Light Chemical, End the Chemical Medicine Death,
Identical Image of Christ, The Words of Christ, The Mother of Christ,
The Nature of Christ, The Magnets of Christ, The Nature of Matter,
Energy Centre of America, English Centre of America,
Jewish Centre of America, Nuclear Centre of America,
Unclear Centre of America, Unclear Centre of a Atom, Cross Centre of Circle,
Nuclear Centre of Nato, The Nuclear Bomb of Nato, Numbers and Letters,
Electric Field Current, Electric Thought Field, Electric Ohm Current,
North Data & South Data, North Lie & South Lie, The Pendulum of I Ching,
The Chronicles of America, The Birthdays of America, The Birthdate of
People,
The Birthday of the Child, Sixty-Nine of I Ching, Plain Truth of Ma and Pa,
Eighth Fold Path of Circle, The Devil and the Beast, The North And South,
The Mind Over Matter, The Matter over Mind, The Pure Mind Matter,
The Pure Mind Sciences, The Prince of Darkness, The Alphabet of Theory,
The Centre of Darkness, The Centre of Mirror, Theory of the Centre,
The Illuminati, Yin and Yang Knowledge, Historical Knowledge,
A Historian Knowledge, A Standard Life Knowledge, Perpetual Knowledge,

Published History, History's Print, History Matters, Master's Combination,
Holy Day of Judgement, Pure Ark of Judgement, Bible Vow of Judgement,
Holy Serpent of Life, Police Story of Jail, Police Story of Life,
Police Agenda of Control, Control of Numbers, Control of Electron,
Story of Numbers, Magnet Understanding, Pure Understanding,
Understanding Order, Understanding Word, Active Understanding,
The Relativity Law, Volt Relativity, People Relativity, Animals Relativity,
Darwin Relativity,

*211 = The New Testaments, The News Statement, The War Statements,
The War's Torture, Symbolism of the Bible, Symbol Key of the Bible,
Pharoah's Key of The Bible, Pyramid Key of The Ark, Slowing Down Light,
Falling of Hollywood, Hollywood Records, Hollywood Armageddon,
Pandora's-Box Records, Nelson Mandela's Records, Discriminating Sense,
Miscarriage of Justice, Darrell's Millennium, Darrell's Prophesy,
Darrell's Umbilical Cord, Darrell's Umbilical Mind, Darrell's Cyber Text,
Darrell's Mind Records, Darrell Comes Like a Thief, Darrell's Implosion,
Darrell's Invention, Adam and Eve's Invention, Eating the Umbilical Cord,
Eating the Umbilical Food, Eating the Umbilical Mind, The Shadow and the
Light,
Jesus Christ's Key, Jesus Christ's Mom, Jesus Disciple's Clue,
Space-Time Travelling, Travelling Brain Omen, Travelling Brain Time,
Window to the Sky, Outcome Base Education, Hollywood's Dead Logo,
Hollywood's Saint, Woodpecker From Space, The Ark of the Covenant,
The "10" Basic Commandments, The God Head Commandments,
The "10" Basic Information,

*212 = The Spirit of Silence, "W.W.W. World Wide Web", The Beginning of Matter,
Theoretical Knowledge, Egyptian's Knowledge, Election Ninety-Nine,
Computer System, Opposite Direction, The Holy Star of David,
The Word Science of Mind, The Divine Laws of David,
"I am the Beginning and the End", The Black Cross of Satan,
The Noble Eight Fold Path, Electronic Magnetic Field, Electronic Money
Law,
Big-Brother Money Law, Marxist Money Law, Subtract Money Law,
The Sacrifice of the Devil, The Sacrifice of the Earth, Democratic Revelation,
Democratic South Africa, Photosynthesis, Resurrection of God,
The Phases of the Moon, The Logos of the Moon,

*213 = A Word is Technology, News is Technology, The Light Technology,
The Past Technology, Virus Technology, Parasite Technology,
Gate Keeper's System, Name Keeper's System, Aids Keeper's System,
The Secular System, The Words System, The Magnets System,
Rotate the System, Rotate Aids System, Aids Journey to Hell,
The Journey to Hell, The Signs of the Zodiac, The Logos of the Zodiac,
The Language of the Zodiac, The Language of the Science,
"I am the Way and the Light", 'I am the Atom and the Light',
Master of the Wisdom, Master of The South, Salvation in Christ,
King Solomon's Chart, Coming Forth by Night, Extraterrestrial, Virtual
President,

The Esoteric Teachings, "I am the Born and the Created", Destroying Matter,
Premature Knowledge, Newspaper Knowledge, Published Newspaper,
Planetary System, Planetary Magnetism, Planetary Word Key,

*214 = A Planetary Skeleton, His Eyes are Opened Wide,
His Images are God and Satan, His Chemical are Star War,
His Love are Science War, His Chemical are 'New Science',
His Chemical is An Atom Bomb, His Chemical is Mustard,
His Chemical is Thallium, His Chemical is New Chemical,
His Chemical Key is a Chemical, His Chemical Key is Sky,
His Chemical Key is Cloud, His Chemical Key is Heaven,
His Chemical Clue is Escom, His Chemical Home is Escom,
Electrical Speed of Light, Electrical Atom of Light, Electrical Logo of Light,
Electrical Danger of Light, The Electrical Law of OHM, Electrical Neutrons,
Electrical Positron, Electrical Face of the Moon, Electrical Light Shadow,
Electrical Light Stop, A Electrical Light Volt, North and South Mode,
His Chemical 'Air-Hydrogen', His Chemical 'A-Base' = A. Einstein,
An Atom Bomb's Isotope, The Scientist's Brain, Concentrates the Brain,
Scientist Knowledge, The Brain's Scientist, Faculties Scientist,
The Genetic Scientist, Electrical Nature of Data, Electrical Nature of God,
Begotten Nature of God, Begotten Words of God, The Electrical Body of God,
A Begotten Mystery, A Begotten Solution, A Complex Solution,
A Blue-Blood Mystery, Mind Logo Mystery, A Nameless Solution,
A Di-Electric Solution, A Sanity Solution, A Life & Light Solution,
A Hormone Solution, A Fungus Solution, The Divine Scientist,
The Godly Scientist, The Diety Scientist, Published Scientist,
The Odessa Scientist, A Newspaper Society, A Newspaper Binary-code,
A Newspaper's Nazi-Race, Prints a Newspaper, A Published Newspaper,
Newspaper Story, Newspaper Control, Publishing Control,
Borne in Mind Control, Atom Quark Control, Atom's Logo Control,
Language Logo Control, Language Logo Story, Diabolical Logo Control,
Diabolical Logo Story, Decipher Logo Story, Decipher Logo Control,
Ageless Logo Story, The Logo Story Image, German-Jew Scientist,
Same German Scientist, The Brain's Isotopes, The Conscious Brains,
Concentrate The Sight, Concentrate On Hand Text, Barriers to Success,
Bill...Bill...The Science Guy, Bill...Bill...the Science Legacy,
Bill...Bill...the Grave Science, Stop!...The Coffin Science,
Stop!...The Albert Legacy, Premature Control, To Break the Umbilic Cord,
To Break the Umbilic Line, To Break The Umbilic Mind,
To Break the Child Kingdom, To Break the Child Paradise,
The Formula of Parent, The Formula of Child Balance,
The Formula of Child Change, The Formula of Child Death,
The Formula of Same Child, The Formula of Alike Child, Control of Destiny,
Story of Coincidence?, Virtual Computer, Virtual Witch-Craft,
Human-Body Computer, Computer Satellite, Computer Politics,
Computer Mercury, Integrated Electrons, Body-Birth Witch-Craft,
Computer Human-Body, Computer Human-Hero, Human-Body Witch-Craft,
The Demons Witch-Craft, The Demon's Voodoo-Bag, Computers Jargons,
Computer Cancel Centre, Computer Cancel White, Computer White Balance,
Computer White Death, Synoptic's Energy, Synoptic's Gospel,

Numerical Dictionary, Dictionary in Number, The Brain's Dictionary,
The Diety Dictionary, A Language Dictionary Code,
A Language Code Dictionary, A Planet Dictionary Code,
A Logos Dictionary Code, Divine Energy Matter, Godly Jesus Christ,
Divine Holy Spirit, Divine Word Theory, "I Love Jesus Christ",
'I Love The Lucifer God Head', The Brother of Jesus, The Pyramid of Jesus,
The Pyramid Hierarchy, The Pyramid Masters, The Voodoo Masters,
Modern Psychology, Animals Psychology, The Child Psychology,
The Law Psychology, People Psychology, Digital C.D. Psychology,
Red-Tape Psychology, Text Psychology, Message Psychology,
"I Believe" Psychology, Judicial Psychology, Primal Psychology,
Numerology Text, Numerology Binary, Proto-Plasm Romance,
Logo Characters Text, Published Logo Text, Millennium Text End,
Zero Codex Nasaraeus, Zero Communication, Israel Communication,
Israel Space Programme, Israel Brain Programme, Alphabetical Zero Order,
Israel Bio-Technology, Zero Understanding, Poor Understanding,
Lazy Brain Programme, Infant Bio-Technology, Zion Bio-Technology,
The Symbol of Energy, The Formula of the Omega, The Formula of Messiah,
The Formula of Lucifer, The Formula of Nuclear, The Formula of Parent,
The Formula of Gematria, The Formula of English, Formula of Jewish Name,
Brother of Jewish Name, Brother-Hood-Brother, Congregation Brother,
Congregation Voodoo, The Master's Pyramid, The Light's Identity,
The Light's Arithmetic, Magneto Hydro-Dynamic, Theoretically Grasp,
Androgynous(-+) News, The Actor of T.V. News, News Reformations,
Nuclear Word Reactor, Energy Word Reactor, Magnet Energy Reactor,
News People Not Real, News Message Not Real, News Text Not Real,
News Essay Not Real, News Text Harness, Atomic Text Harness,
Atomic Albert Einstein, Albert Einstein's Radar, Albert Einstein's T.V.,
Father Einstein's Bomb-Bag, Einstein's War Science, Einstein's New Science,
Einstein's New Calendar, Einstein's Star War, Einstein's New Micro,
German's New Einstein, Geman's New Hierarchy, Adolf's Book Hierarchy,
Jew's Book Hierarchy,

*215 = Thralldom of 'Not-Self', Not Human of Self Body, Logo of Human-Fish Body,
Logo of Human-Fish Branch, Logo of New Human Body,
Atom Of New Human Body, Family Human Meat Ties, Fishes Shark-Meat Ties,
Artificial Human-Meat Gene, Human Vulture Meat, Artificial Gene Characters,
Artificial Gene Prints, Blue Blood Gene Prints, Policeman Gene Prints,
Numbers Classic 'Catch-22', Words Classical 'Catch-22', Master's Vocabulary,
Christian's Hierarchy, Master's Chemistry, Unidentified Hierarchy,
The Planet's Hierarchy, Communism Hierarchy, ILLuminati Hierarchy,
Zodiacal Logo's Master, Zodiacal Language Master, Zodiacal Sign's Master,
Electronic Computer, Electronic illusion, Electronic Witch-Craft,
Electronic Children Change, Electronic Children Death,
Electronic Children Balance, Electronic-Calculation, Electronic Pictures,
Electronic Human-Voice, Electronic Moon-Voice, Electronic Obituary,
The Electronic Embryo, The Electronic Genesis, The Big-Brother Genesis,

Electronic Moon & Sun, Human Chemical Existence, Human-Love Experience,
Human-Chemical Experience, Human-Love Observer, Micro Soft Control,
Blue-Movie...Chemical Human, Blue-Movie...Chemical Balances,
Blue Movie...Porno-Aids, Blue-Movie Rouses Ma, Blue Movie Rouses Dead,
Mind Movie Rouses Ma, Future Technology, Nineteen Ninety-Nine,
The Light of the World, The Past of The World, Parasite of the World,
Parasite of the Origin, Parasite of the Money, Mirror Technology,
Technology Theory, Technology Objective, Technology Honour,
Hitler's Technology, An Instrument of God, An Instrument of Data,
The Image in the Mirror, The Naked in the Mirror, The Image in the Darkness,
The Mirror in the Eye, The Mirror in the Image, Middleway of Deliverance,
Middle Year of Deliverance, Year Time of Deliverance,
Logo Time of Deliverance, Deliverance of Time Speed, The Pyramid's of Light,
The Pyramid's of Past, The Betrayal of Christ, Christ Judges Himself,
The Judgement Wisdom, Fair Armageddon Judgement, The Current Light-Code,
The Current Gas-Light, The Judge's Inner Light, The Judge's Pure Light,
The Judge's Police Past, The Judge's Police Light, Big-Brother Computer,
Mad-Brother Computer, Brother Head-Computer, Pharaoh's Computer Head,
A Judges Scale of Justice, A Judge's Mind of Justice, A Judge's Rape of Justice,
A Unique Mind of Judges, Judas Judges Iscariot, Judges Christ Himself,
Ancient Civilization, Ancient illumination, Ancient Astrologers, Ancient Astrolatry,
Outcome Based Education, Information High-Way, The Skeleton High-Way,
The Skeleton Life Logo, The Skeleton Life Speed, The Skeleton (M/C)2 Speed,
Alphabet Logo Magnetism, Alphabet Logo Magnet Key,
Alphabet Logo Word Key, Earth-Mars and Saturn,

*216 = The Hitler Computer, The Hitler Witch-Craft, The World Illusion,
The Magnetic illusion, The World Computer, The First Computer,
The Genesis World Seed, The Genesis First Bird, The Genesis Chicken-Birds,
The Genesis Earth-Axis, The Genesis Cyber-Birds, Push with either Hands,
Zero with either Hands, Mother's Umbilical Law, Mother's Umbilical Child,
Nature's Primate Law, Mary...The Mother of God, The Human Nature of God,
The Human Words of God, The Human Words Monad,
The Human Nature Epoch, The Holy Circumference, The Pure Circumference,
The Word Circumference, Editorial Circumference, Truth Commission,
Justice Commission, Hollywood Justice, Hollywood Natural,
A Statue Commission, Pandora's Unique Box, Pandora's Unique Key,
Pandora's Unique Camera, Pandora's Ceremonial Magic,
Bishop's Ceremonial Name, Bishop & Knight Liars, Bishop & Knight Dogmas,
Rome's Court Bishop, The C.N.A. Bishops Court, The A.N.C. Bishop's Court,
Kaffir Bishop Court, Bishop Tutu Centre, Red-Bishop's Court Act,
Bishop's Brother-Hood, Bishop's Brother War, Bishop's New Brother,
Bishop's Court Agendas, Bishop's Court Cells, Bishop's Court Lifes,
A Communist's Bishop, Token Bishop Tutu, Alphabet Text Records,
The Alphabet Law Records, The White Law Records, Beyond Bishop Tutu,
Holy Desmond Tutu, Holy Inquisition, Police Inquisition, Diocese Inquisition,

A Liars Inquisition, A Idols Inquisition, A Slave Inquisition, A Aryan
Inquisition,
A Liars Characteristics, Pure Subjective Mind, Black Subjective Land Dogma,
Star War Chemical Valence, New Science Polarity, Phenomenal Universe,
Phenomenal Brain Text, Phenomenal Space Message, The Vine of The
Words,
The Vine of The Sword, Wisdom of the Words, Wisdom of the Nature,
Wisdom of the Magnets, Wisdom of the Mother, The Virgin Birth of God,
The Nature Birth of God, The Stomach Birth of God, The Caesar Stomach
Birth,
The Secular Birth Time, The Secular Birth Legend, The King of Revelation,
The Key of Revelation, The King of South Africa, The Home of South Africa,
Energy of South Africa, Nuclear of South Africa, Cross of the Vision,
Vision of the Messiah, "Six Roman Numerals",Compendiums of the Bible,
Two Parts of the Bible, Nuclear Science of the Bible,
Unclear Science of the Mafia, Unclear Science of Genetic,
Lost Octave of the Bible, Ancient Octave of the Bible,
The Whole Genetic of Law, The Divine Genetic of Law,
The Human Genetic Plant, The Key of Revelation, The Key of the Vision,
The Vision of Jesus, The Nuclear of Vision, A Position of Power,
Current Newspaper, Current Torture, Vivi-Sectomy Chemical,
Ape Life Vivi-Sectomy, Ape Vivi-Section Agenda, The Deep Things of Satan,
A Nuclear News Reactor, Albert Einstein's Brain, Androgynous Diety,
Nuclear Medicine Reactor, Head Scientist Reactor, Mad Scientist Reactor,
The Time's Mathematician, The Beast's Torture, The Monad's Torture,
A Radio Psychologist, Evil Psychologist, Sex Psychologist, Blood
Psychologist,
Crime Psychologist, Star War Chemical Valence, Nuclear Chemical
Messages,
Sun's Nuclear Text, Children's Immunity, Children's Definitions,
Numbers Definitions, Darrell's Childrens Image, Children's Technology,
Children's Polarities, Children's Cosmology, Children's Hierographs,
Children's Text in Life, The Children's Change of Life,
The Children's Jail of Death, The Children's Jail of Africa,
The Children's Agenda of Africa, A Sacrifice of South Africa,
Parent of South Africa, South Africa Hierarchy, F.W. De Klerk & South
Africa,
Bi-directional F.W. De Klerk, The False F.W. De Klerk Path,
Oscillating Hierarchy, Twisting Hierarchy, Mandela's Hierarchy of Land,
Cash Wealth of Hierarchy, Land Wealth of Hierarchy, Land Labour of
Hierarchy,

*217 = Computer Programme, Computer Net-Work, Computer Team-Work,
Positive and Negative, Darkness on the Screen, Theory on the Screen,
The Reflection of Light, Reflection of the Light, Reflection of the Past,
The Energy of the Past, Mirror on the Screen, The Truth Control,
Chemistry Control, Unidentified Story, Vocabulary Control, Vocabulary
Story,
The Planet's Story, The Planet's Control, Orderly Vocabulary,
A Numerical Vocabulary, A Uniform Vocabulary, The Number Zero Omen,

The Zero Count Time, Zero the Count Epoch, The Israel Children Legend,
Count the Israel Monad, Sacrifice the Israel Monad, Reflection of Life and
Death,
The Cross of Religion, The Parent of the Black Race, Reflection of Memory,
Mystic of the Messiah, Sequence of Quantum, Sequence of The Nuclear,
Anatomy of the Nuclear, The Light of the Nuclear, Shadows of the Nuclear,
Albert Einstein's Lies, Current Scientist, Scientist Atom Graph,
Scientist Logo Graph, Scientist Logo Chart, Scientist Thought,
Concentrate Thought, Conscious Thought, Scientist Judgement,
Ancient Retribution, Retribution Judges, Mankind Retribution,
Energy and Matter Monad, The Dead Energy and Matter,
Moves Time and Stands, Holy Spirit's Epoch, Jesus Christ and John,
Jesus Christ and the Dead, Seer and Jesus Christ, Seers Holy Spirit,
Seer's Word Theory, Seer's Magnet Theory, Seer's Active Theory,
The Wages of Sin is Death, The Wages of War is Death,
The Wages of Self...is Africa, The Wages of A King...is Gold,
Glamour and illusion, The Divine Principles, The Public's Principle,
Published Principles, The Letters Come Alive, The Letter's Logo Law,
The Law Scale of Justice, The Master of Justice, The Justice Mind of Law,
Secret Computer Law, Secret Computer Chip, Stop!... Witch Craft Law,
Stop!...The Crucified Law, A Concentrated Micro-Chip,

*218 = Experience & History, Marxist History, Electronic History, Computer Soft-
ware,
Jerusalem History, Big-Brother History, Jerusalem Historian,
Human History Past, Marxist Mutation, Perverted Pervert, Perverted
Existence,
Perverted Blue Movie, Perverted Experience, The Bottomless Pit,
South African Broad Cast, South African Mind Cast, South African Film Cast,
Television Vision, Conventional Weapon, Conventional Nuclear,
Conventional Dialogue, Famous People Dialogue, The Famous People Joke,
"No-body People Energy", Electric Energy People, Digital-Electric 'D/C'
Energy,
Electric Digital C.D. Energy, Digital C.D. Electric Analogy,
Analogical Digital C.D. Ruler, Incoming Information, Information Harness,
The Skeleton Harness, Repeats Information, The Half Human Skeleton,
The Human Skeleton Code, Human Information Code,
Human Race Information, Newspaper Magnetism, Newspaper Skeleton,
Newspaper Vis-a-Vis, Newspaper Blasphemy, Newspaper Division,
Newspaper Compound, Doubtful Newspaper, Newspaper Identikit,
Immortal Newspaper, In-accessible Newspaper, Cycle of Life News Shit,
Red-Tape Newspaper Agenda, Grave-yard of Atlantis, Grave-yard of Society,
White Blood Cell Count, White Blood Cell Sacrifice, White Life Children
Cycle,
White Children Life Blood, White Children Logo Echo, Abstract Information,
"I am Who I am on The Screen", 'Am I Who I Am on The Screen?,
The Holy Bible's Analogue, The Computer Gematria, The Jewish Computer,
The English Computer, Hierographical Messages, Hierographical Vision,
Mysticism Complex, Mysticism Doctrine, Nameless Mystic King,
Pythagorean Doctrine, Pythagora's Doctrine, Hippocrate's Doctrine,

Altered Vision State, White Vision Altered, Electrical Industry,
Volts Electrical Charge, New Electrical Vision, New Electrical Photon,
New Electrical Logo Ten, Electronic Vision Data, Astrologer Vision,
Pythagora's Angle Logo (3>4<5), Pythagorean Complex,
Pythagorean Di-Electric, Natural Development, Languages' Development,
Development of God Mind, Development of Time Scale, Unique Development,
Unique Intuition, Mind Intuition of Data, Intuition of God Mind,
Parallel-o-gram of Dual-Man, Pairs of Opposites, Opposite Colours,
Genetic Finger Prints, Divine Finger Prints, Published Prophesy,
Mush-Room Atomic Image, News Room Atomic Image,
News Room News Image, News Room News Eye, Atomic News Room Image,
Editorial Mystery?, Editorial Solution?, Coloured Mystery?, Child Birth Mystery?,
Human Child Mystery?, Human-Law Mystery?, Umbilical Cord Prints,
Umbilical Mind Knowledge, King and Queen in-Common, Children's Hypnosis,
The Lost Children's Race, The White Children's Call,
Complementary Angles (-><+), Complementary Science, Recurring all the Time,
The Age of Jesus Christ, The I.D. of Jesus Christ, Age of The Holy Spirit,
Exist With God and Law, Exist With God and Child, With Christ God and Child,
Christ's Pyramid Law, Tutankha Pyramid Field, Tutankhamun's Trap,
Tutankhamun's Dead-Key, Tutankhamun's Dead-Box,
Tuth's Medical Aids Circle, Tuth's Medical Name Circle,
Tuth's Medical-Aids Drug, Tuth's Medical Drug Name, Tuth's Medical Monkey,
Tuth's Medical Wisdom, Tuth's the Dead Monkey, The Dead Monkey Vision,
Monad Monkey Vision, Medical Monkey Pain Cycle, Medical Monkey Mind Cycle,
Medical Monkey Sex-Rape, Medical Monkey Anatomy, Medical Monkey Memory,
Medical Monkey Di-Electric, Medical Monkey Dynamics, Omen Monkey's Text,
Monkey's Medical Verse, The Dead Monkey Fungus,
Dead Monkey Aids Fungus, Ma Monkey Nameless Aids,
The Ape and Monkey News, Planets of the Ape's Law, Justice of the Court,
Languages of the Court, The Court of Justice, The Court of Twelve,
The Lotus of Court, The Person of Court, The Justice of Christ,
Exist with God and Tao, Dowism Monad Lao Tsu (**Founder of Taoism..."Yin &
Yang"...600 years B.C.), Genetically Modified Food, Mind Modified Genetically,
Bush Plant Food Modified, Food & Drug Genetic Centre,
Food & Drug Plant Centre, Food & Drug Brother-Hood,
A Communist Mind Drug, The Genetic-code of Parent,
The Genetic code of Jesus, The Holy Bible of Jesus, The Holy Ark of Jesus,

Letters of the Alphabet, Letters of Alpha and Omega, Thought of God
Himself,

*219 = The Holy Originator, The Word Originator, Editorial Originator,
Coloured Originator, First Chemical Coloured, World Coloured Chemical,
Magnetic Coloured Love, A Yellow Chemical Origin, A Yellow Magnetic
Sun,
Garden of the Human Genome, Draft of the Human Genome,
Logo of the Human Genome, Atom of the Human Genome,
Pill of the Human Genome, Aids Pill of Human Genome,
Aids Pill of Human Slave, Aids Danger of Chemical Valence,
America's Space Programme, America's Brain Programme,
America's Cancer Programme, Provincial Hospital, Artificial Gene Hospital,
Current Chemistry, A Artificial Baby Hospital, Blue Blood Gene Hospital,
Hospital Vulture, Policeman Gene Hospital, Family Hospital Ties,
Family Hospital Grave, The Voodoo Hospital, The Hospital for the Dead,
The Hospital-Team Monad, The Hospital-Team Epoch, Hospital Confession,
Undeniable Hospital Agenda, A Genetically Modified Mind,
A Genetically Modified Dogma, The Theory of Energy, The Fission of
Energy,
The Fission of Nuclear, The Genealogy of Messiah, The Genealogy of Jesus,
The Genealogy of Lucifer, Genealogy of The God Son,
Genealogy of the God Tree, God's Paradise Tree of Life,
God's Sacrifice of the Beast, The Final Expression, illusion of Glamour,
illusion of Nothing, God's Children of the Time, The Formulae of Nuclear,
The Formulae of Parent, Christian Scientist, Christian Conscious,
Conscious Skeleton, Conscious Magnetism, The Electro-Magnetic Field,
The Electro-Static Field, The Electro-Static Bone, The Twisting of Space,
Twisting of the Brain, The Mount of Olives, The Forgiveness of God,
The Solar Energy of God, The Chemical Reaction Time,
The Circumference of Self, Attempt a World Task,

*220 = The Symbol of the Beast, The Symbol of the Time, The Pyramid of the Beast,
The Tri-Angle of the Beast, The Tri-Angle of the Time,
The Voodoo of The Epoch, The Missile of Real Space,
The Formula of Real Space, The Formula of Real Brain,
The Formula of Child Brain, The Look and Learn Method,
The Beginning of Creation, The Beginning of Biology,
The Beginning of The Earth, Bottom of the Beginning, Matrix of the
Beginning,
The Riddle of the Beginning, The Data Beginning Him-and-Her,
The Data Beginning Her and Baby, The Reversal of Cain and Abel,
The Reversal of Mankind, The Reversal of Dual-Man, The Reversal of
Woman,
The Reversal of Queer, The Reversal of the Name, North meets South,
North under South, "Arse-hole under Puss", Monkey under Doctor,
The Reversal of the AIDS, Ancient Evidence of the Seed, Evolution of the
Seed,
Evolution of Mankind, Evolution of Dual-man, Evolution of Queer,
Ancient of Evolution, The Chemical Evolution, The Love Evolution,

The Sun Evolution, Donour Evolution, Natural Evolution, In-breeding Evolution,
Unique Evolution, Languages Evolution, Person Evolution, Lotus Evolution,
Justice Evolution, In-breeding Government, Government Aids Search,
Government Seed Search, Government Name Search, Prisoners Justice,
Natural Homosexual, Homosexual Priest, Homosexual Justice,
The Homosexual Love, Homosexual AIDS Chemical,
Government AIDS Chemical, Mad Government Bi-Science,
Government Head Bi-Science, Prisoner's Back a Bi-Drive?,
Head Prisoner's Judicial?, Theory for Reality?, The Human Meat Theory,
The Human H.I.V. Theory, The Human H.I.V. Fission, Philosophical Taoism,
Philosophical Matter, Killing People in Chemical, Secret Sacrifice Matter,
World Wide Web Matter, The Forbidden Aids Chemist, The Chemist Aids Elixir,
Taken the Liars Aids Oath?, Ten Commandments of God,
The 'Ten Skeleton' of God (1+0), The Skeleton Team of God,
Medical-Aids Skeleton Team, The Pyramid Skeleton, The Pharoah's Skeleton,
The Grave Information, The Coffin's Dead Skeleton,
A Draft of the Human Genome, A Logo of the Aryan Jews,
A Atom of the Aryan Deaths, Hate Logos of Aryan Adolf,
Hate Language of Aryan Jew, Language of the 'SS' Police,
A Basic State Security, A Basic White Vocabulary, German-War Vocabulary,
New German Vocabulary, New Science Chemistry, War Science Unidentified,
Star-War Initiation, Primary Chemistry, ILLuminati Time Machine,
Parousia Chemistry, A Unidentified Oval Model, A Clinic Chemistry Pill,

*221 = Substitute for God, White Substitute, Alphabet Substitute, Music Substitute,
The Life Substitute, Substitute the Cell, The Jail Substitute,
The Numerical Life Order, The Numerical Cell Order, The Holy Numerical Life,
The Pure Numerical Life, New Miracle Dictionary, New News Dictionary,
Electronic Publishing, Electronic News Paper, Marxist Newspaper,
Big-Brother Newspaper, Electronic Testament, Electronic Statement,
Newspaper Observer, Torture Observer, New Church Dictionary,
Electronic Mathematician, Electronic Film Stars, Liars Electronisc Science,
Lethal Electronic Dogmas, Electronic Muse Dogmas, Big Brother Borne in Mind,
Digital T.V. Hierographic, Communicated Radar Star, Communicated Tele-Micro,
The Signs of the Times, The Language of the Times,
The Logos of African Radio, The Language of African Radio,
Decipher the African Radio Beam, Diabolical African Radio Chemical,
Diabolical African Radio Voice, Decipher African Radio Voice,
Decipher the Dead African Voice, Decipher African Legend Voice,
Ageless African Radio Voice, Ageless African Radio Chemical,
Soldiers of Fortune, Soldiers of Judgement, Millennium Judgement,
Prophesy Judgement, Current Prophesy, A Revelation Judgement,
A South Africa's Criminal, Without Attachment, Without the World,
To Cut The Umbilic Cord, To Cut The Red-Tape Line,

The Stomach Umbilic Cord, The Stomach Umbilic Food, The Secular Mind Text,

The Mother Binary Line, The Mother Binary Mind, The Stomach Kingdom Come,

The Stomach Kingdom Child, Mother's Ancient Birth, The Mother's Birth Seed,

Thirty Nine Steps, Thirty New Steps, Thirty New Vows, Thirty War Battles, Thirty Nine Mortal,

*222 = Religious Theology, Knowledge of the World, Knowledge of the Origin,
Knowledge of the Magnetic, Money of the Economics,
The First Born of The Dead, The First Born of Time,
The Magnetic Logo of Doom, The Static Atom of Force,
The Static Atom of Radio, The Box of the Covenant,
The Clue of the Covenant, The Key of the Covenant, Messiah of the Covenant,
Jesus of the Covenant, Covenant of the Cross, Covenant of the Parent,
Covenant of the Gospel, Micro-chip of the Nuclear, The Dream of the Covenant,
The Key of Saint Peter, Cross of Saint Peter, Gospel of Saint Peter,
Gematria of Saint Peter, Heaven's of Saint Peter, Hade's Seal of Saint Peter,
Occult of Saint Peter, Fish-Life of Saint Peter, New Life of Saint Peter,
Messiah of Saint Peter, Seven Golden Lamp Stand, Concisely as Possible,
Mystery Story, Father and Son Story, Father and Son Control,
The Holy Life Story, The Police Cell Story, The Police Jail Control,
Coloured Jail Control, Regulated Jail Amnesty, Physical Life Control,
Ancient Jail Race Control, Editorial Life Control, Pure Propaganda Text,
Pure Red-Tape Propaganda, The Lost Circumference, The Key of Symbolism,
Symbolism of Occult, Symbolism of Energy, Symbolism of Jesus,
The God Son Trinity, Satan and the Trinity, The Beast of Revelation,
The Omen of South Africa, The Legend of South Africa,
The Doom of South Africa, The Darkness of Matter, The Twisting of Time,
The Twisting of The Monad, The Twisting of The Dead, Time Consciousness,
A Political Group Monad,

*223 = The Synoptic Charts, The Synoptic Circles, The Synoptic Text,
The Synoptic Message, The Bi-directional Text, The Revelation Text,
The Synoptic Beholder, The Judicial Revelation, The South African Sky,
The Micro Controller, The Science Controller, The Star Controller,
Darkness Controller, Fission Controller, Prison Controller,
A Brief History of Time, A Brief History of The Dead, A Brief History of Doom,
A Frequency Scale of Radio, A Mind Frequency of The Dead,
A Mind Frequency of Radio, A Radio Frequency of Mind,
A Prisoner of Justice, The Voice of A Prisoner, Languages of a Prisoner,
Time Scale of a Prisoner, Aryan Prison Number, Liars Prison Number,
Peter Lost the Keys, The Nought's Symbol, The Creation Symbol,
The Life Word of Christ, The Life Keys of Christ, The Holy Life of Christ,
The Pure Life of Christ, King Solomon's Keys, The Genesis of Darkness,
The Genesis of Prison, Computer of Genealogy, The Theory of Genesis,

The Witch Craft of Science, Science of The Computer, Theory of Aids Genesis,

*224 = Highly Intelligent Man, Intelligent Worded Man, Code Written Messages,
Hand Written Messages, The Word Development, The Pure Development,
The Crucifixion Vow, The Ancient Mystery, The Judges Mystery,
The Monads Solution, The Twin Mystery, The Cain and Abel Mystery,
Exclusion Principle, The Disciples of Jesus, The Knowledge of Jesus,
The Key of Gontierism, Nuclear of Gontierism, Gontierism Hierarchy,
Hollywood Hierarchy, Hollywood Masters, The Key of Pandora's Box,
Magnetic Centre of Forces, World's Centre of the Dead, When East Meets West,
Photo of Nelson Mandela, Nelson Mandela Hierarchy,
Captured in Black and White, Vision in Black and White,
The Whole Name Process, Knowledge of Quantum, Knowledge of Photons,
Theology of The Brains, Doctrines of Satanism, Repellent of Knowledge,
Repellent of Judicial Race, Treasure of The Public, Eternal Life of Freemason,
Theological Statement, Theological Newspaper, Theological Testament,
Hormones of Blood Cycle, Eternal Life of Blood Cycle,
Eternal Life of Blood Tree, The Family Tree Stands,

*225 = The Faithful Witness, Unification of Wisdom, Unification of Germany,
The Vision of Germany, Unification of Gestapo, Mind Cycle of the Monkey,
Vision of the Monkey, Unification of the Bush, Unification of the Circle,
Unification of the 'I Ching', Unification of Dowism, Intuitive Knowledge,
The Intuitive Brains, Your Inner Souls, Your Magnet Formula,
Magnets Magnet Formula, The Law of Polar Union, Outer manifestation,
Future Information, The Divine's Purpose, Mirror Information,
Your Inner Compass, Human Immuno Deficiency,

*226 = The Infra-Structure, Government Policy, Poorest of the Poor,
Roman and Greek Culture, Poorest of Control, Poorest of Story,
The Horror of the Beast, The Numbers of the Beast, The Numbers of the Judge,
The Number of the Times, The Sacrifice of the Judges,
The Children of the Judges, The Children of the Ancient,
The Children of Judgement, Arithmetic of Judgement,
Judgement of Initiates, Chronicles of Judgement?, Court-Roll Numbers?,
Convicted by a Numbering? Poor Judgement of Self, Poor Record Judgement,
The Crucified Trinity, The Unforgivable Sin, The Numbers of the Seer,
The Electron of the Radio, The Roman Catholic Church,
The Roman Temple Church, A Combustible Substance,
Roman Catholic Doctors, A Roman Catholic Editorial, A Catholic News Editorial,

*227 = Modes of Communication, A Mad Mode of Communication,
Phones Communication, Light of Communication, Alphabetical Order of Light,
Rings Around the Sun, The Disciples of Christ, The Knowledge of Christ,
The Knowledge of the God Head, The Myth of the Cross,

The Myth of the Messiah, The Myth of the Occult, It is Human...yet Divine,
It is Human...yet Godly, The Ascension of Jesus, The Ascension of
Muhammad,
The Judgement of Jesus, The Current of Energy, The Thought of Jesus,
The Symbol of Truth, The Pyramid of Truth, The Symbol of Energy,
The Spirit of the Lord, The Fission of the Atom, The Fission of the Logo,
"A Time...and Times...and half a Time", Umkhonto we sizwe (**The African
National Congress=*271), Invariance in Geometry, The Degrees in Geometry,
Geometry in The Brains, Pictured in Geometry, The Brains in The Skull,
Mysterious Sight, Delusions of Grandeur, Delusions of Vision,
Delusions of Brain-Space, Brain Delusions of Brain, Conscious of Vision,
Scientist of Marijuana, Begotten of Scientist, Scientist of Blue-Blood,
Scientist of Mind Cycle, Conscious of Live Mind, Scientist of Di-Electric,
Conscious of Sanity, Conscious of the Laws, Scientist of the Laws,
Conscious of Doctrine, Delusion of Apostle, Delusion of Empathy,
Scientist of Life & Light, Isotopes of Volts, Time Barrier of the Laws,
Space Energy of the Sky, Remaining Anonymous, Life Symbol of Life &
Light,
The Human Saint Lucifer, The Saint Lucifer Birth,

*228 = The Baby of God's Judgement, The Day of God's Judgement,
The Judgement of God's Bible, Electronic Technology, Marxist Technology,
Big Brother Technology, Digital T.V. Technology, Digital Radar Technology,
New Digital Technology, Signalling Technology, Jesus Christ is Lord,
Atom is Energy Matter, Department of Prison, Missing White Children,
One's Highest Thought, To Control Society, To Control The Public,
To Control the Skies, To Control Port-Base, To Control the Brains,
Save Your Life-Stop,

*229 = Sexual Intercourse, The Wisdom of Numbers, The Wisdom of..."I am who I
am",
The Picture of Wisdom, The Kingdom of God is at Hand, Micro Soft
Computer,
The Sacrifice of God is Blood, The Sacrifice of God is a Beast,
The Holy Dream of Jesus, Individual Unfoldment, Individual Technology,
The World Technology, The Magnetic Technology, The First Technology,
The Money Technology, Genetic Finger Printing,

*230 = The Holy Dead Sea Scrolls, The Key to Revelation, The Key to South Africa,
The Key to the Vision, The Written Vision, Written Revelation,
The World's First Chance, Collective Technology, Mathematical Technology,
Arithmetic Technology, Technological Century, A Technological Time Loop,
A Man-Power Technology, Black Power Technology, Bureacracies Mystery,
Holographical Bureacracies, Hierograph Mystery, Holographical Pyramids,
A Pyramid Shadow Kingdom, The Famous People Mirage,
The Famous People Legacy,The Famous Grave People,
The Famous Pandora Legacy, The Famous Ghost Legacy,
The Doctor 'Tuth' Legacy, Desert Pyramid's Chemical, Desert Pyramid's Sun,
Desert Pyramid Kingdom, Temple Pyramid Kingdom, Googol Pyramid
Number,

Orion's Pyramid Bodies, My Pyramid Soul Mate, My Voodoo Soul Mate,
Voodoo Rouses The Dead, Pharoah's the True Monad,
Pharoah's The True Judge, Pharoah's the Israel Force,
Pharoah Controls The Dead, Pharoah's the God of Israel,
Imaginary Pyramid Rock, Pyramid Mark of the Beast, Pyramid Mark of the
Time,
False Missile of the Monad, False Pyramid Skeleton,
Pharoah's False Body Bones, Pharoah's False Identikit,
The Electrical Lode-Stone, The Lode-Stone's Volt, The Ascension of Christ,
The 'Up-Right' of Christ, The Letters of Christ, The Sacred Logo of Christ,
The Fishes of Christ, The Christ of Judgement, The Current of Judgement,
The Electrical Supply, The Judgement of Christ, The Court of Judgement,
The Compendium of the Bible, Twenty-four Elders, Electronic Computer
Face,
An Electronic Computer, Digital T.V. Computer Face, Marxist Computer
Face,
Big-Brother Computer Face, Computer's Face Script,
Biological Computer Faces, Jerusalem's Doctrines, Jerusalem's Theology,
Big-Brother's Eternal Life, Marxist Doctor's Life, Marxist's "No-Body" Life,
Marxist's Black-Hero Agenda, Big-Black Brother's Start,
Big Black-Brother's Genesis, Ageless Black-Government,
See Government Logos, Black Lord's Government,
A Black-Noble's Government, Mafia's Noble Government, Government
Control,
Government Amnesty, Government Story, Government Serpent,
Present Government, Government Echo-Marker, Government Land Marker,
Government Gene Marker, A Government Coincident?, Evolution Story?,
Prisoner's Control, Prisoner's Story, Prisoner's Amnesty?,
Supreme Government, A Supreme Controller, A Individual Unfoldment,
A Individual Technology, A Technological Individual, The Last Nail in the
Coffin,
The Last bone in the Chicken, Biological Bone in the Chicken,
Bottom-bone in the Chicken, The Bone Riddle in the Chicken,
The Bone Riddle in Voodoo, Text Riddle in Pyramid, Snakes Riddle in
Pyramid,
Volt Riddle in Pyramid, Worm Riddle in the Grave,

*231 = "Is the Bible the Word of God"?, "The Bible is the Word of God"!,
The Bible is the Vow of God, Bible is the Editorial of God,
The Bible Editorial is of God, "I am the Way of the World",
'I am the Logo of the World', "I am the Lord of the World",
'I am the Lord of the Origin', The Lord of the Hierarchy,
"I am the Logo of the Re-born", The Black-Cross of Jesus,
See!...the Cross of Jesus, The Origin of Symbols, Symbols of the World,
Opposite Directions, Chemical Valence Combination, Egyptian's Genetic
Coding,
Robben Island Chemical Valence, Robben Island Voice Valence,
Mandela's Robben Island Time, Mandela's Robben Island Legend,
Sun-Moon and Earth Echo, Perpetual Publishing, Perpetual Newspaper,
Perpetual Film Stars, Newspaper History, Ancestor's Testament,

Constantly Remembered, Policeman Killing People, People Killing Policeman,

Policeman Killing the Law, Policeman Killing the Child, World Wide Web Vision,

First and Last Vision, Justice...Stuck in Time, Justice...Time Control,
Supreme Judge Justice, Supreme Justice Monad, Natural Time Control,
Unique Judge Control, Different Monad Control, Famous Justice Bishop,
Justice of the False Judge, Justice of the Holy Bible,
Genetic Code Name of Justice, The Divine Hand of Justice,
Judge Character of Convict, Judge Character of Statue,
The Pope came After Christ, The Mirror Reflection, Meta-physical Current,
Temptation of Christ, Justice in South Africa, Balance a Physical Current,
Change a Editorial Current, A Editorial Death Current,
The Cutting-Edge of Medicine, Cross Cloning Deficiency,
Cross-Cloning a Primate, Clinical Psychologist, End Clinical Psychology,
End Clinical Life Mutation, The Chicken-cock Mutation,
End Clinical Manipulation, National Psychology, The Grave Psychology,
A Patient Psychology, A Cosmic Psychologist, Brain's Psychologist,

*232 = Human Consciousness, Birth Consciousness, The End of the Millennium,
The End of the Prophesy, The End of the Mush-Room,
The End of the Implosion, The End of the News Room,
The End of Atomic News, The End of the Umbilical Cord,
The End of the King and Queen, Physical Mind Current,
Physical Mind Thought, Editorial Dogma Current, The Forbidden Fruit Tree,
The Forbidden Parent Tree, The Symbol of Numbers,
The Formula of Numbers, The Crucifixion of The Dead,
The Development of Time, The Key to the Holy Bible, Parent to the Holy Baby,

King Solomon's Charts, King Solomon's D.N.A. Chart,
King Solomon's Biblical Idea, The Theory of Justice, Planetary Systems,
Spiritual Movement, Mystery Movement, The Holy Key of Christ,
The Magnet Key of Christ, The Word Key of Christ, Editorial Key of Christ,
President Bill Clinton, Ultimate Humiliation, The Future Generation,
The Mirror Generation, The Hitler's Generation, The World's Funerary,
The D.N.A. Magnetic Sequences, First & Last Magnetic Field (1+0 or A + O),
World & Earth Magnetic Field, World and Earth Sequence,
World and Earth Mystic, Since the Beginning of Time,
Wisdom...Beginning of Time, Master's of the Wisdom, Master's of the South,
Virtual Presidents, Hollywood's Human-Race, The Ancient Mysteries,
Current Mysteries, Physical Mind Thought, Destroying Mafia Judges,
To Remain Anonymous, To Remain Saint Lucifer, To Remain Nondescript,
To Remain A Missing Link, To Remain a Missing Body,
Photographic Knowledge, The Photographic Saint,
Pandora's Cosmic Box-Camera, Photographic Knowledge,
Photographic Mind-Light, Photographical Wisdom, Photographical Psychic,
Photographic Faculties, We are Computer People, We are the Computer Chip,

*233 = The Souls in Darkness, The Souls in Prison, The Convict in Prison,
Trying to Catch Darrell, Trying to Catch A Ghost, Virtual Computers,

Human-Body Computers, Satellite Computers, Integrated Computers,
Amana Hendrina Maria Gontier, The Third Born of the Fire,
The Third Born of the Death, Resurrection of The Dead, The Triple Six of
Doom,
The Three Sixes of Legend, Triple Six of the Beast, Enunciated by the Christ,
Published by the Christ, Binary-code by the Christ, Magneto Hydro
Dynamics,
Magneto Hydro Messages, Critical Electrical Stop, Infra-red Policeman Stop,
Doctor's Chemical Reaction, Doctor's Chemical Signal,
A Doctor's Atomic Chemical, Train Driver's Revenge, Train Driver Hierarchy,
Train Driver's Master, Train Driver's Brain Cell, Driver's Perspective,
Convicted Train Driver, Revenge is My Honour, Revenge is My Objective,
Revenge is My Balance of Life, Revenge is My Prison, Prison is my Revenge,
Darkness is my Revenge, Yin-and-Yang Family Ties, Ancestors Family Ties,
Ancestors Family Grave, Ancestors Blue Blood Gene, Historical Family Ties,
A Black and White Artificial Gene,

*234 = After Christ...Devil Comes, After Devil...Christ Comes,
The Second Born of the Death, The Vow Born of the Balance,
The Police Records of Africa, The Police Records of Death,
The Police Records of Gold, The Police Records of Change,
The Law Logo Department, Judicial Logo Department,
The Symbol of Death and Hades, The Symbol of Death and Hell,
The Brother of Death and Hell, The Formula of Death and Hell,
Psychological Sequence, Manipulation Sequence, A Psychological Vision,
A Policeman Psychology, A Mind Crime Psychology,
A Psychological Mind Cycle, A Psychological Mind Sex, Positions of Power,
The Theory of Religion, The Spirit of Religion, The Future of Religion,
Your Future is Here!, The Son of the Living God, The Cycle of the Living
God,
The Blood of the Living God, The Keys to the Kingdom, The Theory of the
Light,
The Electrical Resistance, The Theory of the Past, The Light of the Darkness,
The Light of the Mirror, The Fission of the Light, Hologram of the Mirror,
Sequence of the Mirror, The Tree of Astrology, The Cycle of Astrology,
Self Must be Lord of Self, Right Angles to the Body, Vocabulary to Words,
Chemistry To Words, ILLuminati's Police Eye, Alternating Dead Current,
A Direct Electric Current, A Direct Analogical Thought,

THE EPILOGUE:

Suffice to say, We have arrived at the end of the First Edition of this Publication. The continuation of this Numerical Dictionary will be included in Volume No:"2". Although every endeavour has been taken to avoid the miscalculation of every word value inserted in their respected Numerical Slot, mistakes are bound to have crept_in along the way. You are therefore advised to calculate the value of each word and sentence prior to accepting the veracity of its Numerical Value. To assist You in this endeavour, a special calculator has been included in this Edition. The best way to get the full value of the Numerical Dictionary is to start at the beginning (*9) and read Your way through to the last numerical insertion (*234).

The observant reader will notice a Synoptic Message begin to unwound its self before their very Eyes. If You are a Student of any given Science or Research, Hi-light only that which is related to Your given Science or Research, then re-read the whole Numerical Dictionary once more...noting only 'that'...which You Yourself have Hi-lighted.

VOLUME No:"2".

*235 = The Way to God's Kingdom, The Master of Symbols, Kingdom would never end,
        Paradise would never end, The Master of the World, The Origin of the Master,
        The Letters come to Life, Three Sixes come to Life, The World's Illusion,
        The World's Computer, The First Computers, The Computer's Origin,
        Computer Technology, Complex Conjugate Wave, The Origin of the Species,
        The Devil Came Before Christ, Christ Came Before The Devil,
        Child Protection Unit, Zero Law Protection, The Devil of Man is Sound,
        Biological Man is of Sound, Man is of Biological Sound,
        Man is of Biological Number, Biological Number of Light,
        President John Kennedy, The Grave-yard of Atlantic,
The Grave-yard of the Omen, The Grave-yard of the Beast,
        Star-war Protection, Hospital Protection, Boundary Protection,
        New Science Protection, Field Unit Protection,
        Ohm & Watt Protection,

*236 = The Holy Blood of Jesus, The Holy Son of Jesus, The Holy English Text,
        The Symbol of Knowledge, The Symbol of Freemason, The Symbol of
Society,
        The Symbol of Economics, The Symbol of Judicial Code,
        The Brother of Satanism, The Voodoo of Satanism, The Pyramid of Tutankha,
        The Said Grave of Tutankha, The Said Grave of Atlantis,
        The Magnet Cycle of Energy, The Word Cycle of Dialogue,
        The Revelation to John, Before the Birth of Jesus, Political Correctness,
        Intelligence Quotient

*237 = The Doctor's of Religion, The Doctor's of The Light, The NEWS of Prophesy,
        Prophesy of the NEWS, Prophesy of the Church, In-between Space and
Matter,
        In-between Brain and Matter, Harmonic Proportion, Everyone...must Die
once,
        History and Experience, History and Big-Brother, Marxist Government,
        Electronic Government, Big-Brother Government, Conventional Weapons,
        A Psychiatrist...*On-line, Relativity Knowledge, Cosmic Consciousness,
        The Symbol of Equity, Symbol of Mysticism, Symbol of Altered State,
        Symbol of Pythagoras, Tri-angle of Pythagoras, Time-Angle of Pythagoras,
        The Dead Angle of Pythagoras, Brother of Hippocrates, Voodoo of Hippo-
crates,

White Children's Blood Cell,

*238 = "I am the Light of the World", Supply Commission, The Reflection of Matter,
    The Reflection of Adam Kadmon, The Christ of the Cross, Cross-Fertilization,
    Doctor Nkosazana Zuma, The Four Faces of the Moon, The Four Faces of
Birth,
    New Technique of Living, New Technique of Children,
    New Technique of Number, New Technique of Sacrifice,
    African National Congress, African Brother Congress, Big-Brother
Information,
    Big-Brother Reformation, End Big-Brother Formation,
    A Big-Brother Government, Distorted Busy-ness, This Day in Hollywood,
    Brother in Hollywood, Voodoo in Hollywood, Voodoo in Pandora's-box,
    Pyramid in Hollywood, Electronic Information, Electronic Reformation,
    Eating-off the Umbilical-cord, The day after my birthday,

*239 = The Key of King Solomon, The Mine of King Solomon,
    The Dream of King Solomon, The Clue of King Solomon, Cross of King
Solomon,
    Gematria of King Solomon, Dialogue of King Solomon, English of King
Solomon,
    Indisputable word of God, Everlasting Word of God, Septuagint Vow of God,
    Holy Septuagint of God, God's Destroying Angels, Chronological word of
God,
    Pure Chronology of God, Pure Time Chronology, Success of Gontierism,
    Ruling North & South, Doctrine of Mysticism, Contemplated Witch-craft,
    Contemplated the Crucified, Contemplated the Genesis,
    Contemplated Computer, Physical manifestation, Physical Darre'l Gontier,
    Physical Consistency, "I am not an old Physical Man", The Physical
Resistance,
    The Editorial Resistance, The News Media Resistance,
    The News Media standard agenda, The Physical face of Christ,
    Hologram of Gontierism, Esoteric Psychology, Esoteric Numerology,
    World Wide Web *W.W.W-Code, World Wide Web Binary-Code,
    World Wide Mafia code of Blood, World Wide Mafia Judicial Code,
    The Head of John the Baptist, Hologram of Nelson Mandela,
    President Nelson Mandela, Hologram of Hollywood,
    Hologram of Pandora's Camera, A Big-Brother War Pentagon,
    One-Big-Brother Skeleton,

*240 = A Wolf in Sheep's Clothing, History Repeats Itself, The Wisdom of Solomon,
    The Dowism of Solomon, The Gifted Life of Solomon,
    The Magic I Ching of Solomon, The Magic Circle of Solomon,
    Riders of the Apocalypse, The Rise of the Third Reich,
    The Rise of The Aryan Reich, Zonderwater Prison, The Planetary Hierarchy,
    The Centre of Revelation, The Centre of the Vision, Look left...then "eye"
Right,
    Left-Wing Monad Control, See the Shadow and the Light,
    See the Shadow and the Wolf, See Miscarriage of Justice,
    Miscarriage of Black-Justice,

*241 = News-paper Technology, Technological Newspaper, Information Provider,
   Theory of Gontierism, "And the Word was with God", Six hundred and
Sixteen,
   The Planetary Knowledge, The Planetary and the Brain,
   Psychology and the brain, Dagne Aud Gontier and the Brain,
   Dagne Aud Gontier and the Cancer, The Brain's Judge of Character,
   Cell Mutation and the Brain, The Brain cell's Mutation,
   The Cancer cell's Mutation, The Magic Creative Numbers,
   Zeus...and the word...muse, Moses and the word...science,
   Father Moses and the Word, The Lost Circumference,
   Atlantean Zodiacal Records, Atlantean Zodiacal Primate,
   The Mode of Communication, Seven Golden Lampstands,
   The Law of Retribution, The Law of Jesus Christ, The Field of Energy Matter,
   The Field of Nuclear Energy, Holy Spirit of the Law,
   God's Vision of Truth, God's Vision of Justice, God's Immanuel of Truth,
   God's Policeman of Justice, God's Begotten of Justice, Consistency of Energy,
   Consistency of Dialogue, Consistency of English, Consistency of data-cycle,
   Masters Consistency, The Human Physiology, The Moon Physiology,
   Reversed Psychology, Psychological Knowledge, Psychological in Number,
   Numerical Psychology, Numerology in Number, Natural Science in Number,
   Natural Psychological Science,

*242 = The History of Jesus, The History of the King, The History of Messiah,
   The History of Lucifer, The History of Energy, The History of Nuclear,
   The UN-clear of History, The Year Two Thousand, Pope John Paul the
Second,
   Computer Development, Witch-craft Development, Picture of Hollywood,
   Picture of Nelson Mandela, Electron of Electricity, Oscillation of Electron,
   Vibration of Electrons, Out-going Information, Theory of Pythagoras,
   Department of Man-Power, Ignorance of Esotericism,

*243 = Computer Controller, The Square-root of David, The Square-root of Mind,
   Window's Ninety-eight, The Unholy Trinity, In the Beginning of Creation,
   Darrell and his thoughts, Darrell and his Dictionary, Darrell and his Voodoo
life,
   Darrell and his Voodoo = (M/C)2, Darrell and his end of the dream,
   The Balance of Jesus Christ, The Balance of Energy & Matter,
   Super Natural Power, Exclusion Principles, The Death of Jesus Christ,
   The many Faces of Human Lies, Stand in Spiritual Being, Stand-in Spiritual
hell,
   To Serve his God and Father, To Serve his God and Science,
   To serve under Christ, Unity in Diversity, Biting-off the Umbilical Cord,

*244 = The Life of Darrell Gontier, Consistency of matter, Consistancy of the God-
Head,
   The Life of Mother Nature, The Life of North & South,
   The Agenda of Darrell Gontier, The Three Dimension of Life,
   The Light Dimension of Life, The Past Dimension of Eve,

The Life of the Forbidden Son, The Life of the Mystery, The Life of the Solution,
Master's of the Hierarchy, The Falling of Hollywood, The News of Hollywood,
The New Hollywood Film, The Hollywood war film, The Hollywood War Dogma,
The New Hollywood Liar, The Life of the Forbidden Craft,
The Life of the Forbidden Blood, The Life of the Forbidden Tree,
The Life of the forbidden Trade, The cutting edge of Madness,
The cutting edge Published, Principle of similitude, Past-Present-&-Future,
The miscarriage of Justice, Discriminating Hierarchy,
A Cross-cloning Hierarchy,

*245 = In search of the lost chord, In search of the lost Son,
In search of the Yin and Yang, In search of Past & Future, The History of Christ,
The History of the God-Head, The middle path of Judgement,
The middle path of Current, The Electronic Magnetic Field,
The Electronic Magnetic-chip, Electronic Magnetic People, Synchronisity of God,
Synchronisity of Data, Time-Synchronisity, Monad Synchronisity,
Virtual Time Process, Time's Phases of the Moon, Computer Information,
The Skeleton Witchcraft, Hollywood's Secret Code, Hollywood's Secret Race,
The Horror of Judgement, The Electron of Judgement,
Chemical Electron Current, The 'I am who I am' of Judgement,
The Symbol of Masonry, The Pyramid of Masonary,
The Pyramid of the World, The Compass of the World, World Sports Awards,
Aspiration & Realisation, The Numbers of Judgement, A Principle of Similitude,
Gontierism's Secret Code,

*246 = Harmonic Relationships, The Coming Science of the Mind,
The Coming Science of the Buddha, Hypnotic Suggestion,
Modes of Communications, The Key of Jesus Christ, Dialogue of Jesus Christ,
English of Jesus Christ, Cross of Jesus Christ, Gematria of Jesus Christ,
The Prophesy of Darrell, Vacuum of Nothingness, Mind-Key of Nothing-ness,
Mind-key of Human Justice, Cross of Energy-&-Matter,
Energy Inside a Computer, Lucifer Inside a Computer,
God inside a Live Computer,

*247 = The Numerical Dictionary, The Dictionary in Number,
The Life Symbol in Number, The Numerical Life Symbol,
The Numerical Time Barrier, The Symbol of the Cross, Revelation Gospels,
Tomorrow and Future, Tomorrow's Future, Radio Activity Theory,
Radio Radiation Activity, Radio Fission Activity, The Radio Science Activity,
Radio Lode-Stone Formulae, Asteroid Radio Activity,
Don't Mix Speed with Greed, Computer Generated Actor,
Computer Generated Human, North & South is a Magnet,
Darrell Gontier's Robot, The North & South Light, Past the North & South,
Past the Bermudha Tri-angle, The Mystic Light Eclipse,

Darrell Gontier & The Light, Darrell Gontier's Shadow, The Control of Society,
The Control of the Public, The Control of Army Team,
The Control of Human Meat, The Control of Judicial-code, The Control of Courts,
The Control of Economics, The Control of Inter-web,
The Control of Web-Net Code, The Control of Knowledge,
The Control of the Law Code, The Control of the Record,
The Control of the Odessa, Control of The Nazi's Code,
Control of the Nazi's Race, The Control of Bandit's Code,
The Control of Warder-code, Control of Human World, Story of Human World,
Story of World Birth, That is all I Want From God.

*248 = South African Broad-Casting, Radio and T.V. Solar Energy, Radio and Tele.
Hydrodynamic, Radio and Radar Chemical Reaction,
Radio and Radar Solar Cross, The Dead and the Living Skull,
The Dead and the Living Doctor, Invariant Eight-fold Path, Top-Sport Holy Vehm,
Magnetic Field's Excitation, World's Sixty-Nine Law, World's Ninety-Six Law,
The Release of Gontierism, The Release of Pandora's Box,
The Release of Pandora's Camera, Free Release of Pandora's Film,
Free Release of Buddha's Ghost, The Middle-way of Deliverance,
The Release of Same Honour, Righteous Compromise, Underground Movement,
S.A. Missing White Children, White S.A. Children Missing,

*249 = The Six Roman Numerals, Rhythms of the Cosmos, Rhythms of the Alphabets,
Alphabet of the Computers, The Roman Pope's Numeral,
The Roman Temple God Father, The Roman Temple Lecture,
The Roman Temple Lawyer, The Tree of Knowledge and Life,
The Cycle of Knowledge and Life, The Knowledge of Crime and Jail,
The Knowledge of Blood and Life, The Knowledge of Sex and Life,
My Personal Computer, My Personal Witch-craft, My Personal Divine Tree,
The Jesus Christ Centre, The Holy Spirit Centre, Twenty-two and Seven (22/7),
Reformation of the Church, Reformation of the News, News of the Reformation, A Under-ground Movement,

*250 = The Middle-way of Delivery, The Balance of North & South,
The Change of North & South, The Way of Familiar Approach,
The Balance of Quantum Wave, The Balance of the Energy Wave,
The Balance of the Cross Wave, The Balance of the Mystery,
The Fire of Darrell Gontier, The Change of North & South,
A Shadow of North & South, The Inverted & The Diverted,
Volt...Amps and Resistance, Mechanism of Expression, Mommy's Justice Today,
Present World Problem,

*251 = The Actor of Self is a Ghost, South African Television, The Actor of Self is Darrell, The Age of the Holy Spirit, The I.D. of the Holy Spirit, Body of the Holy Spirit, Dove of the Holy Spirit, The Dove of Jesus Christ, Manipulating Brain Waves, The Pairs of Opposites, Knowledge of Opposites,

Knowledge of the Skeleton, The Knowledge of Magnetism,

Which is Built Upon a Hill, Which is built upon Self,

The Wide Difference in Nature, The Wide Difference in Words,

Christ Himself in Nature, Christ Himself in Words, In the Inner-Light Nature,

Photography in Nature, Photo-Electric in Nature, Photo-Electric in Words,

Illumination in Nature, Words in Illumination, Eternal-Energy in Nature,

Eternal Dialogue in Words, Splitting Image in Nature, Splitting Image in Mother, Splitting Eye in Mother, Holy of Holies in Nature, A Scale of Justice in Words, A Scale of Justice in Nature, A Mind of Justice in Nature,

Key of Justice in Nature, Electrical Charges in Magnets,

Knowledge of Information, Knowledge of Reformation,

Newspaper Information, Statement Information, Testament Information,

Testament Reformation, Newspaper Reformation, End Newspaper Formation,

*252 =

www.ingramcontent.com/pod-product-compliance
Lightning Source LLC
Chambersburg PA
CBHW081656270326
41933CB00017B/3193